THE
EARLY
INTERVENTION
DICTIONARY

A Multidisciplinary
Guide to Terminology

Jeanine G. Coleman, M.Ed.

WOODBINE HOUSE • 1993

Published by: Woodbine House, 5615 Fishers Lane, Rockville, MD
20852/800–843–7323.

Copyright © 1993 Jeanine G. Coleman

Cover illustration: Liz Wolf

Library of Congress Cataloging in Publication Data

Coleman, Jeanine G.
    The early intervention dictionary : a multidisciplinary guide to
terminology / by Jeanine G. Coleman.
        p.   cm.
    ISBN 0–933149–62–X (pap.) : $16.95
    1. Developmentally disabled children—Terminology. 2. Early childhood
education—Terminology.
HV891.C63   1993
362.1'968—dc20   93–8993
                                                   CIP

Manufactured in the United States of America

10 9 8 7 6 5 4 3 2 1

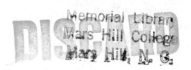

DEDICATION

*This Book is Dedicated with Love to the Memory of
My Mom, Lillian C. Tancredi,
Who Understood the Magic of Children
and
Made Me Feel Magical*

Table of Contents

Advisory Board

Stephanie Renee Booth, M.D., earned the degree of Doctor of Medicine from the University of Southern California School of Medicine. She completed her internship and residency in pediatrics through the University of California at Irvine Medical Center. Currently, Dr. Booth is practicing general pediatrics in Long Beach, California.

Karen Ezaki, P.T., M.Ed., earned a Bachelor of Science degree in Physical Therapy from the University of California, San Francisco Medical Center and a Master's degree in Education from Cal Poly University, Pomona, California. Currently, Ms. Ezaki works in several capacities within the field of Early Intervention. She is a Physical Therapy Consultant for Head Start and State Preschool Programs in Southern California, an Adult School instructor for preschool and adult education, a college instructor and workshop presenter on subjects related to child development and the child with special needs, and an Infant Educator working with infants with developmental disabilities.

Thomas Roccapalumbo, D.O., earned the degree of Doctor of Osteopathy from the College of Osteopathic Medicine of the Pacific, Pomona, California. He completed his internship at Pacific Hospital in Long Beach, California and is currently practicing occupational medicine and family practice in Lakewood, California.

Acknowledgements

There are many people who influence our lives, who in gentle and strong ways contribute to who we are and who we become. I am blessed with some very special people who have enhanced my life and who encourage me to believe in myself and to follow my dreams. This book and its creation have benefitted from the encouragement I have received over the years. I now have the unique opportunity and privilege to thank the people who directly and indirectly helped make this project a reality.

Thank you to my Tancredi/Basiago/Vergara and Coleman/Conover families and to my friends for your enthusiasm and support—how fortunate I am to have your love and encouragement as we embrace this adventure called life!

Thank you to Dale for your endless words of encouragement, for easing my mind with your sound advice and objectivity, for your sensitive understanding of what this book means to me, and most of all for being the love of my life and for the treasures your friendship brings me.

Thank you to Michelle, Julie, and Tom for all your hard work and thoughtful suggestions, for your encouraging words and your infectious laughter, for caring about me so much, and for believing in me and dreaming with me.

Thank you to Mom and Dad for always believing in me and making me feel special, and to Jonathan and Kevin for the joy and inspiration you naturally give.

Thank you to Stephanie Booth, M.D.; Tom Roccapalumbo, D.O.; Karen Ezaki, P.T., M.Ed.; Chris Basiago, D.D.S.; and Diane Hinds, M.S. for your time and effort, and for the care and expertise you gave to this book.

Thank you to Sister Mary Dennis Peters, O.S.B., M.L.S., and to all the very helpful staff members of Wilson Library at the University of La Verne. Your knowledge, assistance, and consideration made my research environment feel like a "home away from home."

Thank you to the team at Woodbine House for your commitment to *The Early Intervention Dictionary*. Especially, I would like to thank Susan Stokes, Editor, for the many ways this book has benefitted from your skill and talent and for making the publication process such a pleasant experience.

Finally, I would like to express my thanks for the many ways God has guided and blessed my life.

Introduction

Early intervention, much like the young children on whom we in the field focus our energies, is an evolving, hopeful discipline with unlimited potential for growth. It is an expansive, multidisciplinary field comprised of a host of medical, therapeutic, and educational professionals who join in a collaborative effort to deliver the most effective programs for children. It is well documented that infants and young children with special needs, and their families, need comprehensive services delivered by well-trained early interventionists. One of the challenges of implementing such a comprehensive multidisciplinary service delivery system is to develop a better understanding of the various disciplines, each with its own system of unique and specialized interventions. It is vital that early interventionists understand the terminology of the various disciplines so we can support each other's efforts and truly provide effective and comprehensive programs to infants and young children with special needs.

My goal in writing *The Early Intervention Dictionary* was to identify and comprehensively define early intervention terminology, making it accessible and understandable to parents and all professionals. As with any dictionary, this book is not intended to provide the total of in-depth information the parent or early interventionist may need to know about the various medical, therapeutic, educational, or psychological terms which are defined. Rather, the intent of *The Early Intervention Dictionary* is to clarify many of the more frequently seen terms, to provide a starting point in the search for more in-depth information, and to provide its readers with a better foundation for understanding the early intervention process.

The entries included in the dictionary were selected from current articles and literature; medical, therapeutic, educational, and psychological reports on individual children; and from discussions with professionals working with the early intervention population. Certainly there are other terms (for conditions, evaluation tools, drugs, etc.) that pertain to early intervention and which are not included; however, I attempted to include the most common. The disciplines represented in the dictionary include pediatric medicine, child development, early childhood education, early childhood special education, physical therapy, occupational therapy, speech and language therapy, audiology, counseling, social work, child life, education of the hearing impaired and the visually impaired, and special education.

It is a rare individual who joins an early intervention team already fully trained and knowledgeable in all areas of early intervention. Further, even this unique person must continuously strive to keep up with the growth of the field. The majority of us do have room for expansion of our knowledge base. It is my hope that *The Early Intervention Dictionary* will help the committed early intervention practitioner acquire the learning that is necessary to provide compassionate and effective early intervention services and to help connect professionals of varying disciplines. As with any type of learning, the more knowledgeable and comfortable we are with the "tools of our trade," the more capable we are of utilizing our resources and integrating our learning into concrete practices that will benefit the young children and families we endeavor to serve.

Finally, as we explore and respond to some of the more challenging aspects of our work as early interventionists, it is my hope that we always appreciate the amazing children who inspire and motivate us to reach *our* potential.

Notes to the Reader

• The definitions in this dictionary are written as they apply to early intervention or to the care and development of infants and young children in general. Many words have other, equally accurate, definitions which are not included because they do not pertain to the early intervention population. For the same reason, not all available information about a condition, drug, evaluation tool, etc., is included. (The reader will note that some terms which pertain to special education of children above five years of age *are* included, as these terms may be encountered in helping children make the transition from early intervention to special education.)

• In order to accurately describe the children who make up the early intervention population, I have alternated the use of masculine and feminine pronouns by letter (i.e., masculine pronouns are used for words beginning with A, feminine pronouns for words beginning with B, etc.).

• Within definitions, I have used terminology that emphasizes that children with special needs are children first, not their conditions. While it is important to understand a child's diagnosis, it is equally important to avoid labeling children. First of all, a diagnosis does not fully describe the child and capture his or her uniqueness and potential; nor is a diagnosis always accurate and/or comprehensive. Secondly, our focus of time and energy must be on children, not on their labels. We teach Michael and Beth who have Down syndrome, not two Down's kids named Michael and Beth.

• Entries are alphabetized by the letter-by-letter method; that is, disregarding spaces and punctuation. For example:

> IAC
> IAL
> I and O
> -iasis
> iatr—

• All but the most common words used within a definition are also defined in the book. The definition for a word is provided in the following manner:

—defined in full at its own entry (it may also be printed in italics within a definition for another word as a reminder to the reader that additional related information is available)
or
—defined briefly in parentheses within the definition of another word if it is integral to comprehension of that definition.

• The causes of medical/developmental conditions are provided if they are known. Sometimes the only information regarding how a disorder occurs is the pattern of inheritance (and this is not always known, either).

• The ages provided at entries describing acquisition of skills and emergence of behaviors are only approximations (and then only for typically developing children).

• Drugs are defined at the generic (official) names of the drugs. Brand names are indicated by the notation of ™ (trade mark) after the name.

• The instruction *"Refer to . . ."* listed at the end of some definitions indicates entries that contain information on related topics. For example, at "Toxicology Screen" I have suggested *"Refer to **Prenatally Exposed to Drugs."***

• *"Compare to . . ."* is listed to indicate terms which are opposites of the word defined or one of several in a sequence of related terms. For example, at "Ductus Arteriosus" I have suggested *"Compare **Patent Ductus Arteriosus"*** and at "Scoliosis" I have suggested *"Compare to **Kyphosis** and **Lordosis"*** (other types of spinal curvature).

• *"Also known as . . ."* lists additional formal and/or informal names of conditions, supplies, agencies, etc. For example, at "Down syndrome," I have listed, *"Also known as **Trisomy 21.**"*

Pronunciation Key

—/a/ as in "pat"
—/ay/ as in "baby"
—/ah/ as in "ahh"
—/ar/ as in "car"
—/b/ as in "boy"
—/ch/ as in "chew"
—/d/ as in "dog"
—/e/ as in "pet"
—/ee/ as in "feet"
—/f/ as in "finger"
—/g/ as in "gag"
—/h/ as in "hot"
—/i/ as in "infant"
—/ie/ as in "tie"
—/j/ as in "jabber"
—/k/ as in "kiss"
—/kw/ as in "quick"
—/l/ as in "learn"
—/m/ as in "mom"
—/n/ as in "new"
—/ng/ as in "thing"
—/o/ as in "pot"

—/oe/ as in "go"
—/oi/ as in "toy"
—/oo/ as in "boot"
—/or/ as in "more"
—/ou/ as in "out"
—/p/ as in "papa"
—/r/ as in "run"
—/s/ as in "sand"
—/sh/ as in "shoe"
—/t/ as in "toddler"
—/th/ as in "throw"
—/u/ as in "cup"
—/yoo/ as in "use"
—/uh/ as in "about"
—/ur/ as in "turn"
—/v/ as in "voice"
—/w/ as in "win"
—/x/ as in "X-ray"
—/y/ as in "you"
—/z/ as in "zoo"
—/zh/ as in "vision"

A

$\overline{a}$

The abbreviation for before.

a-

A prefix meaning away from, not, without, or lack.

AAMD

The abbreviation for American Association on Mental Deficiency (now known as American Association on Mental Retardation).

AAMR

The abbreviation for American Association on Mental Retardation.

ab-

A prefix meaning away from.

Abdomen (AB-doe-men or ab-DOE-men)

The area of the body located between the chest and the pelvis.

Abdominal (ab-DOM-i-nuhl)

Referring to the stomach area, the area of the body between the chest and pelvis.

Abduct (ab-DUKT)

To move away from the midline of the body.
  Compare Adduct.

Abduction

The act of moving apart, as in leg or arm muscles, away from the midline of the body.
  Compare Adduction.

Abductor

One of several muscles that pulls a part of the body away from midline. For example, abductor muscles pull the thumb away from the other fingers.

ABO Incompatibility

The differences in blood type (O, A, B, or AB) between mother and baby. This incompatibility can result in anemia and *jaundice* in the baby.

Abortion

The delivery of an embryo or fetus with no chance of survival. Spontaneous abortion refers to a miscarriage and elective abortion refers to a deliberate, medically induced termination of pregnancy.

Abortus (uh-BOR-tus)
A fetus with no chance of survival.
Refer to **Abortion**.

ABR
The abbreviation for Auditory Brain Stem Response.

Abrachia (uh-BRAY-kee-uh)
Congenital absence of arms.

Abruptio Placenta (uh-BRUP-she-oe pluh-SEN-tuh)
A life-threatening condition in which the placenta separates prematurely from the wall of a pregnant woman's uterus. Severe bleeding can result, making it dangerous for both the mother and the fetus.

Absence Seizure (AB-sens or uhb-SAHNS)
A form of *generalized seizure* that causes a brief clouding or loss of consciousness. The child stares blankly, and sometimes his eyes blink or roll upward. The child recovers quickly from this type of seizure. Absence seizures may occur many times a day and can be brought on by hyperventilation.
Also known as a **Petit Mal Seizure**.
Refer to **Epilepsy**.

Absorption
The process by which substances pass into body tissues, such as when digested food is absorbed into the walls of the intestines.
Refer to **Nutrition**.

ABSR
The abbreviation for Auditory Brain Stem Response.
Refer to **Auditory Evoked Response**.

Abstract Thinking
The ability to grasp concepts, principles, or processes that cannot be experienced directly through the senses; to draw relationships (such as between like and unlike things); and to derive meaning from symbols.

ac
The abbreviation for the Latin words meaning before meals.

Accommodation
The ability of the eye to adjust its shape for vision of near objects.

Accutane™ (AK-yoo-tayn)
Refer to **Retinoic Acid**.

Acetabulum (as-i-TAB-yuh-luhm)
The hip socket holding the head of the femur (thigh bone).

Acetaminophen (uh-see-tuh-MIN-uh-fen)
A drug used to relieve pain and reduce fever.

Acetazolamide (as-et-uh-ZOL-uh-mide)
A drug used to treat *edema*, to reduce eye pressure in *glaucoma*, and to treat certain seizure disorders.

Acetylcholine (as-e-til-KOE-leen)
A *neurotransmitter*, or chemical in the body that transmits messages from one nerve cell to another, or between nerve and muscle cells.

Achilles Tendon (uh-KIL-eez)
The tendon of the calf muscles.
   Also known as the "Heelcord" or Calcaneal Tendon.

Achilles Tendon Lengthening
A surgical procedure in which the Achilles tendon is cut to lengthen the tendon and to correct *contractures*. The procedure helps the child place his foot in a neutral position (toes forward, foot flexed), and to walk on his whole foot rather than on his toes.
   Also known as Heel Cord Lengthening.

Achondroplasia (uh-kon-droe-PLAY-zee-uh)
An *autosomal dominant disorder* in which bones fail to grow normally due to abnormal conversion of cartilage to bone. This causes extreme shortness of the arms and legs, resulting in a child who is dwarfed. Achondroplasia is also characterized by *macrocephaly*, mild *hypotonia*, *lordosis*, and, usually, normal intelligence.

Acidemia (as-i-DEE-mee-uh)
   Refer to Acidosis.

Acidosis (as-i-DOE-sis)
An excess of acid in the blood and body tissues, which can lead to disruption of the chemical processes within the body. There are two types of acidosis: metabolic acidosis and respiratory acidosis. Metabolic acidosis may develop due to illness such as *respiratory distress syndrome* of the premature infant, kidney failure, *diabetes mellitus*, or severe diarrhea. Respiratory acidosis occurs when the body is not able to remove carbon dioxide from the lungs due to illness such as respiratory distress syndrome of the premature infant or bronchitis. It may also occur due to an obstruction in the respiratory tract.

Acoustic Nerve
   Refer to Auditory Nerve.

Acoustic Neuroma
A benign tumor of the auditory nerve (located within the auditory canal) that may cause hearing impairment, headache, balance disturbance, pain or numbness of the face, and a ringing or buzzing noise within the ear or ears.

Acquired
Referring to a feature, state, or disease that happens after birth. (Acquired conditions are not inherited, but rather a response to the environment.)
Compare Congenital and Inherited.

Acquired Immune Deficiency Syndrome (AIDS)
A disorder caused by the *human immuno-deficiency virus* (HIV). Symptoms in children include damaged immune system, recurrent infections, poor growth, and possibly brain disease resulting in developmental delay. AIDS is usually fatal.

Acrocephalosyndactyly (ak-roe-sef-uh-loe-sin-DAK-til-ee)
Refer to Apert Syndrome.

ACTH
The abbreviation for Adrenocorticotropic hormone.

Active Learner
Refer to Kinesthetic Learner.

Activities of Daily Living (ADL)
Normal, everyday actions, such as eating, dressing, or brushing the teeth.

Acuity
The level at which a child sees images or hears sounds.

Acute Illness
Referring to a condition that occurs suddenly and is usually short in duration.
Compare Chronic Illness.

ad-
A prefix meaning to or toward.

AD
The abbreviation for the Latin words meaning right ear.

ADA
The abbreviation for Americans with Disabilities Act.

Adactyly (ay-DAK-ti-lee)
A birth defect in which one or more fingers or toes are missing.
Compare Polydactyly.

Adaptive
Normal or useful.

Adaptive Behavior
The ability to adjust to new situations and to apply familiar or new skills to those situations. For example, a two-year-old is displaying his ability to adapt when he says, "Mine!" to the child who is attempting to take his toy. A five-year-old shows adaptive behavior when he is able to use the same table manners he uses at home at a friend's house.

Adaptive Switch
A switch that can be added to an electronic or battery-operated toy or other device (such as a light or television) to allow a child who has severe motor impairment to better control his environment. Activating an adaptive switch does not require precise motor skills.

ADD
The abbreviation for Attention Deficit Disorder.

Adduct (uh-DUKT or a-DUKT)
To move toward the midline of the body.
   Compare **Abduct**.

Adduction
The act of moving a limb toward the midline, as in the arm or leg muscles toward the middle of the body.
   Compare **Abduction**.

Adductor
One of several muscles that pulls a part of the body toward midline. For example, adductor muscles pull the thigh toward the midline of the body.

adeno-
A prefix meaning gland.

Adenoid (AD-e-noid)
One of two masses of lymph tissue high on the back wall of the throat, behind the nose.

Adenoidectomy (ad-e-noid-EK-toe-mee)
Surgical removal of the adenoids.

Adenopathy (ad-e-NOP-uh-thee)
Swelling of lymph nodes.

Adenosis (ad-e-NOE-sis)
A disease or abnormal growth in a gland, especially a lymph gland.

ADHD
The abbreviation for Attention Deficit Hyperactivity Disorder.

Adhesion (ad-HEE-zhun)
A formation of scar tissue that binds together two surfaces that are normally apart. Adhesions develop most commonly in the abdomen as a result of inflammation or surgery.

adip-
A prefix meaning fat.

Adipose (AD-i-pose)
Fatty.

Adjusted Age
Refer to **Corrected Age**.

ADL
The abbreviation for Activities of Daily Living.

Adrenal Gland (uh-DREE-nuhl)
The organ that sits on top of each kidney and produces hormones that assist with body metabolism, chemical balance, immune system functioning, and response to stress. The adrenal glands also produce male sex hormones, and, to a lesser degree, female sex hormones. The adrenal glands are essential to life.

Adrenaline (uh-DREN-uh-leen or uh-DREN-uh-lin)
Refer to **Epinephrine**.

Adrenocorticotropic Hormone (ACTH) (ad-ree-noe-kor-ti-koe-TROP-ik)
A hormone made by the pituitary gland to stimulate growth and function of the adrenal cortex (the outer layer of the adrenal glands). ACTH is also commercially made and is used to treat *endocrine* and *rheumatic disorders* and *infantile spasms*.
Also known as **Corticotropin**.

Adventitious (ad-ven-TISH-uhs)
A condition that is *acquired* through illness or accident, such as adventitious deafness.

Advocate
An individual who represents or speaks out on behalf of another person's interests (as in a parent with his/her child).

AEP
The abbreviation for Auditory Evoked Potential.
Refer to **Auditory Evoked Response**.

AER
The abbreviation for Auditory Evoked Response.

Aeration
1. The exposure of blood to air and oxygen that takes place in the lungs. (Carbon dioxide is exchanged with oxygen.)
2. The charging of a liquid substance with air, oxygen, or carbon dioxide.

af-
A prefix meaning to.

AFDC
The abbreviation for Aid to Families with Dependent Children.

Afebrile (a-FEB-ril or ay-FEB-ril)
Without a fever.
   Compare **Febrile**.

Affect (AF-fekt)
The outward signs of a child's feelings, such as a smile or grimace.
   Compare **Flat Affect**.

Afferent (AF-er-ent)
Moving from the surface of a body organ to the center, as in blood vessels, lymph channels, and nerves.
   Compare **Efferent**.

Affricate (AF-ri-kit)
A speech sound produced when the breath stream is completely stopped and then released at articulation. The /ch/, /g/, and /j/ sounds are affricates.

AFO
The abbreviation for Ankle-Foot Orthosis.

AFP
The abbreviation for Alpha-fetoprotein.

AGA
The abbreviation for appropriate (or average) for gestational age.

Agenesia Corticalis (uh-je-NEE-see-uh kor-ti-KAL-is)
A condition in which some of the embryo's brain cells do not grow, causing loss of motor function and severe mental retardation in the infant.

Agenesis (uh-JEN-e-sis)
The complete or partial absence of an organ or part at birth, due to a lack of embryonic development.

Agenesis of Corpus Callosum
A condition in which the *corpus callosum* of the brain fails to form (leaving the two cerebral hemispheres unjoined) or forms incompletely. A child with this defect may have difficulty transferring information from one cerebral hemisphere to the other, which affects language abilities. Since the two hemispheres of the brain are capable of functioning independently of each other, agenesis of the corpus callosum does not seriously impair intellectual abilities.

Agnosia (ag-NOE-zee-uh)
Sensory impairment caused by damage to the brain. The impairment results in a loss of ability to recognize either visual, sound, olfactory (smell), tactile, or taste stimuli.

AIDS
The abbreviation for Acquired Immune Deficiency Syndrome.

Aid to Families with Dependent Children (AFDC)
A federally and state funded financial assistance program that provides money to qualified individuals who have children under age 19. The AFDC check is sometimes referred to as the "welfare" check.

Akinetic Seizure
*Refer to **Atonic Seizure**.*

Albinism (AL-bin-izm)
A congenital condition characterized by partial or total lack of pigment in the skin, hair, and eyes. Certain eye disorders (*astigmatism, photophobia,* and *nystagmus*) may be associated with albinism.

Albumin (al-BYOO-min)
A protein that expands the volume of blood and is used for treating *hyperbilirubinemia* and other disorders.

Albuterol (al-BYOO-ter-ol)
A *bronchodilator drug* used to treat asthma and bronchitis.

Aldactone™ (al-DAK-tone)
*Refer to **Spironolactone**.*

-algia
A suffix meaning pain.

Alimentary (al-e-MEN-tar-ee)
Pertaining to food or a nutritive substance, or to the organs of digestion.

Allen Test
A visual acuity test in which the preschooler is asked to name pictures.

Allergen (AL-er-jen)
A foreign substance that can cause an allergic response in susceptible people. Examples of allergens include airborne pollens, molds, and animal dander; and foods such as dairy products, cereals, and strawberries.
  Compare Antigen.

Allergenic (al-er-JEN-ik)
Capable of causing an allergic response in susceptible people.

Allergy
A sensitivity to a generally harmless substance. Exposure to an allergen causes symptoms of allergic reaction (an adverse physical reaction) in susceptible people, but causes no response in others, and may be mild in some (such as a runny nose), and severe in others (such as shock).

Alpern-Boll Developmental Profile
  Refer to Developmental Profile II.

Alpha-fetoprotein (AFP) (AL-fuh fee-toe-PROE-teen)
A protein produced by the fetus that flows from the amniotic fluid to the mother's blood. An unusually low level of AFP has been found in women who gave birth to children with Down syndrome. An abnormally high level of AFP has been associated with neural tube defects, twin pregnancies, or threatened or actual miscarriages.

Alport Syndrome
An *autosomal dominant disorder* characterized by *congenital* progressive *sensorineural hearing impairment*, kidney malfunction, and occasionally ocular (eye) defects.

Alprostadil (al-PROS-tuh-dil)
A drug given to newborns who have certain types of heart defects to help with blood flow.

Alupent™ (AL-yoo-pent)
  Refer to Metaproterenol.

alve-
A prefix meaning channel or cavity.

Alveolar Ridge
The ridge of the *hard palate* just back of the upper teeth.
  Refer to Hard Palate.

Alveolars
Speech sounds produced when the tongue touches or approximates the *alveolar ridge*. The /t/ and the /d/ sounds are examples of alveolar speech sounds.

Alveoli (al-VEE-oe-lie)
1. Tiny air sacs in the lungs where carbon dioxide leaves the blood and oxygen enters the bloodstream.
2. Tiny sacs in the milk glands of the breast where nutrients from the mother's bloodstream are converted to milk.

Alveolus (al-VEE-oe-lus)
Singular of alveoli.

Amblyopia (am-blee-OE-pee-uh)
A condition affecting *visual acuity* that can lead to loss of vision in an eye that is structurally capable of seeing. Amblyopia develops when corresponding images are not formed on the retinas of both eyes. The brain suppresses vision in one eye to prevent blurred or double vision. Over time, this suppression causes permanent visual impairment in that eye. Vision can be maintained if the underlying cause (usually *strabismus*, a *cataract*, or *astigmatism*) is corrected while the child is young (before eight years of age).

Ambulate/Ambulatory
Able to walk or move about.

Amelioration (uh-meel-yoe-RAY-shuhn)
The process of lessening pain or improving symptoms.

American Association on Mental Deficiency (AAMD)
Refer to American Association on Mental Retardation (the new name for the AAMD).

American Association on Mental Retardation (AAMR)
A professional organization established to promote research in *mental retardation* and development of services for individuals with mental retardation. Information regarding preventable mental retardation is made available through the AAMR.

American Sign Language (ASL)
A method of communicating by using hand signs. Each sign represents either one word or a concept that is typically expressed with several spoken words. For words that do not have a sign, *fingerspelling* is used.

Americans with Disabilities Act (ADA) (Public Law 101–336)
A law that took effect in 1992 which defines "disability" (a substantially limiting physical or mental impairment which affects basic life activities such as hearing, seeing, speaking, walking, caring for oneself, learning, or working) and prohibits discrimination by employers, by "public accommodations" (any facility open to the general public), and by state and local public agencies that provide such services as transportation.

Amino Acids
Chemicals that, when linked together, form proteins essential for growth and health. The body produces some amino acids, which are called nonessential amino acids. Other amino acids, which must be obtained through the diet, are called essential amino acids.

Aminoaciduria (uh-mee-noe-as-i-DYOO-ree-uh)
The excessive excretion of amino acids in the urine, often the result of an inherited metabolic disease. Aminoaciduria results in *failure to thrive* and is not treatable.

Aminophylline (uh-mee-noe-FIL-in)
A *bronchodilator drug*.

Amniocentesis (am-nee-oe-sen-TEE-sis)
A prenatal test in which a needle is inserted into the pregnant woman's abdomen and uterus and amniotic fluid is withdrawn. The fluid is analyzed to detect metabolic and chromosomal disorders, to measure *alpha-fetoprotein* levels, to assess the maturity of the baby's lungs, and to determine the fetus's age and sex.

Amniotic Fluid (am-nee-OT-ik)
The fluid surrounding the fetus in the uterus.

Amoxicillin (uh-moks-i-SIL-in)
A type of penicillin (antibiotic) drug used to treat infections.

Ampicillin (am-pi-SIL-in)
A type of penicillin (antibiotic) drug used to treat infections.

Amplification
The process of increasing or enhancing sound.

Amyotonia (ay-mie-oe-TOE-nee-uh)
A muscle defect characterized by loss of tone, weakness, and wasting due to disease of the nerves that send signals from the brain to the muscles.

an-
A prefix meaning not, without, or lack.

Anabolic Steroid (an-uh-BOL-ik)
Refer to Steroid.

Anaclitic Depression
A disorder in infants that occurs after sudden separation from the mother or primary caregiver, characterized by tension, fear, withdrawal, incessant crying, and sleeping and eating problems.

Anal Atresia
*Refer to **Imperforate Anus**.*

andr-, andro-
Prefixes meaning man or male.

Anemia (uh-NEE-mee-uh)
A condition in which the hemoglobin in the blood is too low. Symptoms of anemia include fatigue, dizziness, headache, pale coloring, and heart palpitations. There are several types and causes of anemia, which, along with the speed of development of the anemia, can affect the severity. The most common type of anemia is caused by iron deficiency.

Anencephaly (an-en-SEF-uh-lee)
A birth defect in which all but the most primitive part of the brain, spinal cord, and overlying bones of the skull are absent, due to failure of the neural tube to close during early fetal development. A baby born with this defect will not survive the newborn period.

Anergy (AN-er-jee)
1. A lack of activity or energy.
2. A condition of the immune system in which the body does not mount a normal sensitivity reaction to a substance that would usually be *allergenic.*

Anesthesia (an-es-THEE-zee-uh)
Medication that causes loss of sensation. Local anesthesia causes loss of feeling, thereby obstructing pain, in the area where it is injected. General anesthesia can be injected into the bloodstream or inhaled prior to surgery, causing lack of consciousness and loss of feeling throughout the body.

Anesthesiologist (an-es-thee-zee-OL-oe-jist)
A doctor trained to administer anesthesia and to assess and monitor the lungs, heart, and circulation before and during surgery.

angi-, angio-
Prefixes meaning vessel.

Angiography (an-jee-OG-ruh-fee)
An X-ray study that involves injecting contrast materials into blood vessels so the vessels may be visualized. A sequence of X-rays is taken to examine the flow of blood within a particular organ.

Angioma (an-jee-OE-muh)
A harmless tumor, usually present at birth, made up mainly of blood vessels or lymph vessels.

Angular Movement
Movement that creates an angle of varying degree. For example, the angle between the upper and lower leg gets bigger or smaller as the leg is straightened or bent at the knee. Angular movement is one of four basic kinds of movement by the joints of the body.
Compare **Circumduction, Gliding,** *and* **Rotation.**

Aniridia (an-i-RID-ee-uh)
Absence of an iris of the eye at birth, resulting in some degree of visual impairment.

Ankle-Foot Orthosis (AFO)
A short leg brace that provides support at the ankle.
Also known as an **Orthotic.**

ankyl-
A prefix meaning crooked or growing together (such as a stiffening or fixation of a joint).

Ankylosis (ang-ki-LOE-sis)
The stiffening of a joint, usually into an abnormal position, resulting in loss of movement in the joint. It is caused by degeneration of the bone, followed by fusion of the two bone surfaces. Ankylosis may result from injury, infection, or inflammation, or it may be the result of *arthrodesis* (a procedure in which the joint is surgically fused).

Annual Goal
A statement of the desired outcome of early intervention services for a specific child and his family. For example, an annual goal might be for the child to develop mobility skills. Annual goals are selected by the child's parents and early intervention multidisciplinary team and are stated on the *Individualized Family Service Plan*. Objectives, which are more specific and measurable, such as "(child's name) will creep forward on his hands and knees for 10 feet" and "will walk forward with both hands held for 15 feet" may also be stated to provide developmentally appropriate activities and measurement of progress toward attainment of the goal.

Annual Review
An annual report describing a child who is at-risk or has disabilities, including his health status, needs, eligibility for early intervention services, current functioning level, family involvement, family financial situation, rights/legal status, involvement with service providers and physicians, assessment of progress toward meeting the goals stated on the *IFSP*, and discussion of any new areas of intervention from which the child would benefit. Usually, the case manager is the professional who completes the annual review.

Anomalous Pulmonary Venous Return (uh-NOM-uh-luhs PUL-moe-ne-ree VEE-nuhs)
*Refer to **Total Anomalous Pulmonary Venous Return**.*

Anomaly (uh-NOM-uh-lee)
A change or deviation from what is considered normal, such as a malformation of part of the body. A missing finger and an extra finger are examples of anomalies.

Anophthalmos (an-of-THAL-mos)
Absence of an eyeball, occurring either as a birth defect or due to surgical removal.

Anorectal (ay-noe-REK-tuhl)
Referring to the anus and rectum.

Anoxia (uh-NOK-see-uh)
A condition in which there is insufficient oxygen to an individual organ or to the whole body. Anoxia can occur when there is a decreased amount of oxygen to the lungs, when the blood is not able to deliver oxygen to body tissues, or when the tissues are not able to absorb the oxygen from the blood. Anoxia can be life-threatening, such as when the brain receives too little oxygen. Anoxia during fetal development can lead to *mental retardation*.

Antagonistic Muscle
A muscle which acts in opposition to the action of another muscle.

ante-
A prefix meaning before.

Antepartum (an-tee-PAR-tuhm)
Before birth.

Anterior
Front.
*Also known as **Ventral**.*
*Compare **Posterior**.*

Anteversion (an-tee-VER-zhun)
The position of an organ or structure that is abnormally tilted forward.

anti-
A prefix meaning against.

Antibacterial Drug (an-ti-bak-TEE-ree-uhl)
A drug used to treat infections caused by bacteria by destroying or suppressing growth of the bacteria.

Antibiotic Drug (an-ti-bie-OT-ik)
A drug that kills organisms (such as bacteria) or halts their growth.

Antibody (AN-ti-bod-ee)
A protein produced by the body which combats *antigens* (such as those found in viruses, bacteria, and other microorganisms).
> *Also known as* **Immunoglobulin.**

Anticholinergic Drug (an-ti-koe-lin-ER-jik)
A drug that blocks the effect of *acetylcholine* and decreases muscle spasms.

Anticonvulsant Drug
> *Refer to* **Antiepileptic Drug.**

Antiepileptic Drug (an-ti-ep-i-LEP-tik)
A drug that prevents or arrests *seizure* activity, or lessens the severity of the seizures. Antiepileptics work by quieting the abnormally high electrical activity in the brain and preventing the spread of the activity to other areas of the brain.
> *Also known as an* **Anticonvulsant Drug.**

Antifungal Drug (an-ti-FUNG-guhl)
A drug used to treat infections caused by fungi such as *candidiasis*. Antifungal drugs destroy or suppress growth of fungi.

Antigen (AN-ti-jen)
A substance that activates the body's immune system to produce an *antibody*.

Antigravity Activity
An activity that requires a baby to resist gravity, such as sitting up.

Antigravity Position
A position that requires a baby to resist gravity, such as an all-fours position (weight on hands and knees), sitting, and standing.

Antihistamine Drug (an-ti-HIS-tuh-meen)
A drug that decreases the effects of histamine, a chemical made by the body. (Histamines can cause symptoms of allergic reactions.)

Antipsychotic Drug (an-ti-sie-KOT-ik)
A drug used to treat symptoms of *psychosis*.

Antispastic Drug
A drug used to reduce *spasticity*.

antr-
A prefix meaning chamber.

Anus (AY-nus)
The opening at the *distal* end of the rectum through which feces are evacuated from the bowel.

Anvil (AN-vil)
Refer to **Incus**.

Aorta (ay-OR-tuh)
The artery that carries oxygenated blood from the left ventricle of the heart to the rest of the body.
Refer to **Circulation**.

Aortic Coarctation (ay-OR-tik koe-ark-TAY-shuhn)
A defect of the heart in which part of the aorta is narrowed or constricted. This circulatory obstruction may cause blood to be diverted through small vessels of the aorta, resulting in higher blood pressure on one side of the defect and lower pressure on the other side. Surgery is required to repair this birth defect.

Aortic Stenosis (ay-OR-tik ste-NOE-sis)
A defect of the heart in which the aortic valve between the left ventricle and the aorta is narrowed, blocking the flow of blood at the left ventricle into the aorta. Aortic stenosis causes the ventricle to work harder to move blood past the blockage and may result in a decreased output of blood from the heart, and lung congestion.

Aortic Valve
One of four valves in the heart that opens and closes with each heart beat to control the flow of blood. Blood exits each chamber of the heart through one of the valves. The aortic valve is located between the left ventricle and the aorta. The three cusps (small flaps) of the aortic valve close during each heart beat to prevent blood from flowing back into the left ventricle from the aorta.
Compare **Mitral Valve**, **Pulmonary Valve**, *and* **Tricuspid Valve**.

ap
The abbreviation for the Latin words meaning before dinner.

Apathy
Indifference.

Apert's Syndrome (uh-PAYRZ)
An *autosomal dominant disorder* characterized by irregular and premature fusion of skull bones, underdevelopment of facial bones, wide-spaced and bulging eyes, fused or *webbed* fingers and toes, and sometimes *mental retardation*.
Also known as **Acrocephalosyndactyly**.

Aperture
An opening or orifice.

Apex
The top or tip of a body structure.

Apgar Score (AP-gar)
The score given to a newborn to determine overall physical condition. The infant is tested at one and five minutes after delivery on the following: color, heart rate, respiratory effort, *muscle tone,* and reflexes. A score of 0 to 2 is given in each of the five categories with a maximum score of 10. An infant with a score of 0 to 3 is considered to be in severe distress and needing resuscitation, a score of 4 to 6 indicates moderate distress, and a score of 7 to 10 is normal, indicating a well baby.
  *Refer to the **Apgar Chart** in the Appendix.*

Aphakia (uh-FAY-kee-uh)
Absence of the lens of the eye, either at birth or due to surgical removal. Extreme farsightedness results without a lens.

Aphasia (uh-FAY-zee-uh)
A communication disorder characterized by difficulty with producing language (expressive aphasia, or Broca's aphasia) and/or with understanding language (receptive aphasia, or Wernicke's aphasia). Aphasia is caused by *brain damage* that may result from lack of oxygen, severe head injury, or a stroke that causes nerve damage.

APIB
The abbreviation for Assessment of Pre-Term Infant Behavior.

Aplastic Anemia (uh-PLAS-tik)
A form of *anemia* characterized by reduced red blood cell, white blood cell, and platelet cell formation caused by damage to the bone marrow. The bone marrow may be damaged during radiation therapy, or when exposed to certain drugs (including anticancer drugs) or poisonous chemicals. Sometimes the cause of aplastic anemia is not known.

Apnea (ap-NEE-uh)
A pause in breathing that lasts 20 seconds or longer.
  *Compare **Periodic Breathing**.*

Apnea Monitor
A monitor that sounds an alarm when an infant has a period of *apnea*. The apnea monitor can be set for any time period, but is usually set at 20 seconds.

apo-
A prefix meaning detached, without, or separation from.

Appendix (uh-PEN-diks)

A projection from the blind end of the *cecum* (a pouch that forms the first portion of the large intestine). The appendix itself has no known function, but it contains lymphoid tissue (tissue resembling *lymph*, a body fluid that plays an important role in the *immune system* and in absorbing fats from the intestine), which provides a defense against local infection.

Applied Behavior Analysis

Refer to Behavior Modification.

Appropriate for Gestational Age (AGA)

Referring to a baby whose birth weight is between the 10th and 90th percentiles for his gestational age.

Also known as Average for Gestational Age.
Compare Small for Gestational Age and Large for Gestational Age.

Apraxia (uh-PRAK-see-uh)

A loss of the ability to perform voluntary, purposeful movements due to damage to the brain (although there is no actual paralysis). Because of this damage, the brain is unable to make the transfer between the idea of movement to an actual physical response. Examples of apraxia include the inability to perform the movements of a command (such as, "clap your hands"), to repeat words correctly, or to demonstrate understanding of the use of an object. The damage to the brain which causes apraxia may result from a head injury, a brain tumor, an infection, or a stroke.

Apraxic

Refer to Apraxia.

Aqueous Humor (AY-kwee-us HYOO-mor)

The fluid produced in the eye.

Arachnoid (uh-RAK-noid)

The middle layer of the meninges (the membranes that surround the brain and spinal cord). The pia mater is the innermost layer and the dura mater is the outermost layer.

Refer to Meninges.

ARC

A national organization formerly known as the Association for Retarded Citizens which provides advocacy services to individuals with mental retardation and their families, and publishes and disseminates information about mental retardation. The ARC has local and state branches throughout the United States.

Arch Insole Pad

A small pad that can be placed in a child's shoe to provide arch support.

Arnold-Chiari Malformation (AR-noelt KEE-a-ree)

A *congenital hernia* of the brain stem and cerebellum that can block the outflow of cerebrospinal fluid from the ventricles of the brain. This defect often occurs with *spina bifida* or other brain and spine disorders.

Arrhythmia (uh-RITH-mee-uh)

Any change in the rhythm or rate of the heart beat. Arrhythmias occur when electrical conduction to or within the heart fails.

Arterial (ar-TEE-ree-uhl)

Pertaining to an artery or to the arteries.

Arterial Blood Gas

A sampling of blood from an artery that is analyzed to determine its oxygen, carbon dioxide, and acid content.

*Also known as an **Arterial Stick**.*

Arterial Catheter/Arterial Line

A *catheter* placed in an artery to provide continuous access to arterial blood so it can be withdrawn for monitoring arterial blood gases and blood pressure. In a newborn, it is usually placed in the umbilical artery, but may be placed in the arm or the foot.

*Refer to **Catheter**.*

Arterial Stick

*Refer to **Arterial Blood Gas**.*

Artery

Any blood vessel that delivers blood from the heart to the rest of the body. There are two types of arteries: systemic arteries, which carry oxygenated blood to all parts of the body except the lungs, and pulmonary arteries, which carry non-oxygenated blood from the heart to the lungs.

arthro-

A prefix meaning joint.

Arthrodesis (ar-throe-DEE-sis)

A surgical procedure in which a joint is fused to correct a bone deformity, to provide support, or to relieve pain.

*Also known as **Joint Fusion** and **Artificial Ankylosis**.*

Arthrogryposis (ar-throe-gri-POE-sis)

A condition in which the infant is born with multiple joint *contractures* due to some interference with fetal movements. It may be caused by a neuromuscular problem, small muscle fibers, or *congenital muscular dystrophy*.

Arthrogryposis Multiplex Congenita

A severe form of *arthrogryposis*. The exact cause is unknown, but may result from changes in the spinal cord, muscle, or connective tissue. In addition to the joint *contractures*, there are other bone and muscle abnormalities. Intelligence is usually unimpaired.

Arthrosis (ar-THROE-sis)

A joint.

Articular

Pertaining to a joint.

Articulation

1. The ability to produce and connect vowel and consonant sounds. This ability is based on the coordination of movements of the lips, tongue, palate, and jaw and the manner in which they modify the air stream into meaningful speech sounds.
2. A joint, or the site of the junction between two or more bones.

Articulation Disorder

A speech disorder in which speech sounds are omitted or produced incorrectly. An articulation disorder may be caused by a structural defect such as *cleft lip* or *cleft palate*, hearing loss, weakness or lack of coordination of the oral musculature, or language delay.
Compare *Language Disorder*.

Artificial Ankylosis

*Refer to **Arthrodesis**.*

Artificial Respiration

The process of breathing for a child either by mechanical means (a *ventilator*) or by mouth-to-mouth or mouth-to-nose resuscitation when the child is unable to breathe on his own.

AS

The abbreviation for the Latin words meaning left ear.

ASD

The abbreviation for Atrial Septal Defect.

-ase

A suffix meaning *enzyme*.

ASL

The abbreviation for American Sign Language.

Asphyxia (as-FIK-see-uh)

Improper exchange of oxygen and carbon dioxide, resulting in blood with too little oxygen and too much carbon dioxide, and possibly *brain damage*

and death. Asphyxia can be caused by many things, including the stress of labor on an infant, drowning, aspirating vomit, or an airway obstruction.
Also known as **Suffocation.**

Asphyxiation
Refer to **Asphyxia.**

Aspiration (as-pi-RAY-shuhn)
1. The act of inhaling.
2. Breathing a foreign material, such as *meconium,* food, or vomit, into the lungs (which may cause aspiration pneumonia).
3. Withdrawing blood, mucus, or gases from the body by suctioning.

Aspiration Pneumonia
Inflammation of the lungs caused by inhaling a foreign material.

Assessment
Identification of the needs and strengths of the infant/child who is at-risk or has developmental delays, as well as those of his family. Assessment may include both formal and informal procedures to appraise the child's abilities in all areas of development.
Also known as an **Evaluation.**

Assessment in Infancy Ordinal Scales of Psychological Development
An evaluation tool used to measure cognition in infants between one month and two years of age. This test is based on Piaget's stages of cognitive development.
Formerly known as the **Ordinal Scales of Infant Development.**

Assessment of Pre-Term Infant Behavior (APIB)
An assessment (adapted from the "Brazelton Neonatal Assessment Scale") used to evaluate the behaviors of the premature infant. The aim of the APIB is to provide an overall description of the baby, with less emphasis on a score.

Assimilation
1. The process of absorbing and incorporating new concepts or experiences into one's consciousness.
2. The bodily process of metabolizing nutrients constructively.
Refer to **Nutrition.**

Associated Reactions
Increased muscle tension resulting in abnormal patterns of movement or posture in various parts of the body due to movement in other body parts. For example, when the child whose legs are affected by cerebral palsy attempts to maintain a sitting position, the muscle tension in his arms may increase (even though his arms do not usually appear to have increased tone).

Association for Retarded Citizens
The organization now known as the *ARC*.

Asthma (AZ-muh)
A chronic respiratory disorder characterized by coughing, wheezing, and difficult breathing due to bronchospasm (abnormal contraction of the bronchi resulting in temporarily narrowed airways). Asthmatic attacks may be caused by infection, inhaling *allergens* or irritating airborne substances, or exercise, but sometimes it is difficult to determine what triggers a particular attack.

Astigmatism (uh-STIG-muh-tizm)
Defective curvature of the cornea or lens of the eye. Astigmatism is a common condition that causes blurred vision and can usually be corrected with eyeglasses.

Asymmetric
Not equal on both sides.

Asymmetrical (ay-sim-MET-ri-kuhl)
Referring to parts of the body that are unequal in size or shape, or that are different in arrangement or movement patterns.
   Compare **Symmetrical**.

Asymmetrical Tonic Neck Reflex (ATNR)
A normal reflex in infants up to six months in which turning the head to one side causes the arm and leg on that side to extend and the opposite arm and leg to flex.
   Compare **Symmetrical Tonic Neck Reflex**.
   Refer to **Primitive Reflex**.

Asymptomatic (ay-simp-toe-MAT-ik)
Without symptoms.

Ataxia (uh-TAK-see-uh)
Difficulty with coordinating muscles in voluntary movement that may be caused by damage to the brain or spinal cord. The damage may be the result of a *congenital* disorder, birth trauma, infection, tumor, toxin, or head injury. Ataxia may be associated with *extrapyramidal cerebral palsy* and may cause the child to have difficulty with maintaining balance.

Ataxia-Telangiectasia (uh-TAK-see-uh tel-an-jee-ek-TAY-zee-uh)
An *autosomal recessive disorder* characterized by progressive *ataxia* and *choreoathetosis*; dilated capillaries visible on the whites of the eyes, the ears, the face, the neck, and the extremities; and a poorly functioning immune system. Permanent lung damage and respiratory failure can result if the immune system is not able to resist infection.

Atelectasis (at-ee-LEK-ta-sis)

A condition in which part or all of the lungs is collapsed. Babies born prematurely sometimes experience this condition if their lungs do not expand completely at birth. Atelectasis may be difficult to differentiate from pneumonia on a chest X-ray.

Athetoid Movements (ATH-e-toid)

Refer to Athetosis.

Athetosis (ath-e-TOE-sis)

Slow, involuntary, writhing movements, particularly of the wrist, fingers, face, and occasionally the feet and toes, caused by injury to the nerves supplying the muscles or by damage to the brain, as in some types of cerebral palsy.

Also known as Athetoid Movements.

Atlantoaxial Subluxation (at-lan-toe-AK-see-uhl sub-luks-AY-shuhn)

Partial dislocation of the joint between the first two vertebrae in the neck (the atlas and the axis). It is particularly common in children with *Down syndrome.* It may lead to compression of the spinal cord and, in rare cases, death.

Atlas

The first vertebra lying just beneath the skull. It articulates with the occipital bone of the skull and the axis (the second vertebra in the neck).

ATNR

The abbreviation for Asymmetrical Tonic Neck Reflex.

Atonic (uh-TON-ik)

Lacking *muscle tone.*

Atonic Cerebral Palsy

A form of *extrapyramidal cerebral palsy* characterized by floppy *muscle tone.* Atonic cerebral palsy results when there is damage to the nerve pathways that transmit impulses for controlling movement and maintaining posture from the brain to the spinal cord.

Refer to Extrapyramidal Cerebral Palsy.

Atonic Seizure

A generalized *seizure* characterized by a sudden loss of normal *muscle tone* that causes the child to fall. Consciousness is usually lost. An atonic seizure is similar to an akinetic seizure, and the two names are often used interchangeably.

Also known as a Drop Seizure or Drop Attack.
Refer to Epilepsy.

Atony (AT-oe-nee)
A lack of normal *muscle tone* or strength.

Atresia (uh-TREE-zhuh)
A defect in which a normal body opening (such as the ear canal or anus) fails to form or closes prenatally.

Atresia Choanae (uh-TREE-zhuh KOE-uh-nay)
*Refer to **Choanal Atresis**.*

Atria (AY-tree-uh)
Plural of atrium.

Atrial Septal Defect *(ASD)* (AY-tree-uhl SEP-tuhl)
A form of *congenital* heart disease in which there is a hole in the atrial wall that allows blood to pass from the left atrium to the right atrium. The blood passage that occurs with this malformation enlarges the right atrium, the right ventricle, and the pulmonary artery.

Atrioventricular Canal (ay-tree-oe-ven-TRIK-yoo-luhr)
A complex heart defect involving holes between the right and left atria and the right and left ventricles. Sometimes a baby is also born with a defect of the mitral valve (the valve between the left atrium and the left ventricle). This defect occurs frequently in children with *Down syndrome*. The atrioventricular canal is the most severe form of *endocardial cushion defect*.
*Refer to **Endocardial Cushion Defect**.*

At-Risk
Referring to an infant who needs *early intervention* services to prevent or halt illness, delayed development, or death. A baby may be at-risk due to biological factors (such as a *genetic* disorder), environmental factors (such as *prenatal exposure to drugs*, an unstable home environment, or lack of adequate physical care as an infant or young child), or a premature birth.

Atrium (AY-tree-uhm)
A body chamber, such as the atria of the heart.

Atrophy (AT-ruh-fee)
Wasting away of a tissue or organ. Either the number of cells in the body part decreases, or the size of the cells is reduced. Atrophy is often caused by disease, inadequate blood circulation, or lack of physical exercise.

Attend
*Refer to **Attention Span**.*

Attention Deficit Disorder (ADD)
A group of symptoms believed to be caused by slight abnormalities in the brain. These symptoms include a developmentally inappropriate lack of

ability to attend (such as difficulty with listening to and following directions), and possibly impulsivity, distractibility, and clumsiness. Hyperactivity is not a feature.

Compare Attention Deficit Hyperactivity Disorder.

Attention Deficit Hyperactivity Disorder (ADHD)

A group of symptoms believed to be caused by slight abnormalities in the brain. These symptoms include a developmentally inappropriate lack of ability to attend (such as difficulty with listening to and following directions), impulsivity, distractibility, clumsiness, and *hyperactivity*. ADHD occurs in as many as three percent of children, with onset prior to four years of age in fifty percent of cases.

Compare Attention Deficit Disorder.

Attention Span

The length of time a child is able to concentrate on an activity.

Also known as the ability to Attend.

Attenuation

The process of reducing the strength or effect of a virus or bacteria.

Atypical (ay-TIP-i-kuhl)

Unusual or abnormal.

AU

The abbreviation for the Latin words meaning both ears.

Audiogram (AW-dee-oe-gram)

The results of hearing tests, as described on a graph. The audiogram records the child's ability to hear sounds of varying frequency (pitch) and intensity (loudness) in each ear. Sound frequency that is measured ranges from 125 Hz (a low-pitched sound) to 8000 Hz (a high-pitched sound). Sound intensity that is examined ranges from quiet 10 decibel sounds to loud 120 decibel sounds. The audiogram may also record the results of an examination of bone conduction and the child's ability to respond to increasingly loud sounds.

Refer to Hearing.

Audiologist (aw-dee-OL-oe-jist)

A specialist who determines the presence and type of hearing impairment. An audiologist conducts hearing tests and makes recommendations for hearing aids.

Audiology (aw-dee-OL-oe-jee)

The study of hearing and hearing disorders.

Audiometric Testing (aw-dee-oe-MET-rik)

Tests to measure the ability in each ear to hear sounds of varying frequency (pitch) and intensity (loudness), thereby revealing any hearing impairment. Results are then recorded on an *audiogram*.

Also known as **Audiometry**.

Audiometry (aw-dee-OM-uh-tree)

Refer to **Audiometric Testing**.

Auditory (AW-di-toe-ree)

Pertaining to the sense of hearing.

Auditory Brain Stem Response (ABR)

Refer to **Auditory Evoked Response**.

Auditory Canal

The ear canal leading from outside the ear inward to the eardrum. (This is actually the external auditory canal. There is also an internal auditory canal from the opening of the inner ear to the cochlea.)

Refer to **Ear**.

Auditory Discrimination

The ability to detect differences in sounds, including subtle differences between sounds in words, such as /b/ and /p/ or /d/ and /t/.

Auditory Evoked Potential (AEP)

Refer to **Auditory Evoked Response**.

Auditory Evoked Response (AER)

A test that measures the rate of electrical conductivity along the auditory nerve as sound impulses are carried to the brain. A slower rate of brain wave activity may indicate a hearing impairment. This test can be used with newborns since the baby does not need to voluntarily respond to sounds.

Also known as **Auditory Evoked Potential**, **Auditory Brain Stem Response**, **Evoked Response Audiometry**, **Brain Stem Auditory Evoked Response**, **Brain Stem Evoked Response**, *and* **Brain Stem Evoked Response Audiometry**.

Auditory Impairment

Hearing loss, resulting from problems in any part of the ear or of the hearing center of the brain. Auditory impairment refers to a decrease in the range of perception of loudness and/or pitch. Hearing loss (or deafness) may be a birth defect, or it may be caused by disease or injury.

Refer to **Conductive Hearing Loss, Sensorineural Hearing Loss, Mixed Hearing Loss,** *and* **Deafness**.

Auditory Learner
A child who learns best by hearing rather than through other senses such as vision. For example, singing songs in which parts of the body are named and identified may be useful when teaching the auditory learner about body parts.

Auditory Nerve
The nerve that transmits sound impulses from each inner ear to the brain. It consists of cochlear (hearing) nerve fibers and vestibular (balance) nerve fibers.
> Also known as the **Acoustic Nerve** and the **Vestibulocochlear Nerve**.
> Refer to **Ear**.

Auditory Ossicles
The three small bones of the middle ear: the malleus, incus, and stapes. They bridge the gap between the eardrum and the inner ear.

Augmentative Communication
Any method of communicating without speech, such as by using signs, gestures, picture boards, or electronic or non-electronic devices. These methods can help children who are unable to use speech or who need to supplement their speech to communicate effectively.

Augmentin™
An *antibiotic drug* containing amoxicillin.

Aura (OR-uh or AW-ruh)
A "warning" feeling, such as a sensation of movement, light, or warmth, that some children feel just before a seizure. It is similar to a feeling of "deja vu."

auri-
A prefix meaning ear.

Auricle (AW-ri-kl)
> Refer to **Pinna**.

Auscultation (aws-kul-TAY-shuhn)
Listening to sounds in the chest, abdomen, etc., through a stethoscope to assess the condition of the body systems, such as the heart and lungs.

Autism (AW-tizm)
A developmental disorder characterized by disturbances of social, language, and thinking skills. A child with autism may exhibit the following symptoms: avoidance of interactions with others, receptive and expressive language problems, extreme resistance to change, and repetitive, self-stimulatory behavior (self-stimulation). The features of autism are usually apparent by 30 months of age. Autism appears to result from *brain damage*

and may be associated with other disorders, such as *fragile X syndrome*. It is important to note that some children with *mental retardation*, fragile X syndrome, psychiatric disorders, sensory deficits (such as vision or hearing impairment), and some rare neurological diseases exhibit autistic-like characteristics, but are not autistic.

Also known as **Infantile Autism** *and* **Kanner's Syndrome.**
Compare **Pervasive Developmental Disorder.**

auto-
A prefix meaning self.

Automatic Movement Reaction
Refer to **Automatic Reflex.**

Automatic Reflex
One of several involuntary reflexes that develop during the first two years of life and which develop as the *primitive reflexes* are suppressed. The automatic reflexes are necessary postural responses in the infant as he begins to assume new positions, such as sitting, and as he begins to crawl. The main automatic reflexes are righting reactions, which allow the infant to maintain an upright position (for example, the head righting reflex in which the infant holds his head upright even when his body is tilted); equilibrium reactions, which help the infant maintain balance (for example, the balance reaction of extending the arms when balance has been lost); and protective reactions, which protect the infant during a fall (for example, the parachute reflex in which the arms and legs extend to protect the head and body from a fall). Automatic reflexes remain throughout one's lifetime.

Also known as **Automatic Movement Reaction** *and* **Postural Reaction.**
Compare **Primitive Reflex.**

Automatism (aw-TOM-uh-tizm)
Behaviors that occur without conscious volition. These abnormal behaviors look purposeful, although the child is not controlling the behavior on a conscious level. Automatisms are most commonly symptoms of psychomotor *epilepsy*, although they may occur with other conditions, such as certain brain disorders or drug intoxication. Examples of automatisms include making chewing motions or manipulating the buttons on a shirt.

Autonomic Seizure (aw-toe-NOM-ik)
A type of *partial seizure* characterized by a rapid heart beat, anxiety or fear, paleness, sweating, or dilation of the pupils.
Refer to **Partial Seizure** *and* **Epilepsy.**

Autonomy (aw-TON-oe-mee)
The ability to function independently.

Autosomal Dominant Disorder (aw-toe-SOE-muhl)

A *genetic* disorder that a child inherits (via a defective *gene*) from one of his parents, who also has the autosomal dominant disorder. (A single defective gene is all that is necessary to pass on the disorder.) The term "dominant" means that the defective gene of the gene pair (inherited from either the mother or the father) is able to override the normal gene. Each child born to a parent who has an autosomal dominant disorder has a 50 percent chance of inheriting the disorder and, if inherited, a 50 percent chance of passing it on to offspring. (However, if the parent has two defective genes, the child has a 100 percent chance of inheriting the disorder.) Another way a child can be affected by an autosomal dominant disorder is if the defective gene develops as the result of a *mutation* (a change in genetic information that occurs during early cell division). *Achondroplasia* is an example of an autosomal dominant disorder.

Compare **Autosomal Recessive Disorder.**

Autosomal Recessive Disorder

A *genetic* disorder that occurs when the child inherits two defective *genes*, one from each parent. (Either each parent is a *carrier* of the defective gene that causes the disorder, or one parent is a carrier and the other parent has the autosomal recessive disorder.) The term "recessive" means that the defective gene of the parent's gene pair is hidden by the normal gene. When parents who are carriers for the same disorder have children, each child born will have a 25 percent chance of having the disorder (if each parent's defective gene is inherited), a 50 percent chance of being a carrier (if one parent's defective gene and the other parent's normal gene is inherited), and a 25 percent chance that the gene pair will be normal (if each parent's normal gene is inherited). When one parent has the autosomal recessive disorder and the other parent is a carrier, the offspring have a 50 percent chance of having the disorder and a 50 percent chance of being a carrier. If a child inherits only one defective gene (rather than one from each parent), he is known as a carrier. Carriers do not have the disorder but can pass it on to offspring. *Tay-Sachs disease* is an example of an autosomal recessive disorder.

Compare **Autosomal Dominant Disorder.**

Autosomes (AW-toe-soemz)

The 22 (of the 23) pairs of *chromosomes*, not including the pair of sex chromosomes.

Average for Gestational Age (AGA)

*Refer to **Appropriate for Gestational Age.***

Aversive (uh-VUR-siv)

Referring to an avoidance behavior or an unpleasant stimulus that causes avoidance behavior. For example, an aversive such as a medication that induces vomiting might be paired with drinking alcohol in order to eliminate the drinking.

Axilla (ak-SIL-uh)
The armpit.

Axillary (AK-si-layr-ee)
Referring to the armpit.

Axillary Temperature
The temperature reading when the thermometer is placed under the arm. It runs approximately one degree lower than the oral temperature.

Axis
The second vertebra in the neck, lying just below the atlas, or first cervical vertebra.

B

Babbling

Infant vocal play characterized by repetition of consonant-vowel combinations, such as "ba," "ma," or "da." Initially, babbling is non-specific in that the sounds do not have attached meaning. Later the infant babbles with more specific intent and the babbling begins to sound similar to actual speech and varies in intonation like adult speech patterns. Babbling typically begins by six months of age.

Compare **Cooing**, **Jabbering**, *and* **Jargon**.

Babinski's Sign (Reflex, Response) (buh-BIN-skeez)

A response that consists of extension of the big toe and is usually associated with fanning of the other toes. It is elicited when the outer side of the bottom of the foot is stroked from the heel to the ball of the foot. In the child under 12 months, a Babinski response can be normal. In an older child or an adult, this response (Babinski's sign) may indicate brain injury. (The normal response, i.e., a negative Babinski, in an older child or an adult would be for the toes to bend downward.)

Refer to **Primitive Reflex**.

Baby Bird™

A type of *ventilator* used with infants.

Baby Teeth

Refer to **Primary Teeth**.

Backknee

Refer to **Genu Recurvatum**.

Backward Chaining

Teaching the steps of a skill backwards, beginning with the last step. For example, in learning to wash her hands, the child turns off the faucet after it's already been turned on and she's had her hands lathered and rinsed. After she has mastered turning off the faucet she can begin practicing rinsing. This moves the child toward independent completion of the entire task while allowing her to "finish" the task from the very beginning.

Compare **Forward Chaining**.

Baclofen (BAK-loe-fen)

An *antispastic drug* used to relax *hypertonic* muscles.

Bacteria (bak-TEER-ee-uh)
One-celled *microorganisms* that can cause infection.
> *Also known as* **Germs**.
> *Compare* **Virus**.

Bacterium
Singular for bacteria.

BAER Test
The abbreviation for Brain Stem Auditory Evoked Response.
> *Refer to* **Auditory Evoked Response**.

Bag and Mask
> *Refer to* **Bagging**.

Bagging
A method of giving *artificial respiration* in which air and/or oxygen is pumped into a baby's lungs by compressing a bag attached to a mask that covers the baby's nose and mouth.
> *Also known as* **Bag and Mask**.

Balance
The ability to assume and maintain upright body position while sitting, standing, or moving.

Balance Reaction
An automatic response that occurs when balance has been lost in which the arms quickly extend in an attempt to regain upright balance.
> *Refer to* **Automatic Reflex**.

Band
A bundle of fibers (such as an *adhesion*) that binds two parts of the body together, or that encircles a body structure.

Bardet-Biedl Syndrome (bar-DAY BEE-duhl)
> *Refer to* **Laurence-Moon-Biedl Syndrome**.

Barium Enema (BA-ree-uhm)
A procedure in which barium (a chalky contrast material) is administered into the rectum and X-ray pictures are taken as it passes through the large intestine. The barium enema is performed to examine the colon and to diagnose the cause of abnormalities such as rectal bleeding or persistent diarrhea and diseases such as tumors of the colon and *celiac disease*.

Barium Swallow
A procedure in which barium (a chalky contrast material) is swallowed and X-ray pictures are taken as it passes through the esophagus. In variations of the barium swallow (the barium meal and the barium follow-through), the

barium is observed as it passes through the stomach and small intestine. The barium swallow is performed to diagnose the cause of pain or difficulty in swallowing and disorders such as narrowing of the esophagus.

Basal (BAY-suhl or BAY-zuhl)

Referring to the fundamental or base. On an evaluation tool, basal refers to the highest test item passed before the child fails an item. (The child may have other "passed" items later in the test, as well.)

Compare Ceiling.

Basal Ganglia

The interconnected gray masses within the cerebral hemispheres and the brain stem that are involved in motor coordination.

Baseline

Referring to the level at which a child performs before training or intervention.

Also known as Operant Level.

Bath Seat

A special seat placed in the bathtub that secures the child while being given a bath. There are several types of bath seats, each designed to position the child according to her abilities (i.e., sitting independently, maintaining head control, etc.).

Batten Disease

An *autosomal recessive disorder* in which the child develops normally until six months to two years of age, when progressive brain disease becomes apparent. Batten Disease is characterized by *seizures*, *mental retardation*, and blindness, and is fatal. With early onset, the disease usually progresses more quickly.

Also known as Ceroid Lipofuscinosis.

Bayley Scales of Infant Development-II (BSID-II)

A standardized test used to assess the mental, motor, and behavioral development of infants between one and 42 months of age. It consists of three sections, the Mental Scale (the score in this section is called the Mental Development Index, or MDI), the Motor Scale (the score in this section is called the Psychomotor Development Index, or PDI), and the Behavior Rating Scale or BRS. Training on how to administer the Bayley is required. Typically, the Bayley is administered by a professional who holds a Ph.D. in psychology or education.

Bear Walk

A form of locomotion in which the child "walks" on the hands and feet on the floor.

Becker Muscular Dystrophy
A form of *muscular dystrophy* that is milder and develops more slowly than other muscular dystrophies. (Children usually can maintain the ability to walk into adolescence or young adulthood.) Becker Muscular Dystrophy is an *X-linked recessive* disease that starts between eight and 30 years of age.
*Refer to **Muscular Dystrophy**.*

Beckwith-Weidemann Syndrome
A disorder characterized by low blood sugar, overproduction of *insulin*, a large tongue and body, *omphalocele* (intestinal protrusion through an opening in the abdominal wall), and occasional mild to moderate *mental retardation*.

Behavioral Assessment
Gathering (through direct observation and by parent report) and analyzing information about a child's behaviors. The information may be used to plan ways to help the child change unwanted behaviors. When a behavior occurs, as well as the frequency and duration of the behavior, are variables which are noted.

Behavior Modification
A method of controlling behavior by its consequences. A consistent response (of reinforcement of the appropriate behavior or discouragement of the inappropriate behavior) is necessary. For example, behavior modification is being used when the child is told what is expected (such as to sit on her chair while a story is read aloud) and then rewarded (such as with praise or a sticker) when she has behaved according to the expectation.
*Also known as **Applied Behavior Analysis**.*

Behavior Rating Scale (BRS)
A section of the Bayley Scales of Infant Development-II. The BRS is comprised of a Total Scale, and Four Factors: Orientation/Engagement, Attention, Motor Quality, and Emotional Regulation.

Belly Crawl
*Refer to **Crawl**.*

Benadryl™ (BEN-uh-dril)
*Refer to **Diphenhydramine**.*

Benign (bi-NINE)
Referring to a condition that is not harmful or a threat to health.
*Compare **Malignancy**.*

Benzodiazepine (ben-zoe-die-AZ-e-peen)
A *tranquilizer drug* that is also used as an *antiepileptic drug*.

Beta-Adrenergic Drug (BAY-tuh ad-ren-ER-jik)
A drug that may be used to try to stop labor.
Also known as a **Betamimetic Drug** *or a* **Betasympathomimetic Drug**.

Betamethasone (bay-tuh-METH-uh-sone)
A *corticosteroid drug* given to a pregnant woman before delivering prematurely to help the baby's lungs mature and to decrease the chance of the baby developing *respiratory distress syndrome*.

Betamimetic
Refer to **Beta-Adrenergic Drug**.

Betasympathomimetic
Refer to **Beta-Adrenergic Drug**.

bi-
A prefix meaning two.

Bicarbonate (bie-KAR-boe-nayt)
Refer to **Sodium Bicarbonate**.

Bicuspid Valve
Refer to **Mitral Valve**.

bid
The abbreviation for the Latin words meaning twice a day.

Bilabial (bie-LAY-bee-uhl)
Pertaining to both lips.

Bilabial Closure
Bringing the lips together, closing the mouth.

Bilabial Speech Sound
A consonant sound produced by specific movement or positioning of the two lips, such as the /p/ sound when a stream of air is released or the /b/ sound when voice is added.

Bilateral (bie-LAT-er-uhl)
Pertaining to, affecting, or relating to two sides of the body (such as a two-handed reach or both ears).

Bilateral Hearing Impairment
Hearing impairment in both ears.
Refer to **Auditory Impairment**.

Bile
A substance secreted by the liver that removes waste products from the liver and helps break down fats.

Bililights (BIL-i-lites)

Bright fluorescent lights used to treat jaundice.
Also known as **Phototherapy** *or* **Bilirubin Lights**.

Bilirubin (bil-i-ROO-bin)

A pigment by-product of the breakdown of red blood cells that causes the baby's skin to become yellow, or *jaundiced*. A very high level of bilirubin can cause *kernicterus*, which results in *brain damage* and, if untreated, death.

Bilirubin Lights

Refer to **Bililights**.

Binocular Vision (bi-NOK-yuh-luhr)

Normal two-eyed sight that produces a single three-dimensional image.

Biopsy (BIE-op-see)

A procedure to remove living tissue from the body for microscopic examination and to determine a diagnosis.

Birth Defect

A problem present at birth, such as *congenital heart disease* or *cleft palate*. Birth defects can be *inherited* (genetic), occur due to a factor of the pregnancy (such as maternal illness, drug use, X-ray, or physical factors in the uterus), result from a *chromosomal abnormality*, or occur during childbirth.
Also known as a **Congenital Anomaly** *or a* **Congenital Defect**.

Birth Length

The length of an infant at birth. 50 centimeters (about 20 inches) is the average birth length.

Birth Weight

The weight of an infant at birth. 3500 grams (about seven and one-half pounds) is the average birth weight. A baby weighing less than 2500 grams (five and one-half pounds) is considered to be a *low birth-weight* baby.

Bisacodyl (bis-AK-oe-dil)

A laxative drug that stimulates the intestine.

Bite Reflex

Jaw closure when the gums or teeth are stimulated. This reflex is noted in the one- to eight-month-old.
Refer to **Primitive Reflex**.

Bivalved Cast

A removable cast used to correct foot, wrist, or elbow positioning.

Bladder

The organ located in the center of the lower abdomen that functions as a reservoir for urine. It receives urine from the kidneys through the ureters, then passes urine from the body through the urethra.

Bladder Tap

A procedure to withdraw urine by inserting a sterile needle through the abdomen and into the bladder. Urine obtained in this manner (as opposed to normal voiding) is sterile, and can be examined to see if infection exists.

Blalock-Taussig Shunt (BLAY-lok TAH-sig)

An operation performed on the heart in which two arteries are joined to allow more blood to flow to the lungs. This procedure manages one of the four heart defects of *tetralogy of Fallot* until permanent correction can be done.

Blanket Swinging

An activity (similar to swinging in a hammock) for *vestibular stimulation*.

blast-, blasto-

Prefixes meaning bud or embryonic form.

Blindness

A lack or loss of vision due to damage to the organs of vision or to the vision centers of the brain. A child is considered legally blind if she has corrected *visual acuity* of 20/200 (she can at best see at 20 feet what ordinarily can be seen at 200 feet) or less in the better eye, or a *visual field* of no more than 20 degrees in the better eye.

Blinking Reflex

A normal lifetime response of blinking at a bright light or object that shines on or approaches the eye.
    Refer to **Automatic Reflex**.

Blood Count

    Refer to **Complete Blood Count**.

Blood Gas

The partial pressure of gases (oxygen and carbon dioxide) in the blood.

Blood Gas Determination

A test to measure the oxygen, carbon dioxide, and acid content of the blood. These measurements reflect changes in blood chemistry which indicate the severity of respiratory illness.

Blood Group or Type

A classification of blood according to the presence or absence of specific substances (proteins) on the surface of the red blood cell. Each person is either type O, A, B, or AB, and Rh positive or Rh negative (determined by the presence or absence of the *Rh factor*). There are many other less commonly used blood groups as well.

Blood Pressure
The pressure exerted on the walls of the arteries caused by the flow of blood. The blood pressure measurement consists of two numbers. The systolic pressure (top number) is the measurement of the pressure exerted when the heart muscle contracts and blood surges to the body. The diastolic pressure (lower number) is the measurement of the pressure exerted when the ventricles relax between heart beats when the pumping chambers are filling. Blood pressure reflects the elasticity of the blood vessels.

Blood Sugar
A substance in the blood that is necessary for metabolism. Glucose, fructose, and galactose are blood sugars. However, when measured, blood sugar usually refers to glucose in the blood. Both high and low levels of glucose in the blood are associated with certain diseases. For example, increased glucose concentration is associated with *diabetes mellitus* and *hyperthyroidism*. Decreased glucose concentration is associated with *hypothyroidism* and *muscular dystrophy*.

Blood Urea Nitrogen (BUN)
The amount of nitrogen in the blood in the form of *urea* (bodily waste product). Testing BUN levels provides information about kidney function and possibly nutritional status.

BNAS
The abbreviation for Brazelton Neonatal Assessment Scale.

Bobath Therapy
A treatment philosophy designed by Karl and Berta Bobath that is used by physical therapists.
Refer to **Neurodevelopmental Treatment**.

Body Homeostasis
Refer to **Homeostasis**.

Body Image
One's concept of her own body, specifically her physical attributes. This mental picture of one's appearance may be based upon self-observation, develop from others' reactions, or reflect one's experiences. One's body image may or may not be realistic.

Body Measurements
An infant's height, weight, head, and chest measurements.

Body Shell
A *thoraco-lumbar-sacral orthosis* that is worn to treat a progressive spinal defect such as neuromuscular *scoliosis*.

Bolster
Refer to **Roll.**

Bolus (BOE-lus)
A lump of chewed food or medication that is ready for swallowing.
An amount of IV fluid or IV medication that is given all at once.

Bonding
The process by which parents (or primary caregiver) and baby become emotionally attached.

Bone Graft
Transplantation of a section of bone from one area of the body to another.

Bone Marrow
The soft tissue located within bone shafts that is concerned with production of blood cells and hemoglobin.

Bossing
1. A rounded projection, such as on the surface of a bone.
2. A prominence of the forehead.

Bouncing
A technique for providing *proprioceptive* and *vestibular* input, and for increasing *muscle tone*. The child is gently bounced while seated on the adult's lap or on an inflated pillow or beach ball. The child must have adequate head control or support, and be positioned with proper body alignment.

Bowleg (BOE-leg)
Refer to *Genu Varum*.

BP
The abbreviation for blood pressure.

BPD
The abbreviation for bronchopulmonary dysplasia.

Brace
A device used to support a part of the body and hold it in position. Wearing a brace can enable the supported body part to function, such as making standing and walking possible, and can prevent *contractures* or deformities. A brace is one kind of an *orthotic*.

brachi- (BRAYK-ee)
A prefix meaning arm.

Brachial (BRAY-kee-uhl)
Referring to the arm.

Brachial Artery
The principal artery of the upper arm.

Brachial Plexus
A group of nerves that pass from the upper spine and neck down the arm.

brachy- (BRAYK-ee)
A prefix meaning short.

brady- (BRAYD-ee)
A prefix meaning slow.

Bradycardia (brayd-ee-KAR-dee-uh)
A steady but slower than normal heartbeat rate. In a newborn, bradycardia is a heartbeat rate below 100 beats per minute.

Brain
The organ of nerve tissue located within the cranium that controls the activity of the nerves, and regulates the function of many processes, including sensory, reflexive, motor, cognitive, and communication. The main parts of the brain include the *cerebrum*, the *cerebellum*, *midbrain*, *pons*, and the *medulla oblongata*.

Brain Bleed
Refer to **Intraventricular Hemorrhage**.

Brain Damage
Injury to the brain that can be caused by *anoxia*, *hypoxia*, *inborn errors of metabolism*, infection, problems during pregnancy or delivery, head injury, *stroke*, a brain tumor, or *status epilepticus*. Brain damage may result in a lack or loss of cognitive abilities; *epilepsy*; motor, language, or sensory deficits; or *hydrocephalus*.

Brain Death
An absence of brain function (electrical impulses from the brain) resulting in irreversible unconsciousness.

Brain Dysfunction
Refer to **Brain Damage**.

Brain Imaging Techniques
Procedures that produce pictures of the brain, such as *X-ray*, *Computerized Tomography (CT) Scanning*, *Magnetic Resonance Imaging (MRI)*, *Ultrasonography*, *Brain Mapping*, and *Positron Emission Tomography (PET)*.

Brain Injury
*Refer to **Brain Damage**.*

Brain Mapping
A procedure that produces a picture of the brain which distinguishes abnormalities from healthy areas. Brain mapping consists of computerized analysis of EEG (*electroencephalogram*) signals.

Brain Stem
The part of the brain that connects the cerebral hemispheres with the spinal cord. The parts of the brain stem are the *midbrain* (or mesencephalon), *pons,* and the *medulla oblongata.* The brain stem controls basic body functions such as breathing and blood pressure, and contains nerves which control sensory, reflex, and motor functions. The brain stem functions on a reflexive level.

Brain Stem Auditory Evoked Response (BAER)
*Refer to **Auditory Evoked Response**.*

Brain Stem Evoked Response (BSER)
*Refer to **Auditory Evoked Response**.*

Brain Stem Evoked Response Audiometry (BSERA)
*Refer to **Auditory Evoked Response**.*

Brain Wave
The pattern of electrical impulses activated by *neurotransmitters* as they move from one brain cell to the next. Brain waves are detectable by *electroencephalograph*.

Branched-Chain Ketoaciduria (kee-toe-as-i-DYOO-ree-uh)
An *autosomal recessive disorder* in which an infant is unable to metabolize three *amino acids*: valine, leucine, and isoleucine. (This causes the urine to smell like maple syrup.) Without early diagnosis and treatment (restricting dietary intake of the listed amino acids), this disorder will result in *mental retardation* or death.
*Also known as **Maple Syrup Urine Disease**.*

Brazelton Neonatal Assessment Scale (BNAS)
A test used to evaluate the newborn's reflexes, behavior, and interactions with her environment. The infant is observed for her responses to various tasks as she makes the transition from sleep to alert states. Although a score is determined, the aim of the assessment is to provide an overall description of the baby. The pediatrician typically administers the BNAS.

Breech Delivery
*Refer to **Breech Presentation**.*

Breech Presentation
Birth (delivery) of a baby with the buttocks, knees, or feet appearing first in the pelvis.
Refer to Fetal Presentation.

Brethine™ (breth-EEN)
Refer to Terbutaline.

Brigance Diagnostic Inventory of Early Development
A *criterion-referenced test* used to evaluate the *psychomotor*, self-help, speech and language, cognition, and early academic skills of infants and children from birth to six years of age. The results of the Brigance are expressed as the child's *developmental age*. The Brigance is also a curriculum tool. Both professionals and para-professionals may administer the Brigance.

Broca's Aphasia (BROE-kuhz)
Refer to Aphasia.

Bronchi (BRONG-kie)
The main tubes that lead from the trachea to the bronchioles. Air travels in and out of the lungs through the main and the smaller bronchi.
Refer to Bronchial Tubes.

Bronchial Tubes (BRONG-kee-uhl)
The smaller bronchi that lead from the trachea to the bronchioles. Air travels in and out of the lungs through the main and the smaller bronchi.
Refer to Bronchi.

Bronchioles (BRONG-kee-oelz)
Small tubes that branch off from the bronchial tubes (the smaller bronchi). The bronchioles lead to the *alveoli* within the lungs, which is where the exchange of oxygen and carbon dioxide takes place.

Bronchitis (brong-KIE-tis)
An inflammation or infection of the mucous membranes of the bronchial tubes. Bronchitis is usually caused by a viral (and sometimes bacterial) infection, and is characterized by a persistent cough that produces sputum.

Bronchodilator Drug (brong-koe-DIE-lay-tuhr)
A drug that widens the airways by relaxing contractions of the smooth muscles of the bronchioles. This makes breathing easier. Bronchodilators are most commonly used in the treatment of asthma.

Bronchopulmonary Dysplasia (BPD) (brong-koe-PUL-moe-ner-ee dis-PLAY-zee-uh or dis-PLAY-zhuh)
A condition in which tissue of the lungs and bronchioles become damaged due to *respiratory distress syndrome* (common with premature infants) and/or use of the *ventilator*. Breathing problems develop when the

damaged tissue dies and is replaced with scar tissue that narrows the airways. Babies recover from BPD (their lungs heal), but are likely to be vulnerable to respiratory illness as infants and preschoolers. BPD is one form of *chronic lung disease*.

Bronchoscopy (brong-KOS-kuh-pee)
An examination of the bronchi in which a narrow, lighted tube is inserted through the nose or mouth and into the bronchi to view the bronchial tree.

Bronchospasm (BRONG-koe-spazm)
Abnormal contraction of the bronchi resulting in temporarily narrowed airways, which causes wheezing or coughing. The most common causes of bronchospasm include *asthma* (which is the number one cause), respiratory infection, and *chronic lung disease*.

Bronchus (BRONG-kuhs)
Singular of bronchi.

Broviac Catheter™
A type of catheter that is used as a long-term *central line*.

Brow Presentation
Birth (delivery) of a baby in which the face, specifically the eyebrow/forehead area of the head, is the first part to appear in the pelvis.
Refer to **Fetal Presentation**.

BRS
The abbreviation for *Behavior Rating Scale* (a section of the Bayley Scales of Infant Development-II).

Bruit (BROO-ee or brwee or broo-EE)
An abnormal sound or murmur in an organ, vessel, or gland that can be heard through a stethoscope.

Brushfield Spots
Pinpoint speckled pigmented spots on the iris of the eye, often seen on the eyes of children with *Down syndrome*. Occasionally, Brushfield spots are seen in children who do not have Down syndrome. Brushfield spots do not affect vision.

Bruxism (BRUK-sizm)
Unconscious, repetitive grinding of the teeth.

BSER
The abbreviation for Brain Stem Evoked Response.
Refer to **Auditory Evoked Response**.

BSERA

The abbreviation for Brain Stem Evoked Response Audiometry.
*Refer to **Auditory Evoked Response**.*

BSID-II

The abbreviation for Bayley Scales of Infant Development-II.

Bucca (BUK-uh)

The cheek, or fleshy part of the side of the face.

Buccae

Plural of cheek.

BUN

The abbreviation for blood urea nitrogen.

Bunny Hopping

A means of locomotion in which the child with *hypertonia* sits on the floor with her legs in the "W" *position* and then moves forward by placing her arms in front of her body on the floor and swinging her trunk and legs up to the hand placement.

Butyrophenone (byoo-ti-roe-FEE-noen)

An *antipsychotic drug* that affects neurochemicals in the brain and is used to treat *psychosis* and to suppress behaviors such as combativeness and *hyperactivity*.

c̄
The abbreviation for with.

C
1. The symbol for carbon.
2. The abbreviation for Celsius.

Ca
1. The symbol for calcium.
2. The abbreviation for cancer or *carcinoma*.

Cafe au Lait Spots (kaf-ay-oe-LAY)
Light coffee-colored marks on the skin. Cafe au lait spots may occur without an associated disorder, but they are also characteristic of certain diseases, such as *neurofibromatosis*.

calc-
A prefix meaning heel.

Calcaneal Tendon (kal-KAY-nee-uhl)
  Refer to Achilles Tendon.

Calcaneovalgus (kal-kay-nee-oe-VAL-gus)
A foot deformity in which the foot is turned outward, the ankle upward.

Calcaneus (kal-KAY-nee-uhs)
The heel bone.

Calcification
A deposit of calcium in body tissues.

Calcium (Ca)
A chemical necessary for the normal functioning of the nerves and heart, for muscle contraction, for blood clotting, for working with *enzymes*, and for the growth of bones and teeth.

Calcium Gluconate
A calcium salt that is sometimes given to a child with insufficient calcium.

Calvarium (kal-VER-ee-um)
The bones which form the top of the cranium.

Candida Albicans (KAN-di-duh AL-buh-kanz)
A common *fungus* that grows in areas of mucous membrane (such as the mouth and vagina) or on the skin and causes thrush (*candidiasis*) and other

"yeast" infections. Candida growth is encouraged by a warm, moist environment and by drugs that kill the bacteria that would normally keep the fungus from growing.

Also known as **Monilia**.

Candidiasis (kan-di-DIE-uh-sis)
Refer to **Candida Albicans**.

Cannula (KAN-yoo-luh)
A small tube for insertion into a vessel or cavity of the body. A cannula can be used to give or withdraw fluids.

Canthi
Plural of canthus.

Canthus (KAN-thuhs)
Each corner of the eye.

Capillary
A tiny blood vessel that connects the arteries and veins, thereby nourishing body tissues and removing waste products.

Capillary Hemangioma
Refer to **Hemangioma**.

Capitate Bone
The largest bone in the wrist.

Carbamazepine (kar-bam-AZ-uh-peen)
An *antiepileptic drug*.

Carbohydrate (kar-boe-HIE-drayt)
A category of foods that includes sugars and starches and is the main source of energy for all body functions.

Carbon
A nonmetallic element that is essential to body chemistry.

Carbon Dioxide (CO_2)
A clear, odorless by-product of body metabolism that is carried by the blood to the lungs, where it is exhaled.

Carbon Monoxide (CO)
A clear, odorless gas that is formed when there is not enough oxygen for proper burning. Carbon monoxide is highly poisonous and can cause asphyxiation, which may lead to central nervous system damage and death if enough of the gas is inhaled.

carcin-
A prefix meaning cancer.

Carcinogen (kar-SIN-oe-jen or KAR-si-noe-jen)
Anything that is capable of causing or accelerating the development of cancer, such as tobacco smoke or asbestos.

Carcinoma (kar-si-NOE-muh)
Any cancerous (malignant) tumor that arises from inner or outer body surfaces, such as the skin or lungs.

cardi-
A prefix meaning heart.

Cardiac
Referring to the heart.

Cardiac Arrest
A sudden stop in the pumping of the heart. Cardiac arrest in children is most often caused by respiratory failure, but other causes include heart attack (which is the most common cause in adults), shock, blood loss, drug overdose, or *hypothermia*. A person who has suffered cardiac arrest will stop breathing and become unconscious. *Cardiopulmonary resuscitation* is necessary to avoid *brain damage* and death.

Cardiac Catheter
*Refer to **Cardiac Catheterization** and **Catheter**.*

Cardiac Catheterization
A surgical procedure to diagnose and assess a heart condition. A small incision is made in the arm or leg and a *catheter* is threaded through a large blood vessel and into the heart. Blood pressure and blood oxygen levels are measured, and X-rays may be taken to show the inside of the heart as it pumps. If X-rays are taken, a contrast material will first be injected into the heart.

Cardiac Massage
An emergency procedure done during surgery and *cardiopulmonary resuscitation* involving a repeated, rhythmic compression of the heart. The procedure is done when the heart stops beating. Cardiac massage forces the heart to pump blood and may stimulate the heart to beat normally on its own.
*Also known as **Heart Massage** or **Chest Compressions**.*

Cardiologist (kar-dee-OL-oe-jist)
A medical doctor who specializes in the evaluation and treatment of diseases of the heart.

Cardiology
The branch of medicine dealing with the heart and circulation.

Cardiomyopathy (kar-dee-oe-mie-OP-uh-thee)
Any disease of the heart muscle that causes a decrease in the force of the heart's contractions. This leads to an inability of the heart to efficiently circulate blood through the lungs and the rest of the body. The cause of cardiomyopathy is usually unknown, but it may be an inherited condition, or be caused by a virus, a toxin, scarring of the lining of the heart, an abnormality in the chemical activity of the heart muscle cells (the cause of the abnormality is unknown), or a vitamin or mineral deficiency. Drugs may be used to treat the symptoms of cardiomyopathy, but often the heart continues to deteriorate.

Cardiopulmonary Resuscitation (CPR) (kar-dee-oe-PUL-muh-ner-ee)
A method of reviving a person who is not breathing and whose heartbeat is not strong enough to be effective or has stopped. CPR consists of cardiac massage (chest compressions) and mouth-to-mouth (or mouth-to-nose/mouth, in infants) resuscitation (rescue breathing).

Cardiovascular System (kar-dee-oe-VAS-kyuh-luhr)
The heart and blood vessels.
Refer to Circulation/Circulatory System.

Caries (KAYR-eez)
Refer to Dental Caries.

Carolina Curriculum for Handicapped Infants and Infants At-Risk
Refer to Carolina Curriculum for Infants and Toddlers with Special Needs.

Carolina Curriculum for Infants and Toddlers with Special Needs
A *criterion-referenced* evaluation tool used to assess the cognitive, communication/language, fine motor, gross motor, self-help/adaptive, and social-emotional development of the birth to 24–month-old. The Carolina also provides suggested activities for program planning and implementation. The Carolina may be administered by professionals and paraprofessionals. Formerly known as the Carolina Curriculum for Handicapped Infants and Infants At-Risk.

Carotid Arteries (kuh-ROT-id)
The principal arteries that carry blood to the neck and head. The carotid arteries can be felt on either side of the neck and are called the left and right common carotid arteries. These arteries each divide into two arteries, the internal and external carotid arteries.

Carpal (KAR-puhl)
Pertaining to the carpus, or wrist.

Carpus (KAR-pus)
The eight small bones of the wrist.

Carrier
1. A person who carries a specific pathogen (a *microorganism* capable of producing disease) and who is capable of spreading disease, even though he does not show signs of the disease or become ill.
2. A person who carries one *recessive gene* for a particular trait or condition, but shows no signs of the trait or condition himself because he also has a *dominant gene* that overrides the recessive gene. A carrier can, however, pass the recessive trait or condition on if he has a child with someone who also carries the recessive gene and the child inherits the recessive gene from both parents. This is how autosomal recessive disorders such as *Tay Sach's* disease occur.

Cartilage
Connective tissue that provides support to body structures. Cartilage also functions to allow smooth motion and decreased friction of joints.

Case Manager
The individual on a child's *multidisciplinary team* who, under P.L. 99–457, is responsible for coordinating performance evaluations and the development of the *IFSP;* identifying, coordinating, and monitoring service delivery; informing the family of the availability of advocacy services; coordinating with medical and health providers; and facilitating the development of transition planning. Sometimes parents are trained to act as their child's case manager.

cata-
A prefix meaning down.

Cataract (KAT-uh-rakt)
An eye disease in which the lens loses its transparency (becomes opaque), causing partial blindness. Cataract may be caused by an infection during the first trimester of pregnancy, *prenatal exposure to drugs*, certain *genetic* disorders, injury to the eye, or contact with certain poisons or medications. Cataract occurs most commonly during old age. Cataracts can often be removed to restore vision.

Catastrophic Health Insurance
State-offered protection plans against the costs of catastrophic illness or injury. Information on this insurance is obtained through public health and welfare departments.

Categorical Placement

Placement of a child with special needs in a class setting where all the other children have the same disability. For example, placing a child with visual impairments in a preschool class of only children with visual impairments.

Compare **Noncategorical Placement**.

Catheter (KATH-uh-ter)

A flexible tube used to administer fluids to or drain fluids from the body. There are several sites where catheters are used. Examples of types of catheters (based on location) include the *arterial catheter* (a catheter placed in an artery to provide continuous access for withdrawing arterial blood for monitoring arterial blood gases and blood pressure); *venous catheter* (a catheter placed in a vein to give nutrients, medication, or blood, or to withdraw blood); *cardiac catheter* (a catheter that is threaded into the heart via a blood vessel to diagnose and assess heart disease); and *urinary catheter* (a catheter that is inserted into the bladder to drain urine). A catheter is sometimes referred to as a "line," such as a *central line*. When a catheter must be left in place for an extended period of time it is called an *indwelling catheter*.

Catheterization

Refer to **Cardiac Catheterization** *or* **Urinary Catheterization**.

CAT Scanning

Refer to **CT Scanning**.

Cattell Infant Intelligence Scale

An evaluation tool used to assess the mental development (sensory, motor, perceptual, language, and cognitive functioning) and intelligence of infants and young children between three and 30 months of age. The Cattell is typically administered by a professional who holds a Ph.D. in psychology or education.

Cause-and-Effect

The concept that actions will produce certain responses to those actions. Pushing a button on a toy to make a bunny pop up is an example of a cause-and-effect activity.

Cava (KAY-vuh)

A body cavity such as the *vena cava*.

Cavus (KAY-vus)

A condition in which the height of the arch of the foot is exaggerated.

CBC

The abbreviation for complete blood count.

CCS
The abbreviation for Crippled Children's Services.

CDH
The abbreviation for congenital dislocation of the hip.

Cecum (SEE-kum)
A chamber or blind pouch that forms the first and widest portion of the large intestine. At its base is the *appendix*.

Ceiling
The upper limits of a range. On an evaluation tool, ceiling refers to the highest test item the child passes.
   Compare **Basal**.

Celestone™ (suh-LES-tone)
   Refer to **Betamethasone**.

Celiac (SEE-lee-ak)
Related to the abdominal area.

Celiac Sprue
   Refer to **Celiac Syndrome**.

Celiac Syndrome
A malabsorption syndrome associated with gluten (wheat) sensitivity. This disease causes diarrhea, dehydration, vitamin and mineral deficiencies, and loss of weight or failure to gain weight. Children usually respond favorably to a gluten-free diet. Celiac Syndrome may be a *genetic* disorder since it tends to run in families.
   Also known as **Celiac Sprue** *and* **Gluten Enteropathy**.

Cell
The smallest fundamental unit of living organisms (such as the human body) capable of independent functioning.

Celontin™ (suh-LON-tin)
   Refer to **Methsuximide**.

-centesis
A suffix meaning puncture.

Central Line
An intravenous catheter that is surgically placed into a large blood vessel to deliver nutrients or medications, to measure venous pressure (the pressure of circulating blood on the walls of the veins), and to withdraw blood samples. A central line is one type of *indwelling catheter*.
   Refer to **Catheter**.

Central Nervous System (CNS)
The brain and spinal cord. The central nervous system functions to receive sensory information and to initiate the appropriate motor response. It works in conjunction with the *peripheral nervous system*.
  Compare **Peripheral Nervous System**.

Central Venous Nutrition (CVN)
  Refer to **Total Parenteral Nutrition (TPN)**

Central Visual Field
The area seen without moving the head or eyes.

cephal-, cephalo-
Prefixes meaning head.

Cephalexin (sef-uh-LEK-sin)
An *antibiotic drug* used to treat some infections.

Cephalhematoma (sef-uhl-hee-muh-TOE-muh)
A birth trauma characterized by a blood-filled swelling on the newborn's head. This is a benign condition which occurs due to pressure on the infant's skull as it passes through the pelvic bones during vaginal delivery. The skull remolds as the infant's head grows during the first year, and the lump (swelling) becomes less noticeable or not noticeable at all. (The blood is reabsorbed and no treatment is necessary.) Cephalhematoma can develop on one or both sides of the head (bilateral cephalhematoma), and can be quite dramatic with a vacuum delivery.

Cephalocaudal Sequence of Development (sef-uh-loe-KAH-duhl)
Referring to the progression of human development, in that skills develop from the head downward (i.e., head control is achieved before control of the legs).

Cephalopelvic Disproportion (CPD) (sef-uh-loe-PEL-vik)
A condition in which the mother's pelvis is relatively too small for the baby's head to pass through during vaginal delivery.

Cerebellum (ser-uh-BEL-um)
The part of the brain responsible for maintaining balance and for coordinating voluntary movements. The cerebellum functions on a reflexive level. The cerebellum is located behind the brain stem at the base of the skull.
  Refer to **Brain**.

Cerebral Angiography (suh-REE-bruhl or SER-uh-bruhl an-jee-OG-ruh-fee)
Angiography of the brain.

Cerebral Cortex

The surface gray matter of the cerebral hemispheres (cerebrum) of the brain. The cerebral cortex is considered responsible for receiving and analyzing sensory information, for conscious thought, and for movement.
Compare **Motor Cortex.**

Cerebral Hemisphere

One half of the paired portions of the brain. The two cerebral hemispheres make up the largest part of the brain (the cerebrum). Within each cerebral hemisphere is a *ventricle* that contains *cerebrospinal fluid*. The ventricles are surrounded by the nerve cells called the basal ganglia. The next layer consists of nerve fibers, or white matter. The outer layer is called the *cerebral cortex*, which is made up of nerve cells, or gray matter. Each hemisphere is comprised of four lobes: the frontal lobe, which occupies the front third of each hemisphere; the occipital lobe, which occupies the back fourth of each hemisphere; the parietal lobe, which is located in the middle-upper area of each hemisphere; and the temporal lobe, which is located in the lower-middle area of each hemisphere. The two cerebral hemispheres are connected by the *corpus callosum*. The left hemisphere is dominant for speech in most people. Also, the dominant hemisphere determines hand preference. For example, if the left hemisphere is dominant, the child will usually be right-handed.
Refer to **Cerebrum.**

Cerebral Palsy (CP) (suh-REE-bruhl or SER-uh-bruhl POL-zee)

A disorder of movement and posture control resulting from nonprogressive damage to the brain during fetal life, the newborn period, or early childhood. Both *genetic* and *acquired* factors may be involved. Cerebral palsy may be caused by a lack of normal fetal brain development, or by injury to the brain. There are several ways a baby's brain can be injured, including drug or alcohol exposure, an inadequate supply of oxygen to the brain either prenatally or during delivery, maternal infection that is present during pregnancy, an excess of *bilirubin* during the *neonatal* period, infection of the infant's or young child's brain (such as with *meningitis* or *encephalitis*), or head injury. The extent and location of *brain damage* determine the type of cerebral palsy and the associated symptoms (such as abnormal *muscle tone*, involuntary movements, or lack of balance and coordination). The three main classifications of cerebral palsy are *Pyramidal Cerebral Palsy*, *Extrapyramidal Cerebral Palsy*, and *Mixed-Type Cerebral Palsy*. Most children with cerebral palsy have normal or high intelligence, but *mental retardation*, *learning disabilities*, and *seizures* may be included in the diagnosis of cerebral palsy.

cerebro-

A prefix meaning brain.

Cerebrospinal Fluid (CSF) (suh-REE-broe-spie-nuhl or ser-uh-broe-SPIE-nuhl)

Fluid produced in the brain's *ventricles* which circulates around the brain and spinal column. The fluid acts as a buffer and also supplies the central nervous system nutritionally.

Refer to **Hydrocephalus.**

Cerebrovascular (ser-ee-broe-VAS-kyuh-ler or ser-uh-broe-VAS-kyuh-ler)

Pertaining to the blood vessels of the brain.

Cerebrum (ser-EE-brum or SER-uh-brum)

The largest part of the brain. It contains the two *cerebral hemispheres,* which are joined together by the *corpus callosum.* The cerebrum has sensory and motor functions and is the area where most voluntary thought and activity is initiated.

Refer to **Cerebral Hemisphere** *and to* **Brain.**

Ceroid Lipofuscinosis (SIR-oid lip-oe-fyoo-sin-OE-sis)

Refer to **Batten Disease.**

Cerumen (se-ROO-men)

Earwax.

Cervical

1. Relating to the neck.
2. Relating to the cervix.

Cervical Incompetence

A weakness in the cervix which may lead to miscarriage or premature delivery.

cervico-

A prefix meaning neck.

Cervix

The lowest part of the uterus through which the infant passes when born vaginally.

Cesarean Section (C-Section) (see-SER-ee-uhn or suh-SER-ee-uhn)

The surgical delivery of a baby through incisions in the mother's abdominal and uterine walls.

CF

The abbreviation for cystic fibrosis.

Chaining

Refer to **Backward Chaining** *and* **Forward Chaining.**

Chairs (Adaptive)
Chairs that are used to position a child appropriately to promote a specific function. Examples of uses include to improve head and trunk control, to increase muscular expansion and contraction of the chest for better breathing, or to assist with maintaining appropriate posture to encourage learning.

Chalasia (kuh-LAY-zhuh or kuh-LAY-zee-uh)
The abnormal relaxation of the sphincter muscle between the esophagus and stomach. This results in *gastroesophageal reflux* (the contents of the stomach come back up into the esophagus).
   Refer to **Gastroesophageal Reflux**.

Charcot-Marie-Tooth Disease (shar-KOE muh-REE tooth)
An *inherited* disorder in which the child progressively develops weakness and wasting of foot and calf muscles and, later, hand and forearm muscles as a result of peripheral nerve degeneration. The disease usually begins between middle childhood and age 30 and usually progresses slowly. Although the quality of the child's movements will be affected, the resulting disability is usually not completely debilitating (frequently the disease becomes stationary) and the patient usually lives a normal life span.
   Also known as **Peroneal Muscular Atrophy**.

CHARGE Association
An *autosomal recessive* syndrome characterized by *C*oloboma (a cleft, or area of incomplete fusion of part of the eyeball that results in an area with loss of vision), *H*eart disease, *A*tresia chonae (also called *choanal atresia*, which is blockage of the nasal passage), *R*etarded growth and development (*mental retardation* ranging from mild to profound and growth deficiency), *G*enital *anomalies*, and *E*ar anomalies and/or deafness.
   Refer to **Coloboma** *and* **Choanal Atresia**.

CHD
Congenital Heart Disease.

cheilo-
A prefix meaning lip or edge.

Chelation (kee-LAY-shuhn)
A procedure that uses certain drugs to bind (combine with) an ingested poisonous substance (such as lead or another metal) so the body can excrete it through the urine more quickly.

Chemical Dependency
A physical and/or psychological need for a substance such as cocaine.

Chemically Exposed
Referring to the child who has been *prenatally exposed to drugs* or alcohol.
   Refer to **Prenatally Exposed to Drugs** *and* **Fetal Alcohol Syndrome**.

Chest Compressions
*Refer to **Cardiac Massage**.*

Chest Percussion
A method of decreasing a child's respiratory congestion by "pounding" on his chest to help him loosen and cough up mucus so he can breathe easier. Chest percussion may be used in the treatment of *cystic fibrosis*.
*Compare **Percussion**.*

Chest Tube (ct)
A tube that is surgically placed to drain fluid or air, and to enable a collapsed lung to re-expand.

Chewing
Biting and grinding with the gums or teeth. A munching pattern (up and down biting action) is used for chewing food initially (beginning around six to eight months of age), until approximately 18 to 24 months of age, when *rotary chewing* (rotary jaw movement) emerges.

CHF
Congestive Heart Failure.

Chicken Pox
A common, contagious, childhood viral illness in which a generalized, itchy red rash with blisters appears on many parts of the body. Chicken pox is contagious until all lesions become crusted with a scab.
*Also known as **Varicella**.*

Child Abuse and Neglect
As defined by the Child Abuse Prevention and Treatment Act, Public Law 93–247: "The physical or mental injury, sexual abuse or exploitation, negligent treatment or maltreatment of a child under the age of 18 . . . by a person who is responsible for the child's welfare. . . ."
*Compare **Emotional Abuse** and **Sexual Abuse**.*
*Refer to **Mandated Reporter**.*

Child Find
A federal program which requires states to actively locate young children with disabilities who are not receiving any or adequate early intervention services. This state-wide system is responsible for identifying and making timely referrals of infants and toddlers to service providers, such as for case management, infant development, or physical therapy services. The child find system should provide for the participation by primary referral sources, including hospitals, physicians, and child care facilities.

Child Protective Agency
An agency that receives and investigates reports of child abuse or neglect. The Department of Children's Services and the police department are examples of child protective agencies.

Chloral Hydrate (KLOE-ruhl HIE-drayt)
A drug that can be used to sedate a child such as for an EEG (*electroencephalogram*) or *CT scanning*, or for dental work. It is also prescribed to help children with sleeping problems.

Chlorothiazide (kloe-roe-THIE-uh-zide)
A *diuretic drug*.

Chlorpromazine (klor-PROE-muh-zeen)
An *antipsychotic drug*.

Choanal Atresia (KOE-uh-nuhl uh-TREE-zee-uh)
A *congenital* defect in which one or both of the nasal passages is blocked.
   Also known as **Atresia Choanae**.

chole-
A prefix meaning bile.

Cholesteatoma (koe-lee-stee-uh-TOE-muh)
A condition in which skin cells from the *auditory canal* grow inward toward the middle ear, forming a cyst that causes damage to the bones of the middle ear and to the mastoid bone. The growth of the skin cells is usually the result of chronic *otitis media* (middle ear infection) that has caused the eardrum to burst, but cholesteatoma may be a *congenital* condition. The cyst must be removed surgically. Hearing impairment may result.

Choline (KOE-leen or KOE-lin)
A factor found in the vitamin B complex.

chondr-, chondro-
Prefixes meaning cartilage.

Chondroectodermal Dysplasia (kon-droe-ek-toe-DUR-muhl dis-PLAY-zhuh)
   Refer to **Ellis-van Creveld Syndrome**.

Chordee (KOR-dee)
Abnormal curving of the penis.

Chorea (koe-REE-uh)
Purposeless, jerking movements. Chorea is caused by damage to the basal ganglia of the brain.

Choreoathetoid Cerebral Palsy (koe-ree-oe-ATH-e-toid suh-REE-bruhl POL-zee)

A form of *extrapyramidal cerebral palsy* characterized by involuntary movements (relatively slow writhing movements with a jerky component), and by *muscle tone* that fluctuates between low and normal or between low and spastic. Choreoathetoid cerebral palsy results from damage to the nerve pathways that transmit impulses for controlling movement and maintaining posture from the brain to the spinal cord.

Also known as **Choreoathetosis**.
Refer to **Extrapyramidal Cerebral Palsy**.

Choreoathetosis (koe-ree-oe-ath-e-TOE-sis)

Refer to **Choreoathetoid Cerebral Palsy**.

Chorionic Villus Sampling (CVS) (koe-ree-ON-ik VIL-us)

A prenatal technique for diagnosing fetal abnormalities in which a small sample of the chorionic villus (a part of the placenta) is removed so the *chromosomes* can be analyzed.

Chorioretinitis (kor-ee-oe-ret-uh-NIE-tis)

An inflammation of the retina and choroid of the eye that can produce visual loss. Chorioretinitis is usually the result of infection. Chorioretinitis can be so minor that, if treated early, the patient may not even be aware that he has it. If the central area of the eye is involved, more eye damage may result.

Choroid (KOR-oid)

The middle layer of the eyeball between the *sclera* and the *retina*. The choroid lines the white of the eyeball and supplies blood to the retina.

chrom-, chromo-

Prefixes meaning color.

Chromosomal Abnormality (kroe-muh-SOE-muhl)

A *genetic* disorder caused by either too few or too many *chromosomes*, or by chromosomes with extra pieces, missing pieces, or pieces attached to another chromosome. An example of a *chromosomal abnormality* is *Down syndrome* (an extra chromosome 21 is present).

Chromosomal Deletion

A condition in which a piece of a *chromosome* is missing. An example of a disorder caused by chromosomal deletion is *cri du chat syndrome*.

Chromosomal Nondisjunction

Failure of a *chromosome* pair to separate during cell division (prior to conception), resulting in both chromosomes being carried to one *daughter cell* and none to the other daughter cell. For example, *Down syndrome* may result due to nondisjunction of chromosome pair 21.

Chromosomal Translocation

The transfer of part of a *chromosome* to another chromosome, resulting in a change in the *genetic* material within the body's cells. Translocation is a type of *mutation* and can be *inherited* or *acquired* as the result of a new mutation. Often the translocation causes no abnormality, but a parent who is a *carrier* of a translocation can have children who are affected. *Down syndrome* is an example of a disorder that can occur due to chromosomal translocation.

Chromosome (KROE-muh-soem)

The microscopic rod-shaped structures within cells that contain the *genetic* information that determines or influences the individual traits of a child. (Every cell in an individual's body—except for the sperm or egg cells—normally carries the exact same chromosomal material.) Normally, human beings have 46 chromosomes (23 pairs) in each cell.

Chromosome Analysis

A procedure to diagnose *chromosome* disorders in which chromosomal materials (from blood, skin, amniotic fluid, and other tissues) are analyzed by number and structure.

Refer to **Karyotyping.**

Chronic Illness

A sickness that develops slowly and lasts for a long time. Some chronic illnesses persist throughout a person's life.

Compare **Acute Illness.**

Chronic Lung Disease (CLD)

A condition in which there is persistent disruption of the passage of air in and out of the lungs. *Bronchopulmonary Dysplasia* is a form of chronic lung disease.

Chronological Age

An infant or child's age stated in hours, days, weeks, months, or years and months since birth.

Compare **Corrected Age** *and* **Developmental Age.**

CID

The abbreviation for cytomegalic inclusion disease.

Cilia (SIL-ee-uh)

Microscopic hairlike projections on some cells that sway, causing movement of the fluid that surrounds them. An example of cilia are those found on the nerve cells of the *cochlea* of the inner ear.

Cimetidine (si-MET-i-deen)
A drug used to decrease stomach acidity and to reduce inflammation of the esophagus. It is sometimes given to children who experience *gastroesophageal reflux*.

Circular Reactions
Refer to **Primary Circular Reactions** *and* **Secondary Circular Reactions**.

Circulation/Circulatory System
The flow of blood throughout the heart and blood vessels. Blood circulates in this manner: the left *atrium* (upper chamber) of the heart pumps oxygenated blood to the left *ventricle* (lower chamber), where the blood is then forced through the *aorta* to many other *arteries* and even smaller arteries called arterioles to get the blood to the rest of the body. The body organs receive blood from the arterioles, which branch off into the *capillaries* of body tissues, where oxygen and nutrients are exchanged with carbon dioxide and other waste products. From here the blood, which is now deoxygenated, flows through the tiny veins called venules, the *veins*, and the *venae cavae*, and on to the right atrium (upper chamber) of the heart. The blood continues on to the right ventricle (lower chamber), which pumps it through the *pulmonary artery* to the lungs. Within the lungs the exchange of carbon dioxide and oxygen is again made, only now the carbon dioxide leaves the blood and the blood is re-oxygenated. Finally, the newly oxygenated blood returns to the left atrium of the heart via the *pulmonary veins* and the cycle continues.
Also known as the **Cardiovascular System**.
Compare **Fetal Circulation** *and* **Persistent Fetal Circulation**.

circum-
A prefix meaning around.

Circumduction Movement
The motion of the head of a bone in its socket, such as a shoulder joint when the *distal* end of the arm moves so as to outline an arc. Circumduction is one of the four basic kinds of movement by the joints of the body.
Compare **Angular**, **Gliding**, *and* **Rotation**.

-clasia
A suffix meaning breaking.

Clavicle
The collarbone. It articulates with the sternum (breast bone) and the scapula (shoulder blade).

Clawfoot
Refer to **Pes Cavus**.

Clawing
The action of an infant's toes pressing against the floor while standing, trying to maintain balance.

CLD
The abbreviation for chronic lung disease.

-cle
A suffix meaning small.

Clean Intermittent Catheterization
A procedure to drain urine from the bladder. A *catheter* is periodically passed through the urethra, then into the bladder, not left in place permanently.

Cleft Lip
A birth defect that occurs between the third and tenth weeks of fetal life when the upper lip doesn't fuse together, leaving one or more vertical openings that may extend up to the nose. Some babies born with a cleft lip also have a *cleft palate*. Cleft lip is a *multifactorial genetic disorder*. (Interaction between genetic and environmental factors is the cause.) Cleft lip can be repaired surgically.

Cleft Palate
A birth defect that occurs between the third and tenth weeks of fetal life when the palatal tissues don't fuse together. There is an open space in the roof of the mouth, either extending through both the hard and soft palates, or only part way through. Some babies born with a cleft palate also have a *cleft lip*. Cleft palate is a *multifactorial genetic disorder*. (Interaction between genetic and environmental factors is the cause.) Cleft palate can be repaired surgically.

Click
A brief, sharp sound. A click can be heard during *systole* (heart contraction), and be indicative of various heart conditions. Also, a click may be felt in a child with *congenital hip dislocation* when the leg is moved into certain positions.

clin-, clino-
Prefixes meaning slant.

Clindamycin (klin-duh-MIE-sin)
An *antibiotic drug*.

Clinical Type
Any type of disability (especially one that causes mental retardation) that can be readily identified by the physical characteristics of individuals who

have that disability. *Microcephaly, Down syndrome,* and *fetal alcohol syndrome* are examples.

Clinodactyly (klie-noe-DAK-ti-lee)

A *congenital* condition in which a baby is born with incurved fifth fingers (the smallest finger on each hand).

Clonazepam (kloe-NAZ-uh-pam)

An *antiepileptic drug.*

Clonic Seizures (KLON-ik)

Seizures characterized by fast, jerky movements (repeated muscle contraction and relaxation).

Clonus (KLOE-nuhs)

The abnormal repeated muscle contraction and relaxation that occurs when a muscle is stretched (for example, when the foot is bent upward at the ankle). Clonus is an indication of damage to the nerves that transmit impulses from the brain to a muscle.

Clorazepate (kloe-RAZ-uh-payt)

A *tranquilizer drug* that is also used as an *antiepileptic drug.*

Clubbing

Broadening and thickening of the soft tissues of the ends of the fingers or toes.

Clubfoot

A birth defect in which the foot is twisted in an abnormal position. It is believed that clubfoot has a *multifactorial* pattern of inheritance. The most common form of clubfoot is *talipes equinovarus.*

   Also known as **Talipes.**

CMV

The abbreviation for cytomegalovirus.

CNS

The abbreviation for central nervous system.

CO_2

The abbreviation for carbon dioxide.

Coarctation of the Aorta (koe-ark-TAY-shuhn)

A narrowing of the *aorta* that causes the heart to work harder to get blood to the lower half of the body (the body parts supplied by the aorta past the constricted section). Because the heart has to pump harder, the blood pressure above the narrowed part of the aorta is raised. (The blood pressure below the narrowed part is lowered or normal.) This *congenital* heart defect must be repaired surgically. The cause of coarctation of the aorta is unknown.

Coccyx (KOK-siks)
The tailbone. The last vertebra of the spine.

Cochlea (KOK-lee-uh)
The spiral-shaped cavity of the inner ear that makes hearing possible. The cochlea functions by transforming sound vibrations into signals that are transmitted to the brain along the auditory nerves.

Refer to **Ear**.

Cochlear Implant (KOK-lee-ar)
A device to treat severe *sensorineural hearing impairment* in which one or more electrodes are surgically implanted in the inner ear to electronically stimulate any undamaged inner ear nerves.

Cockayne Syndrome (kok-AYN)
An *autosomal recessive disorder* characterized by poor growth *(short stature)* with long extremities and large hands and feet, *mental retardation*, hearing loss, visual impairment, skin that is sensitive to sunlight, and premature aging. Cockayne syndrome usually results in death by adolescence or early adulthood.

Coffin-Lowry Syndrome
An *X-linked disorder* characterized by mild growth deficiency, downslanting eyes, coarse facial features, *hypotonia* (decreased muscle tone), tapering fingers, and severe *mental retardation*.

Cognition
Thinking skills, including the ability to receive, process, analyze, and understand information.

Cognitive
Referring to the developmental area that involves thinking skills, including the ability to receive, process, analyze, and understand information. Matching red circles and pushing the button on a mechanical toy to activate it are examples of cognitive skills.

Colace™ (KOE-lays)
Refer to **Docusate**.

Cold
The common cold is usually a viral infection caused by one of many viruses. (A cold can also be a mixed infection or an allergic reaction.) It is usually spread by airborne droplets that are inhaled or land on surfaces which are touched (then transferred to the eyes, nose, or mouth by the hand). Symptoms include a runny nose, congestion, a sore throat, a cough,

muscle ache, and headache. There is no cure for the common cold, and treatment centers on alleviating discomfort.

Colic (KOL-ik)
Sharp abdominal pain that some infants experience during the first three months of life. (It may last longer than three months.) The cause of colic is unclear, but some doctors attribute it to intestinal spasms possibly caused by swallowed air, excessive gas in the intestines, or an allergic reaction to the baby's formula. Babies who have colic cry excessively and are difficult to console, but are otherwise healthy.

Collagen
A fibrous protein that helps hold together the body's cells and tissues such as the ligaments and tendons. Collagen is the most common protein in the body.

colo-
A prefix meaning large intestine.

Coloboma (kol-uh-BOE-muh)
A *birth defect* that occurs in early fetal development when incomplete fusion of the eyeball results in a space, or cleft, of part of the eyeball. (Sometimes the eyelid is also involved.) This causes an area of lost vision within the *visual field* surrounded by an area of vision.

Colon (KOE-luhn)
The large intestine. The colon moves fecal matter to the anus to be evacuated.

Colonoscopy (koe-lon-OS-koe-pee)
A procedure to examine and diagnose problems of the colon in which a long, flexible, lighted tube is inserted into the rectum so the inside of the colon can be viewed.

Color Vision
The ability to perceive and recognize colors. Color vision is possible when light waves are focused on the light-sensitive cone cells in the retina, which emit electrical impulses that are transmitted to the brain via the optic nerve.
  Refer to **Vision**.

Colostomy (koe-LOS-toe-mee)
A surgically created opening to allow the colon to pass feces directly through the abdominal wall, bypassing part of the digestive tract. To collect the waste, a colostomy bag is attached to the skin at the point where the colon is brought through the abdominal incision.

Coma
A state of unconsciousness caused by damage to the brain regions responsible for maintaining consciousness. Coma may be due to brain disease, drugs, hypoxia (a lack of sufficient oxygen in the body cells or blood), metabolic disorders, trauma, or disturbances of the respiratory or circulatory systems.

Combat Crawl
Refer to **Crawl**.
Compare to **Creep**.

Commando Crawl
Refer to **Crawl**.
Compare to **Creep**.

Commissurotomy (kom-i-shyoor-OT-oe-mee)
A surgical procedure that divides (by cutting) any fibrous ring of tissue connecting parts of a body structure, especially that which surrounds a heart valve. This relieves excessive tightness of the valve and allows for a more normal flow of blood.

Common Cold
Refer to **Cold**.

Communicable Illness
Disease that is transmitted person to person via a *microorganism* or parasite.

Communication
The developmental area that involves skills which enable people to understand (receptive language) and share (expressive language) thoughts and feelings. Waving "bye-bye," using spontaneous single-word utterances, and repeating five-word sentences are all examples of communication skills.
Also known as **Language**.

Communication Aid
A nonverbal form of communication such as gesture, *sign language, communication boards,* and electronic devices (for example, computers and voice synthesizers).

Communication Board/Book
A board or book with pictures that a child can point to for expression of his needs.

Communication Disorder
Difficulty with understanding and/or expressing messages. Communication disorders include problems with *articulation, voice disorders, stuttering, language disorders,* and some *learning disabilities*.

Compensatory Movements

Actions carried out to make up for inabilities. For example, if a child cannot raise his arm all the way up over his head, he may tilt his body in order to extend his reach.

Complete Blood Count (CBC)

Tests to measure the number and types of cells in the blood. Both red and white blood cells are counted. Platelet count is also determined, as well as hemoglobin concentration.

Complex Partial Seizure

A seizure similar to a *simple partial seizure*, except that the seizure also spreads into the brain areas responsible for maintaining consciousness, which usually results in the child losing consciousness. If the seizure spreads to involve the whole brain, it is called a secondarily generalized seizure.

*Also known as a **Psychomotor Seizure** or a **Temporal Lobe Seizure**.*
*Refer to **Partial Seizure** and **Epilepsy**.*

Compression

Approximation (bringing together) of the bones of a joint, while they are in extension, to promote stability of that joint. Compression encourages contraction of the muscles that support the joint and increases *proprioception* in the joint. Compression is typically done by a physical therapist.

*Also known as **Joint Compression**.*

Computerized Axial Tomography

*Refer to **CT Scanning**.*

con-

A prefix meaning with or together.

Concha (KONG-kuh)

1. A small shell-shaped bone found along the outer side of the nasal cavity.
*Also known as the **Turbinate Bone**.*
2. The hollow part of the external ear.

Conditioned Orientation Reflex (COR)

*Refer to **Visual Response Audiometry**.*

Conductive Hearing Loss

Hearing impairment caused by problems transmitting sound vibrations to the brain, either because of obstruction in the ear canal or because of disorders of the eardrum or middle ear, such as *otitis media* (infection in the middle ear) or a *perforated eardrum*. This type of hearing loss can usually be resolved with medicine or surgery, and thus may not be permanent. Conductive hearing loss can occur *congenitally* or be *acquired*.

*Compare **Mixed Hearing Loss** and **Sensorineural Hearing Loss**.*

Congenital (kuhn-JEN-i-tuhl)
Referring to a condition present at birth that may be *hereditary* (a genetic disorder), may be the result of a problem during pregnancy (such as a maternal infection), or may occur due to injury to the fetus prior to or at the time of birth.
Also known as a **Birth Defect.**
Compare **Acquired** *and* **Inherited.**

Congenital Anomaly
Refer to **Birth Defect.**

Congenital CMV
Refer to **Cytomegalic Inclusion Disease.**

Congenital Defect
Refer to **Birth Defect.**

Congenital Dislocation of the Hip (CDH)
A condition present at birth in which the head of the thigh bone may be totally out of the hip socket or it may move in and out of the socket. This condition is most correctable when it is discovered very early.

Congenital Heart Disease (CHD)
Heart disease that is present at birth. Examples of congenital heart disease include defects such as *patent ductus arteriosus* and *tetralogy of Fallot.*

Congenital Herpes
Refer to **Herpes Simplex Virus** 2.

Congenital Hypothyroidism
A disorder present at birth that occurs due to *congenital* lack of thyroid secretion. The baby with untreated congenital hypothyroidism may have retarded growth, *mental retardation,* a large tongue, and *floppy muscle tone.* Thyroid hormone can be replaced by taking a daily supplement; thus these consequences can be avoided.
Also known as **Cretinism.**

Congenital Infections
Diseases that occur either before birth or when passing through the birth canal by exposure to viral, bacterial, or other *microorganisms.* Examples of infections acquired before birth include *rubella* and *cytomegalovirus.* Examples of infection obtained during birth include *conjunctivitis, herpes,* and possibly *meningitis.*

Congenital Megacolon
Refer to **Hirschsprung Disease.**

Congenital Rocker-Bottom Foot
A birth defect in which the bones of the foot are positioned in such a way that the bottom side is rounded in a rocker shape. This condition is common in *Trisomy 18*.
Also known as **Vertical Talus**.

Congenital Rubella
A viral infection that produces mild symptoms (slight fever or other signs of upper respiratory infection) and rash in a child, but can cause severe birth defects in the fetus of a woman who is infected during the first four months of pregnancy. The earlier in pregnancy that a woman is infected, the more likely she will either miscarry or have a baby with serious *congenital* problems such as deafness, heart disease, *mental retardation*, eye disorders, and *cerebral palsy*.
Also known as **German Measles** (*however, Rubella is not all that similar to measles*).

Congenital Scoliosis
A sometimes progressive birth defect caused by a spinal abnormality. The spine has a C-shaped or an S-shaped curve which requires treatment if it is severe or worsens.

Congenital Syphilis
A sexually transmitted infection that may be passed to the fetus, possibly causing *jaundice*, *anemia*, damage to the bones, blindness, deafness, and *mental retardation*. Congenital syphilis can be fatal to a fetus or newborn. Good prenatal care should include maternal screening for syphilis.

Congenital Toxoplasmosis
Refer to **Toxoplasmosis**.

Congestive Heart Failure (CHF)
The inability of the heart to pump enough blood to the lungs and the rest of the body. CHF is treated by determining its cause and treating that condition. Many conditions can cause congestive heart failure, including *congenital* malformations, infection, *hypertension*, a heart *arrhythmia*, *cardiomyopathy*, or *pulmonary hypertension*.

Conjugate Gaze
The eyes working in unison.

Conjugation
The act of joining together.

Conjunctiva (kon-jungk-TIE-vuh)
The membranes lining the eyelid and covering the eyeball.

Conjunctivitis (kuhn-jungk-ti-VIE-tis)
Inflammation of the *conjunctiva*. It can be caused by bacteria, a virus, or an allergic response, or be acquired from the mother during birth. Conjunctivitis may be infectious and contagious, and cause redness, an itch, and discharge.

Connective Tissue
Body tissue that supports and holds together various structures within the body. Tendons and cartilage are made of connective tissue, and connective tissue is found in other structures such as bones.

Consanguinity (kon-san-GWIN-i-tee)
Referring to a blood relationship, especially the mating of blood relatives, such as cousins.

Consonant
One of the 21 letters of the alphabet other than the five vowels (a, e, i, o, u). Consonants are produced when air flow that passes over the vocal cords is obstructed (mostly by the teeth and tongue) as it moves through the mouth.
   Compare **Vowel**.

Constipation
Hard, rocklike stools from bowel movements that may be infrequent and painful.

Contagious
Communicable. Referring to a disease that can be passed to another person.

Continuant
A speech sound produced while the speech organs are held in a relatively constant position, such as the /s/, /m/, /f/, and vowel sounds.

Continuous Positive Airway Pressure (CPAP)
A continuous flow of pressurized air (with or without additional oxygen), that assists a baby in keeping his lungs expanded as he inhales and exhales.

contra-
A prefix meaning opposed or against.

Contraction
The brief tightening of a muscle.

Contracture (kuhn-TRAK-chuhr)
A shortening of muscles, tendons, and *fascia* that causes decreased joint mobility. The joint is bent and does not have a full *range of motion*. Contractures may be caused by fibrosis (abnormal formation of fibrous tissue) of the tissues supporting the muscle or joint, by disorders of the muscle fibers

themselves, injury, or arthritis. Contractures can sometimes be prevented by range of motion exercise and by adequate support of the joints.

Convergence
The coordinated turning of both eyes inward to focus on a near point.

Convulsion
A seizure characterized by involuntary muscle contractions.
Refer to Seizure.

Cooing
Vowel sounds produced by the infant in vocal play. The vowel sounds that are made at the back of the mouth with a more open mouth (such as "ahh") are the first sounds a baby creates because they are the easiest. The next sounds that emerge are made with a more closed mouth (such as "ee"). Cooing typically begins around two months of age.
Compare Babbling, Jabbering, and Jargon.

Cookie Insert™
An arch support pad worn inside a child's shoe.

Cooley's Anemia
Refer to Thalassemia.

Coombs Test
A test that detects *antibodies* to red blood cells. It is performed on patients suspected of having *hemolytic disease* (breakdown of red blood cells). In the newborn, hemolytic disease may be caused by maternal antibodies, such as when an Rh-positive baby is born to an Rh-negative mother who produced antibodies to Rh-positive blood. A Coombs test is also run in crossmatching blood (testing to establish blood compatibility before transfusion).
Refer to Rh Incompatibility.

Copy
To draw a design (such as a cross or a circle), with an example to imitate, but without a demonstration of it being drawn.

COR
The abbreviation for conditioned orientation reflex.

cordi-
A prefix meaning heart.

Cornea (KOR-nee-uh)
The transparent, domelike shell covering the front part of the eye.
Refer to Eye.

Cornelia de Lange Syndrome
A sporadically occurring *congenital* disorder characterized by *short stature*, continuous eyebrows, small jaw, *microcephaly*, small or malformed hands and feet, coarse hair growing low on the forehead and on the neck, congenital heart defects, and *mental retardation*.
Also known as **de Lange Syndrome**.

Corner Chairs
Refer to **Chairs (Adaptive)**.

Cor Pulmonale (kor pool-muh-NAY-lee)
A condition in which the right ventricle of the heart becomes enlarged and strained, which may eventually lead to heart failure (a condition in which the heart fails to maintain adequate circulation of blood). It is caused by *chronic lung disease*.

Corpus Callosum (KOR-pus kuh-LOE-sum)
A mass of white matter (nerve fibers) that joins the *cerebral hemispheres* of the brain, allowing them to "communicate" with each other.

Corpus Callosum Agenesis
Refer to **Agenesis of the Corpus Callosum**.

Corrected Age
The age a premature infant would be if he had been born on his due date. For example, a baby born two months prematurely has a corrected age of six months when he is actually (chronologically) eight months old. This is an important consideration when measuring the premature infant's development, because the time missed in the uterus should be a factor in determining appropriate expectations for the baby.
Also known as **Adjusted Age**.
Compare **Chronological Age**.

Correlation
The relationship between variables, such as the relationship between a premature birth and the presence of *respiratory distress syndrome*.

Cortex
The outer layer of an organ or body structure.
Refer to **Cerebral Cortex**.

Cortical (KOR-ti-kuhl)
Referring to the cortex, or outer layer of an organ or body structure.

Cortical Atrophy
Wasting away of the gray matter of the brain.

Cortical Blindness
Visual impairment resulting from an inability of the occipital lobe of the brain to process visual stimuli. (The eye itself is normal.) Cortical blindness can result from an abnormality of the brain, head injury, or infection. Depending on the cause of the damage (for example, an infection of the brain), visual impairment may improve.

Cortical Thumbing
Refer to **Indwelling Thumb**.

Corticosteroid (kor-ti-koe-STEER-oid)
One of the hormones produced by the *adrenal glands*. Corticosteroids (a type of steroid drug) are also made synthetically and are used to replace natural hormones and to reduce inflammation.

Corticotropin (kor-ti-koe-TROE-pin)
Refer to **Adrenocorticotropic Hormone**.

Costal (KOS-tuhl)
Pertaining to the ribs. There are 12 ribs on each side of the rib cage.

costo-
A prefix meaning rib.

Counterrotation
Rotating in opposite directions, such as when the left shoulder rotates backward and the left hip rotates forward.

Coxa (KOK-suh)
The hipbone and hip joint.

Coxae
Plural of coxa.

Coxa Valga (KOK-suh VAL-guh)
A hip deformity in which the angle created by the head and shaft of the femur (thigh bone) is increased, angling the femur toward the side of the body.

Coxa Vara (KOK-suh VAY-ruh)
A hip deformity in which the angle created by the head and shaft of the femur (thigh bone) is decreased, angling the femur in toward the midline of the body. This causes one leg to be shorter, which makes a child limp.

Coxsackievirus (kok-SAK-ee-vie-rus)
An enterovirus (a virus that thrives mainly in the intestinal tract) that may cause *congenital* heart lesions in the newborn of a woman infected during the first trimester of pregnancy. This type of infection can range from mild to serious when contracted by children.

CP
The abbreviation for cerebral palsy.

CPAP
The abbreviation for continuous positive airway pressure.

CPD
The abbreviation for cephalopelvic disproportion.

CPK, C-PK
The abbreviation for creatine phosphokinase.

CPR
The abbreviation for cardiopulmonary resuscitation.

CPS
The abbreviation for Child Protective Services.

Cradle Cap
Refer to **Seborrheic Dermatitis**.

cranio-
A prefix meaning skull.

Craniofacial (kray-nee-oe-FAY-shuhl)
Relating to the skull and bones of the face.

Craniostenosis (kray-nee-oe-stee-NOE-sis)
A defect in which the bone *sutures* of the skull close prematurely. The presence of *brain damage* depends on which bones close prematurely, and how early they close. An abnormally shaped skull can result when some sutures fuse prematurely and other sutures remain open and allow for expansion of the cranium as the brain grows.

Cranium (KRAY-nee-um)
The part of the skull that encloses the brain.

Crawl
To move by using the arms and legs to propel the body forward or backward with the abdomen resting on the floor.
Also known as **Belly Crawl, Combat Crawl,** *and* **Commando Crawl.**
Compare to **Creep**.

Crawling Aid
A device that supports the child's trunk to enable him to bear weight on his hands and knees.

Creatine Phosphokinase (CPK, C-PK) (KREE-uh-teen fos-foe-KIE-nays)

An enzyme released by damaged brain tissue, heart muscle, and skeletal muscle cells. There is a high level of C-PK in the blood of children with *muscular dystrophy*.

Creep

To move forward or backward on the hands and knees with the abdomen off the floor.

*Compare to **Crawl**.*

Cretinism (KREE-tin-izm)

*Refer to **Congenital Hypothyroidism**.*

Crib Death

*Refer to **Sudden Infant Death Syndrome**.*

Crib-O-Gram

A test that detects deafness in infants.

Cri du Chat Syndrome (kree-dyoo-shah)

A *genetic* disorder that occurs when part of the short arm of *chromosome* 5 is deleted. It is characterized by *microcephaly*, wide-spaced eyes, a catlike cry in infancy (due to a small larynx), *short stature*, and *mental retardation*. In French, cri du chat means "cry of the cat."

*Also known as **5p- Syndrome**.*

Crigler-Najjar Syndrome (KREEG-ler NA-hayr)

An *autosomal recessive disorder* caused by a lack of glucuronyl transferase, an enzyme needed to cause a chemical reaction in the body. Crigler-Najjar Syndrome is characterized by severe *jaundice* and *brain damage*, and is usually fatal in infancy.

Crippled Children's Services (CCS)

A state administered program that was established as part of the Social Security Act of 1935 to provide services to children with handicapping conditions. Individual states receive funding under the Maternal and Child Health block grant, as well as from state and local sources. Financial and diagnostic eligibility and services vary from state to state. Services often include medical and therapy intervention, as well as supplies (such as a walker). Most states now use a name other than "Crippled Children's Services" for the agency that offers the services described above. For example, in California the agency is called "California Children's Services" and in Nebraska the agency is called "Medically Handicapped Children's Program." More information on how to receive assistance for a child with disabilities can be obtained by contacting the local office of the state health agency.

Criterion-Referenced Test

A test that compares a child's performance to specific criteria, thus determining the skills the child possesses. (The child is not measured against norms set by the performance of other children.)
Compare **Norm-Referenced Test** *and* **Screening Test**.

Cross-Eye

Refer to **Esotropia**.

"Cross the Midline"

Movement of a limb that goes past the center of the body.

Croup (kroop)

Inflammation and swelling of the trachea and bronchi, characterized by a barking cough and hoarseness. Croup is a viral infection and affects children up to approximately four years of age. *Laryngotracheobronchitis* (inflammation of the larynx, trachea, and bronchi) is sometimes used interchangeably with the word croup.

Crouzon's Syndrome (kroo-ZONZ)

An *autosomal dominant disorder* characterized by shallow, wide-spaced orbits (the bony sockets in the skull that contain the eyes) which make the eyes bulge; moderate hearing loss; underdevelopment of the upper jaw bone; progressive loss of vision (however, vision is not always severely affected); and craniostenosis (a condition in which the *sutures* between the bones of the skull close prematurely).

Cruising

Moving (stepping) sideways while holding on to a support (for example, walking while holding on to furniture).

Cryptorchidism (kript-OR-kid-izm)

Refer to **Undescended Testes**.

Crystalline Lens

Refer to **Lens**.

C-Section

Refer to **Cesarean Section**.

CSF

The abbreviation for cerebrospinal fluid.

ct

The abbreviation for chest tube.

CT Scanning

Computerized Axial Tomography. This is a diagnostic procedure in which a computerized machine creates pictures of cross sections of the body.

These images of tissues are produced by passing X-ray beams at various angles through the area of the body to be studied.

Also known as CAT Scanning.

Cubitus (KYOO-bi-tus)
The bend of the arm, or the elbow joint.

Cuboid (KYOO-boid)
The small bone of the foot that is shaped like a cube. It is between the heel bone and the fourth and fifth metatarsals (the bones of the foot to which the toe bones are attached).

Cue
Refer to Prompt.

Cued Speech
A method of communication for the hearing impaired. Cued speech supplements the visual aspects of speech (speechreading) with gestures that make it easier to distinguish between similar-appearing speech sounds (such as /b/ and /p/). There are eight handshapes which symbolize groups of consonant sounds and four hand placements around the face which represent groups of vowel sounds.

Culture
A laboratory test in which cells, tissues, or *microorganisms* are grown and studied to determine a diagnosis. Samples of body tissues or fluids are placed in a growth medium that encourages cultivation of the cells, tissues, or microorganisms.

Cuneiform Bones (kyoo-NEE-i-form)
Any of the small bones of the wrist or foot.

Curvature of the Spine
An abnormal condition in which the spine is not in alignment.
Refer to Scoliosis, Kyphosis, and Lordosis.

Cutaneous (kyoo-TAY-nee-us)
Referring to the skin.

Cutaneous Vesicostomy
Refer to Vesicostomy.

Cut-away Cup
Refer to Cut-out Cup.

cuti-
A prefix meaning skin.

Cutis (KYOO-tis)
The skin.

Cutis Marmorata
A brief blue or purple *mottling* (coloring) of the skin, such as that which sometimes occurs when the skin is exposed to the cold.

Cut-out Cup
A flexible plastic cup that has a semi-circular piece cut out of the rim. Since the cup has a cut-out portion, the adult can monitor the child's intake of fluid and adjust the flow rate while holding the cup in a position that allows the child to drink without overextending his neck. The flexibility of the cup enables the adult to bend it enough to fit the child's mouth.

C-V Combination
Combining a consonant and vowel sound, such as "ba."

CVN
The abbreviation for central venous nutrition.

CVS
The abbreviation for chorionic villus sampling.

Cyanosis (sie-uh-NOE-sis)
A blue or "dusky" color to the skin and mucous membranes (most notably the lips, tongue, and beds of the fingernails or toenails) caused by a lack of oxygen in the bloodstream. Cyanosis can be a sign of *congenital heart disease* in the newborn, or of other heart or lung disorders.

Cyanotic
Refer to **Cyanosis**.

Cylert™ (SIE-lert)
Refer to **Pemoline**.

cyst-
A prefix meaning bladder.

Cyst
A closed sac in any organ or tissue that contains fluid or semisolid material and forms a lump. Cysts are generally harmless, but can disturb the functioning of the organ or tissue where they are growing.

Cystic Fibrosis (CF) (SIS-tik fie-BROE-sis)
An *autosomal recessive disorder* characterized by abnormally thick secretions, which contribute to chronic lung damage, and a lack of the enzymes needed to breakdown and absorb fats, which causes malnutrition. Cystic fibrosis is a serious illness that nearly always shortens a child's life expectancy.

cysto-
A prefix meaning bladder.

Cystourethrography (sis-toe-yoo-ree-THROG-ruh-fee)
A procedure to detect *reflux* of urine, performed by inserting a tube through the urethra and into the bladder, injecting contrast material into the tube, and taking X-rays. The picture, or cystourethrogram, will also reveal any abnormalities within the bladder. This procedure is known as *voiding cystourethrography* if X-rays are taken as the patient voids.

cyt-, cyto-
Prefixes meaning cell.

-cyte
A suffix meaning cell.

Cytogenetics
The study of the formation, structure, and function of cells in relation to genetics. Cytogenetic techniques make it possible to diagnose fetal abnormalities as early as 11 to 14 weeks of gestation (after amniotic fluid or placental samples are obtained via *amniocentesis* or *chorionic villus sampling*).

Cytomegalic Inclusion Disease (CID) (sie-tuh-muh-GAL-ik)
A *congenital* infection caused by cytomegalovirus (CMV). Although CMV is a common virus that causes no significant damage to healthy children and adults, it can cause severe damage to the fetus of an infected pregnant woman. CMV can cause *low birth-weight*, *microcephaly*, *jaundice*, *anemia*, liver and spleen damage, hearing impairment, and *mental retardation*.

Cytomegalovirus (CMV) (sie-tuh-MEG-uh-loe-vie-ruhs)
A herpes-type virus that may infect an unborn baby, causing severe illness and birth defects.
   Refer to **Cytomegalic Inclusion Disease**.

D

dactyl-
A prefix meaning finger or toe.

Dantrium™ (DAN-tree-uhm)
Refer to *Dantrolene*.

Dantrolene (DAN-troe-leen)
An *antispastic drug* that works directly on the muscle, relaxing spasms caused by injury to the spinal cord or brain.

Daughter Cell
Any cell resulting from the division of a mother, or parent, cell (a cell that divides and gives rise to two or more cells).

dB
The abbreviation for decibel.

dc
The abbreviation for discontinue.

DCS
The abbreviation for Department of Children's Services.

DD
The abbreviation for developmental disability.

DDST
The abbreviation for Denver Developmental Screening Test.

de-
A prefix meaning remove or decrease.

Deaf-Blindness
A condition involving both *auditory* and visual disability. A child with the two disabilities usually has such a high degree of communication and other developmental and educational problems, that she cannot be effectively served in a special education class solely for children with hearing impairments or visual impairments. Deaf-blindness may be caused by *genetic* factors (such as *Usher syndrome*), maternal illness during pregnancy (such as *rubella*), injury (such as a brain hemorrhage associated with prolonged labor), or illness (such as *spinal meningitis*, which may lead to optic and auditory nerve damage if not treated promptly and effectively).

Deafness
A lack of the sense of hearing or profound hearing loss.
*Refer to **Auditory Impairment**.*

Decadron™ (DEK-uh-dron)
*Refer to **Dexamethasone.***

Decibel (dB)
A unit for measure of sound intensity, or loudness. The child with normal hearing can hear sounds at 20 decibels or less.

Deciduous (dee-SID-yoo-us)
Not permanent. For example, the primary teeth (baby teeth) are also known as deciduous teeth.

Deciduous Teeth
Refer to *Primary Teeth*.

Decoding
The process of analyzing and making sense of sounds, symbols, gestures, or other types of communication. Decoding is a part of understanding the meaning of language.

Decongestant
A drug that relieves nasal congestion by reducing the swelling and inflammation of the membranes of the nose.

Decubitus Ulcer (de-KYOO-bi-tus)
A pressure sore or bedsore.

Deep Tendon Reflex (DTR)
An automatic muscle contraction in response to a tapping (stretching) of the muscle's tendon. Deep tendon reflexes are indicators of the condition of the nervous system.

Defecation
A bowel movement. The evacuation of feces from the digestive tract through the rectum.

Deficit
An area of weakness.

Deglutition (dee-gloo-TISH-un)
The act of swallowing.

Dehydration
The loss of excessive amounts of body water. Symptoms include extreme thirst; decreased and concentrated (dark) urine output; difficulty in forming tears and saliva; sunken eyes; and dry lips, tongue, and skin. Dehydration

is caused by not taking in enough water or by losing body water and not replenishing it (as with perspiration, vomiting or diarrhea, or disease such as *diabetes*).

de Lange Syndrome
Refer to **Cornelia de Lange Syndrome**.

Deletion
The loss of *genetic* material from a *chromosome*.

Denis-Browne Splint™
A bar-type splint in which the child's shoes are attached at varying degrees of separation and angle. This type of splint is often used as part of the treatment of *clubfoot*.

Dental Caries
Cavities or decay of the teeth.

Dentin
The hard substance that surrounds the tooth pulp and is covered by the enamel.

Dentition
The characteristics (type, number, and arrangement) of teeth. Dentition also refers to the eruption of teeth.

Denver Developmental Screening Test (DDST)
A screening test used to evaluate the language, gross motor, fine motor, and personal/social development of the six-week to six-year-old and to identify possible areas of delay. Typically, training on how to administer the test is by a certified master trainer or by a training video.

Deoxyribonucleic Acid (DNA) (dee-ok-see-rie-boe-noo-KLEE-ik)
The principal component of living tissue that contains the *genetic* code responsible for the inheritance and transmission of *chromosomes* and *genes*.

Deoxyribonucleic Acid (DNA) Analysis
A diagnostic procedure done to obtain *genetic* information about a fetus. It is used to diagnose conditions such as *fragile X syndrome* prenatally.

Depakene™ (DEP-uh-kayn)
Refer to **Valproic Acid**.

Depakote™ (DEP-uh-kote)
Refer to **Valproic Acid**.

Department of Children's Services (DCS)
A protective services agency that investigates, evaluates, and monitors cases of reported child abuse and neglect.
*Refer to **Child Abuse and Neglect** and **Mandated Reporter**.*

Department of Public Social Services (DPSS)
An agency that provides public assistance, such as financial help, food, or shelter, to individuals who qualify.
*Also known as **Welfare**.*

de Pezzer Catheter™
A type of urinary *catheter*.
*Also known as a **Pezzer Catheter**.*

Depth Perception
The ability to blend slightly dissimilar images from the two eyes to judge depth and spatial relationships.

derm-
A prefix meaning skin.

Dermatoglyphics (der-muh-toe-GLIF-iks)
The study of the skin ridge patterns (also known as prints, as in fingerprints) on the fingers, toes, palms of the hands, and the soles of the feet. Examining skin ridge patterns is useful in diagnosing some *chromosomal abnormalities*.

Derotation Femoral Osteotomy (FEM-or-uhl os-tee-OT-oe-mee)
A surgical procedure in which the shaft of the femur (the thigh bone) is cut to change the alignment of the head and neck of the femur with the acetabulum (the hip socket).
*Refer to **Osteotomy**.*

DES
The abbreviation for diethylstilbestrol.

Development
The lifelong process of growth to maturity through which an individual acquires increasingly complex abilities.

Developmental Age
The age at which a child is functioning (demonstrating specific abilities), based on assessment of the child's skills and comparison of those skills to the age at which they are considered typical. For example, at the chronological age of 36 months, a child might demonstrate the skills of a 30–month-old, and thus be said to have a developmental age of 30 months.
*Also known as **Mental Age** or **Functional Age**.*

Developmental Delay
The term used to describe the condition of an infant or young child who is not achieving new skills in the typical time frame and/or is exhibiting behaviors that are not appropriate for her age. Some children who are developmentally delayed eventually have a specific diagnosis of a particular developmental disability, while other children with delays catch up to their typically developing peers.

Developmental Disability (DD)
Any physical or mental condition (such as *mental retardation, cerebral palsy, epilepsy, autism,* or a *neurological disorder*) that begins before the age of 18 years, causes the child to acquire skills at a slower rate than her peers, is expected to continue indefinitely, and impairs the child's ability to function normally in society.

Developmental Milestone
A skill that is recognized as a measurement of a child's functioning, or development, and that is typically achieved by a certain age. Taking steps independently is an example of a developmental milestone.

Developmental Profile II (DP-II)
A developmental scale used to assess the physical, self-help, social, academic, and communication development of children between birth and nine and one-half years of age. An interview format is used. Typically, the DP-II is administered by a physical or occupational therapist or an M.D.
   *Formerly known as the **Alpern-Boll Developmental Profile**.*

Developmental Programming for Infants and Young Children
An evaluation tool used to assess the perceptual/fine motor, gross motor, social/emotional, self-care, language, and cognitive development of infants and young children between birth and 36 months of age. The Developmental Programming for Infants and Young Children is also a curriculum tool. Typically, this test is administered by a professional with a minimum of a college degree or by a physical or occupational therapist.

Developmental Quotient (DQ)
A score similar to an *IQ* that describes an infant's developmental level.

Deviation
A moving away from the normal standard or course.

Dexamethasone (dek-suh-METH-uh-sone)
A *steroid* drug that may be used to help reduce inflammation and swelling.

Dexedrine™ (DEKS-uh-dreen)
   *Refer to **Dextroamphetamine**.*

Dextroamphetamine (deks-troe-am-FET-uh-meen)
A *stimulant* drug that may be used to treat *Attention Deficit Disorders* and *hyperactivity*.

Dextrostix™ (DEK-stroe-stiks)
A test that measures sugar levels in the blood, performed by placing a drop of blood on a chemically treated plastic strip (also known as a Dextrostix). It is used in the diagnosis of *hyperglycemia*.

di-
A prefix meaning two.

dia-
A prefix meaning through or between.

Diabetes Insipidus (die-uh-BEE-teez in-SIP-i-duhs)
A disease characterized by excessive urination and excessive thirst. Diabetes insipidus is caused by damage to part of the pituitary gland (possibly from a head trauma), which results in inadequate secretion of antidiuretic hormone. Treatment is by eradicating the injury to the pituitary gland when possible, or by replacing the antidiuretic hormone to control the disease. Diabetes insipidus is more common in the young.

Diabetes Mellitus (die-uh-BEE-teez muh-LIE-tuhs)
A chronic disorder of carbohydrate metabolism characterized by abnormally high sugar levels in the blood and sugar in the urine, excessive urination and thirst, and sometimes by abnormally large intake of food, weight loss, and excessive acidity of body fluids. Diabetes mellitus results from inadequate production or utilization of insulin (a hormone that regulates the metabolism of blood sugar). Some patients with diabetes mellitus are insulin-dependent (because the body produces little or no insulin) and therefore require insulin therapy. (This is referred to as Type I.) Others are non-insulin dependent (the body produces some insulin) and the disease can usually be controlled by diet and medication, although insulin therapy is sometimes needed. (This is referred to as Type II.)

Diagnosis (Dx)
Determination of the nature of a disease or disorder. Prenatal diagnosis is the determination of a baby's illness or *developmental disability* before birth.

Diagnostic and Statistical Manual of Mental Disorders (DSM-III-R)
A reference published by the American Psychiatric Association that lists the criteria for classifying mental and emotional disorders, such as reactive attachment disorders of infancy, developmental learning disorders, and psychoses. The DSM-IV is scheduled to be published in 1994.

Diamox™ (DIE-uh-moks)
Refer to Acetazolamide.

Diaphragm (DIE-uh-fram)
A muscle that assists with respiration. It separates the chest cavity from the abdominal cavity, and is located above the liver.

Diaphysis (die-AF-i-sis)
The shaft of a long bone.

Diastasis (die-AS-tuh-sis)
A separation of two parts of the body that normally are joined together or are in contact.

Diastasis Recti Abdominis
The separation of the two rectus muscles that extend from the lower ribs down the length of the abdomen. This condition can occur as a birth defect due to incomplete development or be the result of injury. It is also occasionally seen in women during or following pregnancy.

Diastole (die-AS-toe-lee)
The period of relaxation when the heart chamber dilates and fills with blood to be pumped to the rest of the body. (The time between heart contractions.) Diastole coincides with the interval between the second and first heart sound.
Compare Systole.
Refer to Blood Pressure.

Diazepam (die-AZ-uh-pam)
A drug that works as a *muscle relaxant* by acting on the central nervous system. It is usually prescribed for its calming effects. Diazepam can be administered rectally, in which case absorption is much faster than by intramuscular injection or by mouth. It is often administered rectally to stop *status epilepticus.*

DIC
The abbreviation for disseminated intravascular coagulation.

Didactic Materials
Educational tools intended for teaching a specific skill or group of skills. Examples of didactic materials include animal picture cards and a shape sorter.

Diencephalic Syndrome of Infancy (die-en-sef-AL-ik)
A disorder that causes *failure to thrive* after initial normal growth in the infant. Babies with this condition usually have a brain tumor that affects the appetite center of the brain (the hypothalamus).

Diencephalon (die-en-SEF-uh-lon)
The part of the brain that contains the hypothalamus and thalamus.

Diethylstilbestrol (DES) (die-eth-il-stil-BES-trol)
A synthetic estrogen (female sex hormone). DES was formerly prescribed to prevent miscarriage; however, its use with pregnant women was stopped when it was linked to cancer and reproductive problems in daughters of women who were given DES during pregnancy.

Digestion
The bodily process by which food is changed into substances that can be absorbed and assimilated. Digestion takes place in the stomach and the intestines.
*Refer to **Nutrition**.*

Digit
A finger or toe.

Digitalis (dij-i-TAL-is)
A drug that is used to treat heart failure and other heart conditions.

Dilantin™ (die-LAN-tin)
*Refer to **Phenytoin**.*

Dimetapp™ (DIE-muh-tap)
An over-the-counter *antihistamine* and *decongestant* combination.

Diphenhydramine (die-fen-HIE-druh-meen)
An *antihistamine drug* used to treat allergic disorders and motion sickness.

Diphtheria
An acute, infectious bacterial disease that can cause fever, pain, sore throat, and sometimes airway obstruction. Diphtheria can cause inflammation of the heart muscle and certain nerves, and can lead to death. Diphtheria is uncommon now due to the routine administration of the *Diphtheria, Tetanus, and Pertussis Vaccine* (the "D" part of the DPT vaccine).

Diphtheria, Tetanus, and Pertussis Vaccine (DTP/DPT)
An *immunization* against *diphtheria*, *tetanus*, and *pertussis*. The primary series for the DTP immunization consists of injections at two, four, and six months. Two boosters are given, one at 18 months of age, and another injection prior to beginning school (at four and one-half to five years of age). Research suggests that consideration should be given as to whether or not the pertussis vaccine should be administered to some children, specifically infants with a non-stable *neurological disorder*, such as *seizures*, or infants who have had a serious reaction to a prior DTP shot.

Diphthong

A vowel sound that is produced when moving from one vowel sound to another within the same syllable, such as the "oy" sound in "boy."

Diplegia (die-PLEE-jee-uh)

Weakness or *paralysis* in the legs and arms caused by disease or injury to the nerves of the brain or spinal cord that stimulate the muscles, or by disease to the muscles themselves. Sometimes the word diplegia is used to describe *cerebral palsy* in which the legs are most affected (although the arms, trunk, and face may be slightly affected).

Refer to **Paralysis** *and* **Pyramidal Cerebral Palsy.**

diplo-

A prefix meaning double.

Diploid (DIP-loid)

Having two of each kind of *chromosome.* Human cells are normally diploid (except for the *sex chromosomes* in a male).

Compare **Haploid.**

Diplopia (dip-LOE-pee-uh)

Double vision.

dis-

A prefix meaning apart.

Disability

As described in the Americans with Disabilities Act (ADA) of 1992, a disability is a substantially limiting physical or mental impairment which affects basic life activities such as hearing, seeing, speaking, walking, caring for oneself, learning, or working.

Refer to **Developmental Disability.**

Disassociation

Refer to **Dissociation.**

Disease

Any change or interruption of the normal structure or function of a body part, organ, or system. Disease is indicated by characteristic signs and symptoms. The cause and prognosis of a disease is not always known.

Dislocated Hip

A condition in which the femur (thigh bone) has popped out of its hip socket. A dislocated hip can be a *congenital* condition, or it can be caused by injury or the unequal pressure of *spastic* muscles at the joint.

Dislocation

The separation of two body parts, usually two bones of a joint, so that they are no longer in contact.

Compare **Subluxation.**

Disorder

An abnormality or disturbance of normal function, such as a speech disorder.

Disorganized Behavior

Referring to the infant's decreased ability to make smooth transitions through various states of alertness. As the infant approaches toddlerhood, disorganized behavior refers to a decreased ability to organize and tolerate certain types and amounts of sensory stimulation.

Displacement

The removal of an organ or structure from its normal position.

Disseminated Intravascular Coagulation (DIC)

A condition in which too much of the blood's platelets and clotting factors is used due to infection, injury, or disease. There is uncontrolled activation of clotting pathways and overproduction of anticlotting substances, which leave the child vulnerable to excessive bleeding.

Dissociation

1. The process of separating into parts.
2. The ability to use selected (smaller) movement patterns rather than gross (large) movement patterns. This allows for independent movement of one body part without movement of another body part. For example, the child is able to move her head in all directions without the rest of her body moving.

Also known as **Disassociation.**

Distal (DIS-tuhl)

Farther from the point of attachment or origin. For example, the fingers are distal to the shoulder, while the elbow is *proximal* to the shoulder.

Compare **Proximal.**

Distance Vision

Distinct vision of objects at a distance, usually 20 feet.

Distractability

A behavioral characteristic in which a child has difficulty focusing her attention on what is important because her attention is easily diverted by inconsequential occurrences.

Disuse Syndrome
Problems that result from lack of use of a part of the body. A *contracture* is an example of a physical problem that results from lack of use of a body part, and memory disturbance is an example of a mental problem that results from lack of mental activity.

Diuretic (die-yoo-RET-ik)
A drug that promotes excretion of urine from the body.

Diuril™ (DIE-yoo-ril)
Refer to **Chlorothiazide.**

DNA
The abbreviation for deoxyribonucleic acid.

DO
The abbreviation for Doctor of Osteopathy.

Doctor of Osteopathy (D.O.)
A fully licensed physician trained to practice *osteopathic medicine.*

Docusate (DOK-yoo-sayt)
A stool softener.

dolicho-
A prefix meaning long.

Dolichocephalic (dol-i-koe-si-FAL-ik)
Referring to having a long head.

Domain
A developmental area. The six main developmental areas are the cognitive, language (communication), gross motor, fine motor (perceptual), social/emotional, and self-help (adaptive) domains.

Dominant Gene
A *gene* that overrides any *recessive gene* it is paired with in determining what characteristic or condition a child inherits from her parents. For example, the gene for brown eyes is dominant over the gene for blue eyes, so a child who inherits one gene for brown eyes and one for blue eyes will have brown eyes.
Refer to **Autosomal Dominant Disorder.**

Dominant Hand
Refer to **Hand Preference.**

Dopamine (DOE-puh-meen)
An *amino acid* that functions as a *neurotransmitter* in certain areas of the brain and central nervous system, enabling electrical impulses to travel

from one *neuron* to another across a *synapse*. Dopamine also affects the myocardium (the middle and thickest layer of the heart wall composed of cardiac muscle) by increasing cardiac output.

Doppler Scanning™ (DOP-ler)
An *ultrasound* imaging technique that can monitor movement of a body structure, such as a fetal heart beat.

dors-
A prefix meaning back.

Dorsal (DOR-suhl)
Referring to a position that is to the back. For example, the back is dorsal compared to the abdomen, which is *ventral*.
   Also known as **Posterior**.
   Compare **Ventral**.

Dorsal Rhizotomy (DOR-suhl rie-ZOT-uh-mee)
A neurosurgical procedure in which certain nerves of the spine are cut to reduce *spasticity*.
   Also known as **Rhizotomy**, **Selective Dorsal Rhizotomy**, *and* **Selective Posterior Rhizotomy**.

Dorsiflexion (dor-si-FLEK-shuhn)
Bending or flexing backward. For example, bending the foot toward the upper surface of the foot.
   Compare **Plantar Flexion**.

Dorsum
The back surface of a body part. In the foot, the dorsum is the top of the foot.

Double Hemiplegia
Weakness or *paralysis* in both the arms, both the legs, the trunk, and the head caused by disease or injury to the nerves of the brain or spinal cord that stimulate the muscles, or by disease to the muscles themselves. Double hemiplegia also describes *cerebral palsy* in which the arms, legs, face, and trunk are affected, with the arms (and often the face) most affected.
   Refer to **Cerebral Palsy** *and* **Pyramidal Cerebral Palsy**.

Down Syndrome
A *genetic* disorder caused by a *chromosomal abnormality*. Down syndrome results when an extra (a third) *chromosome* 21, or extra part of chromosome 21, is in the body's cells. The presence of this extra genetic material can occur several ways: by *nondisjunction*, *translocation*, or *mosaicism*. Nondisjunction is the failure of the chromosome 21 pair to separate in the sperm or ovum (egg), prior to conception. If a sperm or ovum in which the chromosome 21 pair has not separated is involved in forming a fertilized

egg, the resulting baby born will have 3 (a trisomy) chromosome number 21s. (She will have inherited two chromosome 21s from one parent and the usual one chromosome 21 from the other parent.) This is the most common way Down syndrome occurs. Translocation occurs when an extra (a third) chromosome 21 becomes attached to another numbered chromosome, again prior to conception. Mosaicism is the abnormal separation of the chromosome 21 pair, after conception. Because the separation occurs after some cell division has taken place, not all cells will be affected, and thus the characteristic features of Down syndrome will vary. Characteristics of Down syndrome may include *hypotonia*, upward slant to the eyes, *congenital* heart defect, *epicanthal folds*, a small mouth, small stature and facial features, a flattened back of the head, short broad hands with a *simian crease*, *Brushfield spots*, joint hyperflexibility, and varying degrees of *mental retardation*.

Also known as **Trisomy 21**. *Previously known as* **Mongolism** *because the characteristic facial features associated with Down syndrome were considered to look similar to those of Mongolians.*

DP-II
The abbreviation for Developmental Profile II.

DPSS
The abbreviation for the Department of Public Social Services.

DPT/DTP
The abbreviation for Diphtheria, Pertussis, and Tetanus Vaccine.

DQ
The abbreviation for developmental quotient.

Drop Attack
Refer to **Atonic Seizure**.

Drop Foot
A condition in which the foot is bent downward and the toes drag when walking. This condition is usually caused by nerve damage.

Drop Seizure
Refer to **Atonic Seizure**.

Drug Baby
Refer to **Prenatally Exposed to Drugs**.

DSM-III-R
The abbreviation for the third edition of *The Diagnostic and Statistical Manual of Mental Disorders*.

DTP/DPT
The abbreviation for the Diphtheria, Tetanus, and Pertussis Vaccine.

DTR
The abbreviation for deep tendon reflex.

Dubowitz Assessment
An assessment in which the doctor moves and positions the baby to determine her neurological and muscular maturity. It is performed to estimate a newborn's *gestational age*.

Duchenne Muscular Dystrophy (dyoo-SHEN MUS-kyoo-ler DIS-troe-fee)
The most common form of *muscular dystrophy*. This *X-linked recessive disease* is characterized by progressive muscle weakness and wasting, respiratory problems, often mild *mental retardation*, and rarely, heart failure. Duchenne muscular dystrophy affects mostly boys and appears slowly in early childhood. Most children do not survive beyond 20 years.
Also known as **Pseudohypertrophic Muscular Dystrophy**.

Duckfeet
Refer to **Toeing Out**.

Duct
A tube leading from a gland to allow the passage of fluids. The tear ducts are an example.

Ductus Arteriosus (DUK-tus ar-tee-ree-OE-sus)
A blood vessel present in the fetus that connects the aorta with the pulmonary artery in order to bypass most blood away from the baby's lungs. Before birth, the placenta does the job of oxygenating the baby's blood. The blood vessel normally closes within a few days after birth so that blood can flow through the lungs to be oxygenated. Often the vessel does not close normally in premature babies. (This condition is called a *patent ductus arteriosus*, or PDA.)
Compare **Patent Ductus Arteriosus**.
Refer to **Fetal Circulation**.

Ductus Venosus (DUK-tus vee-NOE-sus)
A small channel that develops in the embryonic liver, diverting the fetus's blood through the liver. (The blood flows through the channel in the liver rather than through liver tissue.) Before birth, the placenta does the job of cleansing the baby's blood. After birth, the ductus venosus closes so blood can pass through the liver tissue to be cleansed before returning to the heart.
Refer to **Fetal Circulation**.

Dulcolax™ (DUL-koe-laks)
Refer to **Bisacodyl**.

Duodenal Atresia (dyoo-oe-DEE-nuhl or dyoo-OD-uh-nuhl)
Blockage in the small intestine due to failure of the opening to develop or destruction of the opening.

Duodenal Stenosis
Narrowing (constriction) of a portion of the small intestine.

duodeno-
A prefix meaning duodenum.

Duodenum (dyoo-oe-DEE-num or dyoo-OD-uh-nuhm)
The first and widest section of the small intestine. It is located between the stomach and the jejunum. (The jejunum is the middle section and the ileum is the third section of the small intestine.)

Dura Mater (DYOO-ruh MAY-tur)
The outermost layer of the *meninges* (the membranes surrounding the brain and spinal cord). The innermost layer is the pia mater and the middle layer is the arachnoid.
Refer to **Meninges**.

Dwarfism
Refer to **Short Stature**.

Dx
The abbreviation for diagnosis.

Dynamic Splint
A device used to properly position a joint (such as the wrist) while also assisting other parts of the body (such as the fingers) to engage in purposeful movement.
Compare **Static Splint**.

dys-
A prefix meaning painful, abnormal, or difficult.

Dysarthria (dis-AR-three-uh)
Speech *articulation* problems due to damage to the vocal structures or the nerves that control these structures, resulting in decreased muscle control. Children with dysarthria have language skills (they understand and can formulate language), but have difficulty with spoken expression.

Dyskinesia (dis-ki-NEE-see-uh)
Difficulty in performing voluntary movement, usually due to damage to the basal ganglia of the brain. Examples of dyskinesia include *chorea*, *athetosis*, and *choreoathetosis*. Dyskinesia is usually characterized by extra (involuntary) movements that may affect a specific muscle group or the whole body.

Dyskinetic
Refer to **Dyskinesia**.

Dyslexia (dis-LEK-see-uh)
A learning disability in which the child has difficulty with reading due to difficulty distinguishing written symbols. She may, for example, transpose letters and words (such as reading "top" as "pot").

Dysmaturative Myopathy
A rare form of *muscular dystrophy*.

Dysmature
1. Lacking in development, or having faulty development.
2. Referring to a fetus or newborn who is abnormally small due to failure to gain weight in the weeks before birth.

Dysmetria (dis-MEE-tree-uh)
Difficulty with voluntary movement in which the child is unable to stop the movement at the desired point (either overreaching or falling short of the desired point).

Dysmorphic (dis-MOR-fik)
Referring to a deformed shape.

Dysplasia (dis-PLAY-zee-uh or dis-PLAY-zhuh)
A growth abnormality of a body structure or an individual cell. The size, shape, or number of cells may be a factor.

Dyspnea (disp-NEE-uh)
Difficult breathing.

Dyspraxia (dis-PRAK-see-uh)
Difficulty with planning and performing coordinated movements, although there is no apparent damage to the muscles. For example, a three-year-old with dyspraxia may have difficulty with standing on one foot or stomping her feet on request, even in imitation of someone else.

Dystonia (dis-TOE-nee-uh)
1. Abnormal *muscle tone*, either increased or decreased tone.
2. A *genetic* disorder in which the child experiences severe muscle spasms and exhibits abnormal movements and postures, especially when walking.

E

Ear

The organ responsible for the sense of hearing. The ear consists of the outer ear (external ear), the middle ear, and the inner ear. The outer ear consists of the *pinna* (the part of the ear seen on the outside of the head) and the *auditory canal* (the canal leading from the outside inward to the *tympanic membrane*, or eardrum). The eardrum separates the outer and middle ear. The middle ear consists of the small cavity between the eardrum and the inner ear and the three tiny bones (ossicles) of the ear (the *malleus*, the *incus*, and the *stapes*). Also in the middle ear is the opening to the *eustachian tube* which joins the back of the throat to the ear. The inner ear consists of the *cochlea* and the *vestibular apparatus*. It is through the cochlea that the *auditory nerve* passes as it extends to the brain.

*Refer to **Hearing**.*

Ear Canal

*Refer to **Auditory Canal**.*

Eardrum

*Refer to **Tympanic Membrane** and to **Ear**.*

Eardrum Perforation

A rupture of the eardrum that can be caused several ways, including by acute or chronic *otitis media*, a hard blow to the ear, or puncture with a sharp object. Antibiotics are used to treat infection, but a perforated eardrum usually heals on its own. Once healed, if there is no damage to the bones of the middle ear, normal hearing returns.

*Also known as a **Perforated Eardrum**.*

Early Educator

*Refer to **Infant Educator**.*

Early Intervention

Specialized services provided to infants and toddlers who are *at-risk* for or are showing signs of *developmental delay*. Services emphasize the continued development of basic skills through planned interactions that will minimize the effects of the baby's condition. Several types of qualified professionals may plan and implement early intervention services, provided in conformity with an *individualized family service plan*. These professionals include case managers, infant educators (who use developmental play activities to promote the infant's acquisition of basic skills), physical or occupational therapists, speech and language therapists, audiologists, social workers, or other individuals who are trained to help infants and young children with acquiring new skills and behaviors, or to provide other services such as family training, screening, assessment, or health care. Early intervention services are provided under public supervision and at no cost (except where federal or state law provides for a system of payment by families).

Early Interventionist
An *infant educator* or other professional who is trained to assess and/or plan and implement a program which addresses the infant or young child's developmental needs.

Ear Tube
A small plastic tube that is surgically placed through the eardrum into the middle ear to treat chronic ear fluid or chronic ear infections. The tube is not placed permanently, and usually falls out on its own.
   Also known as a **Tympanostomy Tube**, **Myringotomy Tube**, **Pressure Equalization Tube**, *and* **Ventilation Tube**.
   Refer to **Myringotomy**.

ECG
The abbreviation for electrocardiogram.

Echocardiography (ek-oe-kar-dee-OG-ruh-fee)
An *ultrasound* imaging technique that creates a picture of the heart (*echocardiogram*) produced by the echo of sound waves.

Echolalia (ek-oe-LAY-lee-uh)
Involuntary repetition of another person's words or phrases, including voice tone, usually without comprehension. Echolalia is sometimes seen in children with *autism*, *mental retardation*, or *schizophrenia*. (In very young children, imitating or echoing another's speech is normal, and helps in the development of expressive speech and language skills.)

Echovirus (EK-oe-vie-ruhs)
A usually harmless *enterovirus* associated with many infections.

Eclampsia (e-KLAMP-see-uh)
A serious complication of pregnancy in which the woman who has *pre-eclampsia* also has *seizures* and sometimes *coma*. Eclampsia can be fatal to the pregnant woman, and termination of the pregnancy or early delivery may be necessary if the woman's condition cannot be stabilized.
   Refer to **Pre-eclampsia**.

ect-, ecto-
Prefixes meaning outside.

-ectasis
A suffix meaning dilation.

Ectasis (EK-tuh-sis)
Dilation or distention of any tubular vessel.

-ectomy
A suffix meaning surgical removal.

Eczema (EK-ze-muh)
Inflammation of the outer layer of skin, resulting in an itchy, weeping rash that blisters and scales. The cause of eczema is often unknown; however, it may result from an allergy.

EDC
The abbreviation for estimated date of confinement.

Edema (e-DEE-muh)
Fluid retention in the body tissues that often causes swelling.

Educable
An old term for mild *mental retardation*.

Education for All Handicapped Children Act (Public Law 94–142)
A federal law passed in 1975 that mandates that states provide special education services ("a free appropriate public education in the least restrictive environment") to meet the needs of children with disabilities from ages 5 to 21 years.
Refer to **Individuals with Disabilities Education Act (IDEA)**.

Education of the Handicapped Amendments of 1986 (Public Law 99–457)
A federal law passed in 1986 that amends and becomes a part of PL 94–142. PL 99–457 mandates that states provide preschool education for children with special needs (beginning at age three years). Part H focuses on the development of services to at-risk and handicapped infants and toddlers.
Refer to **Individuals with Disabilities Education Act (IDEA)**.

Edward Syndrome
Refer to **Trisomy 18**.

EEG
The abbreviation for electroencephalogram.

EENT
The abbreviation for ears, eyes, nose, and throat.

ef-
A prefix meaning out of or away from.

Efferent
Directed away from center, such as a nerve impulse that travels from the central nervous system to a nerve or muscle.
Compare Afferent.

Ehlers-Danlos Syndrome (AY-lerz DAN-los)
A *congenital hereditary* disorder characterized by deficiency in the quality or quantity of *collagen*, which may result in very stretchy skin with poor wound healing, fragile tissue, and *hyperextensible* joints that easily dislocate.

EKG
The abbreviation for electrocardiogram.

Electrocardiogram (EKG, ECG) (ee-lek-troe-KAR-dee-oe-gram)
A recording of the heart's electrical impulses.

Electrocardiography (ee-lek-troe-kar-dee-OG-ruh-fee)
A test to study the electrical impulses of the heart. *Electrodes* attached to an electrocardiograph machine are applied to the individual's chest, wrist, and ankles. The machine records the heart's electrical impulses (and thus detects any abnormal electrical activity), which are displayed on a screen or printout. The procedure causes no discomfort.

Electrode (ee-LEK-trode)
A device attached to an adhesive pad that is placed on the body to record electrical activity such as when obtaining an *electroencephalogram* or *electrocardiogram*.

Electroencephalogram (EEG) (ee-lek-troe-en-SEF-uh-loe-gram)
A recording of the electrical impulses of the brain.

Electroencephalography (ee-lek-troe-en-sef-uhl-OG-ruh-fee)
A test to study the electrical impulses produced by the activity of the brain. *Electrodes* attached to a recording machine are applied to the individual's scalp. The machine measures the brain's electrical impulses, which are displayed on a printout. Electroencephalography is useful in diagnosing certain conditions such as *epilepsy* and certain tumors.

Electrolyte (ee-LEK-troe-liet)
A substance that, when dissolved or melted, splits into ions which can conduct an electrical current.

Electromyogram (EMG) (ee-lek-troe-MIE-oe-gram)
A recording of the electrical activity of muscles.

Electromyography (ee-lek-troe-mie-OG-ruh-fee)
A test to study the electrical activity of muscles.

Electronic Communication Aids
Computers, voice synthesizers, printers, and other electrical devices that enable a child with speech difficulties to communicate.

Ellis-van Creveld Syndrome
An *autosomal recessive disorder* characterized by short limbs and stature, extra fingers and occasionally toes, often a cardiac defect, and occasional *mental retardation*.
   Also known as **Chondroectodermal Dysplasia**.

Emaciated
Referring to an extremely lean, wasted condition of the body.

Embryo (EM-bree-oe)
The unborn, developing infant from conception through approximately the eighth week.

Emesis (EM-e-sis)
Vomiting.

EMG
The abbreviation for electromyography.

-emia
A suffix meaning blood.

Emotional Abuse
Continual belittling, threatening, blaming, ignoring, or rejecting of a child that can disable him emotionally and behaviorally. The parent or caregiver who verbally abuses, is always negative, or responds in unpredictable ways toward a child in his care is considered to be maltreating him. Although emotional abuse is difficult to prove, the *mandated reporter* should report any observed or suspected abuse.
   Refer to **Child Abuse and Neglect** *and* **Mandated Reporter**.

Emotionally Disturbed
Having a *learning disability* or behavioral disturbance characterized by an inability to learn and/or maintain normal relationships with peers and with teachers. The child who is emotionally disturbed has no apparent neurological disorder and usually is of average or above-average intelligence, yet is unable to function in the regular classroom.

Encephalitis (en-sef-uh-LIE-tis)
An inflammation of the brain, usually caused by an infection. Encephalitis can be mild, but is more commonly serious, and may result in *seizures*, *paralysis* of one side of the body, *brain damage, coma*, or death.

Encephalocele (en-SEF-uh-loe-seel)
A birth defect in which the brain, *meninges* (the membranes surrounding the brain and spinal cord), or both protrude through an opening in the skull. With this form of *spina bifida*, severe *brain damage* usually results due to the brain tissue exposure.
  Refer to **Spina Bifida**.

Encephalomyelitis (en-sef-uh-loe-mie-el-IE-tis)
An inflammation of the brain and spinal cord, usually caused by a virus. Encephalomyelitis can result in *seizures*, partial *paralysis*, loss of sensation, *mental retardation*, and death.

Encoding
1. The stage of memory when information received through the senses is modified and stored.
2. The process of changing ideas into words or written expressions. Encoding is part of expressing language.

Encopresis (en-koe-PREE-sis)
The inability to hold bowel movements long enough to eliminate in the toilet. (The term encopresis applies to children who are old enough to have gained bowel control.) There is no specific physical cause and the condition rarely occurs after ten years of age. Encopresis usually involves a vicious cycle of stool withholding, constipation and leakage of stool, and painful passage of stool.

end-, endo-
A prefix meaning inside.

Endocardial Cushion (en-doe-KAR-dee-uhl)
Raised areas, or masses, on the atrioventricular canal of the embryonic heart. These raised areas of tissue are concerned with development of the atrioventricular canals and valves.
  Refer to **Endocardial Cushion Defect**.

Endocardial Cushion Defect
A complex heart defect involving one or more parts of the *endocardial cushion*. Endocardial cushion defects occur frequently in children with *Down syndrome*.

Endocarditis (en-doe-kar-DIE-tis)
Inflammation of the inner lining of the heart (the endocardium), including the heart valves. Endocarditis is usually caused by infection and can result in heart damage and/or the need for valve replacement. If left untreated, endocarditis can be fatal.

Endocrine (EN-doe-krin or EN-doe-krine or EN-doe-kreen)
Pertaining to the glands of the endocrine system, or glands that secrete directly into the bloodstream.

Endocrine Disorders
Disorders of the glands that produce hormones and regulate body functions. *Diabetes mellitus* is an example.

Endocrine Gland
Glands that secrete important hormones into the bloodstream and influence metabolism and other body functions. The endocrine glands include the pituitary, thyroid, parathyroid, and adrenal glands, the pineal body, and the gonads.

Endocrinologist
A medical doctor who specializes in treating problems of the endocrine system.

Endoscopy (en-DOS-koe-pee)
A procedure in which a narrow, flexible tube is inserted into a body cavity for visual examination.

Endotracheal (en-doe-TRAY-kee-uhl)
Referring to within the trachea.

Endotracheal Tube (ET Tube)
A narrow plastic tube inserted into the trachea to improve respiration.

Enema (EN-e-muh)
A procedure in which fluid is introduced into the rectum. An enema is given to rid the bowel of feces, to administer medicine, or as part of an X-ray study of the intestines.

ENT
The abbreviation for Ear, Nose, and Throat Specialist.
Also known as an **Otolaryngologist**.

entero-
A prefix meaning pertaining to the intestines.

Enterobius Vermicularis (en-ter-OE-bee-us ver-mik-yoo-LAR-is)
Pinworms.
Refer to **Worms**.

Enterocolitis (en-ter-oe-koe-LIE-tis)
An inflammation of the small or large intestines.

Enterovirus (EN-tuhr-oe-vie-ruhs)
A virus that thrives mainly in the intestinal tract.

Enucleation (ee-noo-klee-AY-shuhn)
Surgical removal of the entire eye.

Enunciate
To pronounce, or speak clearly.

Enuresis (en-yoo-REE-sis)
The inability to control the need to urinate at night, during sleep. Enuresis (commonly referred to as bedwetting) is a condition that can occur in children beyond the age of achieving bladder control. Enuresis is caused by immaturity of the nervous system functions concerned with bladder control, by stress, or by a physical abnormality, such as an infection, spinal cord damage, or an anatomic defect of the urinary tract. Usually children no longer wet the bed after about ten years of age.

Enzyme (EN-zime)
A protein that speeds up a chemical change in the body, such as in the digestion of foods.

EOM
1. The abbreviation for extra ocular muscles.
2. The abbreviation for equal ocular movements.

Ependyma (e-PEN-di-muh)
The lining of the central canal of the spinal cord and of the ventricles of the brain.

epi-
A prefix meaning upon, after, or above.

Epicanthal Fold (ep-i-KAN-thuhl)
A vertical skin fold at the inner corner of the eye.

Epiglottis (ep-i-GLOT-is)
The cartilage flap that covers the trachea when swallowing to prevent food from entering the lungs.

Epilepsy (EP-i-lep-see)
A condition characterized by recurrent *seizures* that are caused by abnormal electrical activity in the brain. Seizures can occur for many reasons, including damage to the brain due to infection, injury, birth trauma, tumor, *stroke*, drug intoxication, and chemical imbalance. Seizures that have a known cause are called *Symptomatic* or Secondary. Seizures that do not have an identifiable cause are thought to occur due to a *genetic* predisposition (but not as an inherited genetic disorder), and are referred to as *Idiopathic* or Primary seizures. There are several types of seizures, classified according to the area of the brain affected and the associated behaviors. Seizures are classified as either *Generalized Seizures* or *Partial Seizures*. Generalized seizures

affect the whole brain and usually cause a loss of consciousness. The types of generalized seizures include *Tonic/Clonic (Grand Mal) Seizures, Absence (Petit Mal) Seizures, Myoclonic Seizures,* and *Atonic (Drop) Seizures.* Partial seizures affect specific areas of the brain (although the electrical disturbance may not remain confined to one area and may spread to the whole brain, thus causing a generalized seizure). The child may retain consciousness during a partial seizure. The types of partial seizures include *Simple Partial Seizures* and *Complex Partial Seizures.* Epilepsy is usually treated with *antiepileptic drugs* to control the seizures.

Epinephrine (ep-i-NEF-rin)
A hormone released by the adrenal glands, along with *norepinephrine,* to increase the heart's ability to work, especially in response to stressors on the body such as exercise or fear. It also relaxes the smooth muscles of the *bronchioles* and intestines and has other muscular and metabolic effects. Epinephrine is also made synthetically.
Also known as **Adrenaline.**

Episodic
An incident, such as a *seizure,* that occurs at intervals.

Epithelial (ep-i-THEE-lee-uhl)
Pertaining to the skin, or lining of other body structures such as the lungs and intestines.

Epithelium (ep-i-THEE-lee-um)
A tissue that covers the internal or external surfaces of the body, such as the skin and the lining of the lungs.

Epstein-Barr Virus
A herpes-like virus that causes infectious *mononucleosis.*

Equilibrium (ee-kwuh-LIB-ree-uhm)
Balance.

Equilibrium Reactions
The ability to restore balance when the center of gravity has shifted. Children learn to compensate for a loss of balance by moving in ways to counteract the pull of gravity.
Refer to **Automatic Reflex.**

Equinovalgus (ee-kwi-noe-VAL-gus)
Refer to **Talipes Equinovalgus.**

Equinovarus (ee-kwi-noe-VAY-rus)
Refer to **Talipes Equinovarus.**

Equinus (EE-kwi-nuhs)
A condition in which the foot is held in extension, which results in toe walking. It is caused by a shortening of the calf muscles and tendons.

ERA
The abbreviation for Evoked Response Audiometry.
  *Refer to **Auditory Evoked Response**.*

Erb's Palsy
A condition in which the *brachial plexus* is injured during delivery, resulting in weakness and paralysis of the upper arm on the damaged side. Functional use of the arm usually improves with treatment, including physical therapy.

Erythema (er-i-THEE-muh)
Inflammation of the skin, resulting in redness. Examples of causes include fever, mild sunburn, or blushing.

erythro-
A prefix meaning red.

Erythroblastosis Fetalis (e-rith-roe-blas-TOE-sis fee-TAY-lis)
Severe *hemolytic anemia* of the fetus or newborn infant that is typically caused by *Rh incompatibility*. Rh incompatibility occurs when a pregnant woman who has Rh negative blood is carrying a fetus with Rh positive blood, and the woman was previously exposed to Rh positive blood (either through a pregnancy in which the woman carried a baby with Rh positive blood or through a blood transfusion of Rh positive blood). Due to this prior exposure to the Rh positive blood, the woman produced *antibodies* to Rh positive blood, which react to the Rh positive blood of the fetus she is currently carrying as a foreign substance and destroy the fetus's red blood cells. Erythroblastosis fetalis results in serious fetal disease (generalized *edema*, enlargement of the liver and the spleen, hemolytic anemia, and *jaundice* that leads to *kernicterus*) or in death.
  *Also known as **Hemolytic Disease of the Newborn**.*
  *Refer to **Rh Incompatibility** and **Rh Factor**.*

Erythrocyte (e-RITH-roe-site)
A red blood cell.

Erythromycin (e-rith-roe-MIE-sin)
An *antibiotic drug* used to treat infection.

eso-
A prefix meaning inside or inward.

Esophagitis (ee-sof-uh-JIE-tis)
Inflammation of the esophagus caused by *reflux* (backflow) of gastric juice from the stomach, infection, or irritation from a tube inserted through the nose to the stomach.

Esophagus (ee-SOF-uh-gus)
The tube that carries food from the throat to the stomach.

Esotropia (es-oe-TROE-pee-uh)
A form of *strabismus* in which one eye turns inward (is convergent) while the other eye focuses straight ahead, resulting in double vision.
Also known as **Cross-eye**.
Compare **Exotropia**.
Refer to **Strabismus**.

esthe-
A prefix meaning perceive or sense.

Estimated Date of Confinement (EDC)
The pregnant woman's estimated date of delivery, or due date.

Ethmoid Bone
A small bone of the skull that forms part of the orbit (the bony socket that contains the eye) and the nose.

Ethosuximide (eth-oe-SUK-si-mide)
An *antiepileptic drug*. It is used most commonly to treat *absence seizures*.

Etiology (ee-tee-OL-oe-jee)
The study of the cause of disease.

ET Tube
The abbreviation for endotracheal tube.

eu-
A prefix meaning good, well, or true.

Eustachian Tube (yoo-STAY-shuhn or yoo-STAY-kee-uhn)
A tube lined with mucous membrane that joins the nasopharynx (the passageway between the nasal area behind the nose and the throat area behind the *soft palate*) with the middle ear. The tube regulates air pressure in the ear, such as when it opens during yawning and swallowing. (The air pressure must be equal on each side of the eardrum for it to function properly.) The eustachian tube also functions as a passageway through which fluids can drain.
Refer to **Ear**.

Evaluation
Refer to **Assessment**.

Eversion
Turning a part of the body outward (for example, turning the foot toward the direction of the little toe).
Compare **Inversion.**

Evoked Potential/Evoked Response
A refined or specialized *EEG* to assess the condition of the visual, auditory, or tactile pathways of the neurological system.
Refer to **Electroencephalogram.**

Evoked Response Audiometry (ERA)
Refer to **Auditory Evoked Response.**

ex-
A prefix meaning out or away from.

Exchange Transfusion
A type of blood transfusion in which the infant's blood is withdrawn in small amounts and replaced with equal amounts of donor blood.

Excrete
To eliminate or discharge waste product from the body.
Compare **Secrete.**
Refer to **Gland.**

Excretion
The process by which the body (beginning at the cell level) gets rid of waste products. Excretion is the final stage of nutrition.
Refer to **Nutrition.**

exo-
A prefix meaning outside.

Exomphalos (eks-OM-fuh-lus)
Refer to **Omphalocele.**

Exophthalmos (eks-of-THAL-mose)
Abnormal protrusion of the eyeball.

Exotropia (eks-oe-TROE-pee-uh)
A form of *strabismus* in which one eye turns outward (is divergent) while the other eye focuses straight ahead, resulting in double vision.
Also known as **Walleye.**
Compare **Esotropia.**
Refer to **Strabismus.**

Expectorant
A drug given to encourage the coughing up of mucus.

Expressive Aphasia
Refer to **Aphasia**.

Expressive Language
The ability to communicate thoughts and feelings by gesture, *sign language*, verbalization, or written word.
Compare **Receptive Language**.

Extension
Straightening of the neck, trunk, or limbs. This movement increases the angle between two bones of a joint.
Compare **Flexion**.

Extensor
Any muscle whose function is to straighten out a joint of the body.
Compare **Flexor**.

Extensor Pattern
A pattern of muscle movement that causes a straightening out of a limb.

Extensor Thrust Pattern
An abnormal pattern of muscle movement in which the child's body becomes rigid and extends (straightens out) while the child is lying on his back.

External Ear
The outer ear.
Refer to **Ear**.

External Rotation
A turning outward or away from the midline of the body. An example of external rotation is turning a leg outward so that the toes are pointed to the side, away from the body's midline.

Extrapyramidal Cerebral Palsy (eks-truh-pi-RAM-i-duhl)
Cerebral palsy that results from damage to the nerve pathways (outside the *pyramidal tract*) that transmit impulses for controlling movement and maintaining posture from the brain to the spinal cord. There are three forms of extrapyramidal cerebral palsy: *choreoathetoid cerebral palsy*, rigid cerebral palsy, and *atonic cerebral palsy*.
Compare **Pyramidal Cerebral Palsy**.
Refer to **Cerebral Palsy**.

Extrapyramidal Tract
The nerve pathways that transmit impulses for controlling movement and maintaining posture from the brain to the spinal cord.
Compare **Pyramidal Tract**.

Extremity
An arm or leg.

Extrusion Reflex
A normal response in infants up to four months, in which the baby pushes his tongue out when the tongue is depressed.
Refer to **Primitive Reflex**.

Extubation (eks-too-BAY-shuhn)
The removal of the *endotracheal tube*.
Compare **Intubation**.

Eye
The organ responsible for vision. The eye consists of the *pupil*, which is the opening in the center of the *iris* (the clear tissue of the eye under which are pigment cells that give the eye its color); the *cornea*, which is the transparent, domelike shell covering the front part of the eye; the *lens* (crystalline lens) which is between the iris and the *vitreous humor* (the gel-like substance of the eye); the *retina*, which is the membrane lining the back of the inside of the eyeball; and the *optic nerve*, which is the bundle of nerve fibers that lead from the retina to the brain.
Refer to **Vision**.

Eye Dominance
Preferring one eye to assume the major function of seeing, such as when using one eye to look through a microscope or door peephole.

Eye-Hand Coordination
The ability to use visual input to assist in manipulation of an object with the hands. For example, seeing a desired object and successfully reaching toward and grasping it.

F

F
The abbreviation for female.

Face Presentation
Birth (delivery) of a baby in which the face area of the head is the first to appear in the pelvis.
Refer to Fetal Presentation.

Facies (FAY-shi-eez or FAY-shee-eez)
The face's expression or appearance. For example, the characteristic facies of *fetal alcohol syndrome* includes small eyes, *epicanthal folds* (a vertical skin fold at the inner corner of the eyes), small jaw, flat midface, indistinct or long philtrum (the grooved area between the upper lip and the nose), thin upper lip, short nose, and short *palpebral fissures* (the opening between the upper and lower eyelids).

Facioscapulohumeral Muscular Dystrophy (fay-shee-oe-skap-yoo-loe-HYOO-mer-uhl)
An *autosomal dominant* form of *muscular dystrophy* that affects the muscles of the face, shoulder, and upper arms, which weaken slowly. This is a relatively benign form of muscular dystrophy.

FACP
The abbreviation for Fellow, American College of Physicians.

FACS
The abbreviation for Fellow, American College of Surgeons.

Fading
A method of teaching a skill in which prompting is phased out as the child begins to show signs of learning.

FAE
The abbreviation for fetal alcohol effects.

Failure to Thrive (FTT)
A condition of infancy and early childhood characterized by lower weight/slower weight gain than that which is expected by comparison to a standardized growth chart. FTT may occur when the baby does not receive sufficient nutrients. This may be due to physical or psychosocial problems.

False Negative
A test result that fails to show evidence of a substance, condition, or disease when it is actually present.
Compare **False Positive**.

False Positive
A test result that shows evidence of a substance, condition, or disease when it is not actually present.
Compare **False Negative**.

Familial (fuh-MIL-yuhl)
Pertaining to a disease that is common to, or occurs in, more members of a family than expected by chance alone.

Familial Disorder
A condition that occurs in more members of a family than would be expected to occur in the general population. Familial disorders are usually, but not always, *hereditary*.
Compare **Hereditary**.

Familial Dysautonomia (fuh-MIL-yuhl dis-aw-toe-NOE-mee-uh)
Refer to **Riley-Day Syndrome**.

Family Dynamics
The interaction and influence of members of a family on each other.

Fanning
The action of an infant's toes extending and separating while standing and trying to maintain balance.

Far-Sightedness
Refer to **Hyperopia**.

FAS
The abbreviation for fetal alcohol syndrome.

fasc-, fasci-
Prefixes meaning band.

Fascia (FASH-ee-uh or FASH-uh)
Fibrous connective tissue in the body that surrounds structures and supports organs.

Fasciculation (fa-sik-yoo-LAY-shuhn)
The involuntary twitching of a single muscle group that is innervated by a single nerve. It can be a symptom of certain diseases, result from fever or dietary deficiency, or occur as a side effect of some drugs.

Fats
One of the categories of essential nutrients. Fats are the body's most concentrated source of food energy and the form in which extra energy is stored.

fauci-
A prefix meaning throat.

Febrile (FEE-bril or FEE-brile or FEB-ril)
Having a fever.
  Compare *Afebrile.*

Febrile Seizure
A *seizure* that is associated with a high fever, occurring especially when the temperature is rapidly rising. Febrile seizures are the most common type of seizure in children under age five. They are not considered to be a form of *epilepsy.*

Feces/Fecal
Referring to the waste material from the digestive tract (bowel movements).

Feeding Tube
A tube placed into part of the digestive tract to feed babies who cannot take food by mouth. Examples include the NG Tube (*Nasogastric Tube*) or the G-Tube (*Gastrostomy Tube*).

Femur (FEE-mur)
The thigh bone.

Fer-In-Sol™
The over-the-counter liquid form of iron (ferrous sulfate).

Ferrous Sulfate (FER-us SUL-fayt)
Iron.

Fetal Alcohol Effects (FAE)
A combination of *congenital* abnormalities that is caused by maternal consumption of alcohol during pregnancy. The effects of alcohol can range from a slightly smaller birth weight to the presence of many of the same anomalies present in a child with *fetal alcohol syndrome (FAS).* Usually the term is used to describe a child who has some, but not all, of the characteristics of a child with FAS. Research shows that children with fetal alcohol effects may be just as affected (have as difficult a time functioning and adapting) as children with FAS or *prenatal exposure to drugs.*
  Refer to **Fetal Alcohol Syndrome.**

Fetal Alcohol Syndrome (FAS)

A combination of *congenital* abnormalities that is caused by maternal consumption of alcohol during pregnancy. Characteristics may include growth deficiency, *mental retardation, attention deficit hyperactivity disorder*, motor delays, and *congenital anomalies*, such as a characteristic facial appearance, including small eyes, *epicanthal folds* (a vertical skin fold at the inner corner of the eyes), small jaw, flat midface, indistinct or long philtrum (the grooved area between the upper lip and the nose), thin upper lip, short nose, ear anomalies, and short *palpebral fissures* (the opening between the upper and lower eyelids).

Fetal Circulation

The unique pattern of blood flow in the fetus in which blood flows to and from the placenta to receive oxygen and nutrients, and to discharge wastes. The fetal lungs are bypassed in the process of circulation.

Compare **Circulation** *and* **Persistent Fetal Circulation**.

Fetal Dilantin Syndrome

Refer to **Fetal Hydantoin Syndrome**.

Fetal Hydantoin Syndrome (FHS) (FEET-l hie-DAN-toe-in)

A combination of birth defects caused by use of *phenytoin* during pregnancy for *seizure* control, resulting in *microcephaly*, small size, facial/finger/toe abnormalities, poor growth, and mild *mental retardation*.

Also known as **Fetal Dilantin Syndrome**.

Fetal Monitor

An electronic device used for monitoring fetal heart rate during pregnancy and labor. Fetal heart monitoring is done by placing an *ultrasound* transmitter on the mother's abdomen or by inserting an *electrode* through the mother's vagina and placing it on the fetus's head.

Fetal Presentation

The body part of the fetus that is first seen in the mother's pelvis at the time of delivery. Types of fetal presentation include vertex (head first, specifically the crown, or top of the head first), brow (head first, specifically the eyebrow/forehead area first), face (head first, specifically the face first), shoulder, and breech (feet, knees, or buttocks first).

Fetoscopy (fee-TOS-koe-pee)

A diagnostic procedure for visualizing a fetus while in the uterus. Fetoscopy involves placing a tube into the mother's uterus to view the fetus or obtain blood or tissue samples.

Fetus

The developing unborn child from the end of the embryonic stage (about the eighth week of pregnancy) until birth.

FHS
The abbreviation for fetal hydantoin syndrome.

Fibrotic (fie-BROT-ik)
Pertaining to the formation of fibrous, thickened connective tissue such as the formation of scar tissue as a reparative response to injury.

Fibula (FIB-yoo-luh)
The outer and smaller of the two bones of the lower leg. (The other bone is the tibia.)

Field of Vision
  Refer to **Visual Field**.

Fine Motor
The developmental area that involves skills which require the coordination of the small muscles of the body, including those of the hands and face. Examples of fine motor skills include stacking small blocks, stringing beads, tracking an object with the eyes, and smiling.

Finger Feeding
Independently picking up small bites of food with the fingers and placing them in the mouth.

Finger Opposition
  Refer to **Opposition Movements**.

Fingerspelling
A form of sign language in which the fingers are used to represent letters of the alphabet. The letters (signs) are strung together to spell words.

Fissure (FISH-uhr)
A crack or groove on the surface of an organ. This may be a normal or abnormal condition. The division between the lobes of the lungs is a normal fissure. A crack in the skin around the anus that may bleed (called a rectal fissure) is not a normal condition.

Fisting
Keeping the hand(s) tightly fisted with the thumb held against the palm and the fingers flexed around the thumb. A baby with *hypertonicity* may keep her hands fisted.

Fistula (FIS-chuh-luh)
An abnormal passage between two hollow organs or between an organ and the surface of the body. An example of a fistula is a *tracheoesophageal fistula* found between the esophagus and the trachea. Fistulas may be *congenital* or may be *acquired* as a result of infection or damage to tissue, such as during abdominal surgery.

Fixation
Directing the eye to an object so its image, in the normal eye, centers on the fovea (the part of the retina that provides the area of most distinct vision).

Flat Affect
Having no visible emotional reaction. A child whose visible expression of feelings varies little in response to his environment, even in situations that typically induce anger or excitement, would be said to have flat affect.
Compare Affect.

Flatfeet
Refer to Pes Planus.

Flexion
To bend, bringing the body parts that a joint connects toward each other. Bending the neck, trunk, and limbs are examples of flexion.
Compare Extension.

Flexor
A muscle that controls flexion of a joint.
Compare Extensor.

Flexor Tone
Muscle tone that tends to keep the arms and legs close to the body ("folded") and never completely extended. (This is normal in a newborn.)

Floppy Infant
Referring to a baby with *hypotonia*.

Flu
Refer to Influenza.

Fluctuating Tone
Muscle tone that fluctuates between low tone ("floppiness," or *hypotonicity*) and high tone (spasticity, or *hypertonicity*).

Fluorescent Treponemal Antibody Test (FTA)
A blood test to confirm the diagnosis of *syphilis*.

Fluoride
A mineral used to prevent tooth decay.

FO
The abbreviation for foot orthosis.

Focal (FOE-kuhl)
Referring to a limited or localized area or part of an organ or of the body.

Focal Motor Seizure

A *simple partial seizure*. (The seizure originates in and remains confined to a localized area of the brain.)

   Refer to **Partial Seizure** *and* **Epilepsy**.

Foley Tube/Catheter™

A type of urinary *catheter*.

Fontanel/Fontanelle (fon-tuh-NEL)

One of the two "soft spots" on the top of the infant's head between the bones of the skull before they completely fuse. The posterior (rear) fontanelle usually closes by two months of age and the anterior (front) fontanelle usually closes by 18 months of age.

Fontan Operation

A surgical procedure done to allow blood to bypass obstruction associated with a heart defect.

Foot Orthosis (FO)

A plastic heel or foot support (brace) that fits into the shoe. It is prescribed by an orthopedic specialist.

Foramen Magnum (for-AY-muhn)

An opening in the *occipital bone* of the skull through which the spinal cord enters the spinal column.

Foramen Ovale

An opening in the wall between the right and left *atria* in the fetal heart. After the newborn takes her first breath the foramen ovale begins to close, which is necessary for her blood to be able to circulate through her lungs for oxygenation. A heart defect results if the opening does not close off.

Forelock

A front lock of hair.

Forward Chaining

A method of teaching a skill in which the skill is broken down into steps. The child receives a reinforcement upon learning step one, then steps one and two, and so on.

   Compare **Backward Chaining**.

Four-Point Position

On the hands and knees.

Fragile X Syndrome

An *X-linked disorder* that often, but not always, causes mild to severe *mental retardation*. Some children with fragile X have average intelligence, with or without a *learning disability*. Other symptoms may include a large head with prominent forehead, nose, jaw, and ears; *attention deficit hyperactivity disorder*; heart murmurs; *strabismus*; and occasional autistic-like behaviors. Boys with fragile X are usually more severely affected than girls. The condition is so-called because *chromosomal analysis* often reveals a partially broken (fragile) site on some X chromosomes. Fragile X is believed to be the most common genetic cause of mental retardation.

Franceschetti's Syndrome (fran-ches-KET-eez)

An *autosomal dominant disorder* characterized by a flattening of the cheek bones, *coloboma* (a space, or cleft of part of the eyeball), lower jaw defects, external ear malformation, hearing loss, and malformed extremities.

Fraternal Twins

Twins formed when two eggs are released and fertilized at the same time. Fraternal twins may be the same or different sexes, and look no more alike than any other siblings.

Frejka Pillow Splint™

A splint consisting of a pillow that is belted between the baby's legs. It is used to correct *dislocated hips*.

Frenulum (FREN-yoo-lum)

A narrow fold of tissue that connects a movable part to an immovable part, such as the mucous membrane that attaches the tongue to the floor of the mouth.

Fricative

A consonant sound that is produced by closing off most of the air flow as it passes through the mouth, such as /f/, /v/, and /z/.

Friedreich's Ataxia (FREED-riks uh-TAK-see-uh)

A *hereditary* disorder involving degeneration of nerves in the spinal cord. This progressive disorder is characterized by unsteadiness and loss of coordinated movement *(ataxia)*, speech impairment, and possible *cardiomyopathy* (heart muscle disease).

Also known as **Spinal Cerebellar Degeneration** *and* **Hereditary Spinal Ataxia**.

Frontal

Pertaining to the forehead.

FT

The abbreviation for full term.

FTA

The abbreviation for fluorescent treponemal antibody test.

Full Inclusion
Including children with disabilities in classrooms with their typically developing peers.

Full Term (FT)
Relating to an infant born between the 38th and 42nd weeks of *gestation*.

Functional Age
Refer to **Developmental Age**.

Functional Behaviors
Behaviors (basic skills, such as meal-time skills) the child has mastered, or needs to master, in order to get along as independently as possible in society.

Fundal Plication
Refer to **Fundoplication**.

Fundi
Plural of fundus.

Fundoplication (fun-doe-plie-KAY-shuhn)
A surgical procedure to correct severe *gastroesophageal reflux* in which the opening from the esophagus to the stomach is tightened by wrapping the upper end of the stomach around the lower end of the esophagus and sewing it in place.
Also known as **Fundal Plication**.

Fundus
The base of a hollow organ, or the part farthest from the entrance.

Fungal
Referring to a fungus.

Fungi
Plural of fungus.

Fungus
A simple parasitic plant (a plant that takes nutrition from a living organism of another species) or a saprophytic plant (a plant that takes nutrition from dead organic matter), such as a yeast or mold, that can produce infections in humans.

FUO
The abbreviation for fever of undetermined origin.

Furosemide (fyoo-ROE-suh-mide)
A *diuretic*.

G

g
The abbreviation for gram.

Gag Reflex
A gagging response elicited when the *soft palate* or back of the throat is stimulated. The gag response is a lifetime reflex, but it is increased in newborns, usually until the ability to chew food develops. *Oral stimulation* (mouthing of safe toys) is important for developing tolerance of various food textures and sensations.

Gait
The manner or style of walking. Walking is normally a progression of *reciprocal movement* in which one foot steps forward and weight is placed on it, then the second foot steps forward (ahead of the placement of the first foot).
   *Compare **Non-Reciprocal Gait**.*

galact-
A prefix meaning milk.

Galactosemia (guh-lak-toe-SEE-mee-uh)
An *autosomal recessive disorder* characterized by the body's *inborn* inability to metabolize galactose (a sugar substance derived from lactose, i.e., milk sugar). This causes high levels of galactose and, if untreated, results in liver and kidney disease, *cataracts*, and *mental retardation*.

Gamma Globulin (GAM-uh GLOB-yoo-lin)
A class of *immune* proteins formed in the blood.

Gantrisin™ (GAN-tris-in)
   *Refer to **Sulfisoxazole**.*

gastr-, gastro-
Prefixes meaning stomach.

Gastrocnemius (gas-trok-NEE-mee-us)
A muscle in the back of the calf of the leg.

Gastroenteritis (gas-troe-en-ter-IE-tis)
Inflammation of the stomach and intestines that results in nausea, diarrhea, and vomiting. Gastroenteritis can be caused by many things, including a virus or bacteria that has contaminated food or water, certain drugs, or ingesting toxic substances.

Gastroenterologist (gas-troe-en-ter-OL-oe-jist)
A doctor who specializes in the study and treatment of problems of the stomach and intestinal tract.

Gastroesophageal (gas-troe-uh-sof-uh-JEE-uhl)
Pertaining to the stomach and the esophagus.

Gastroesophageal Reflux (GE Reflux)
An abnormal backflow of stomach acid and other contents into the esophagus caused by a weakness in the sphincter muscle that closes off the passageway between the esophagus and stomach. GE reflux may cause *esophagitis*. Feeding the infant smaller meals more frequently and in a more upright position may help decrease the vomiting that usually occurs after meals.

Gastrointestinal Disorder
Any illness involving one or more parts of the body related to digestion and elimination. *Gastroesophageal reflux* is an example of a gastrointestinal disorder.

Gastrointestinal Reflux (gas-troe-in-TES-ti-nuhl)
Refer to **Gastroesophageal Reflux**.

Gastroschisis (gas-TROS-ki-sis)
A birth defect in which the abdominal wall fails to close completely. This results in a hole through which the intestines bulge.

Gastrostomy (gas-TROS-toe-mee)
A surgically created opening in the abdominal wall through which a feeding tube is inserted directly into the stomach. A gastrostomy tube (G-tube) may be temporarily or permanently placed, depending on the reason for needing tube feeding. G-tube placement may be necessary if the esophagus is blocked, if the child is not able to receive adequate nutrition orally, or to provide drainage after abdominal surgery.

Gastrostomy Button
A small flexible *gastrostomy* tube with a one-way valve used to tube feed.

Gaucher Disease (goe-SHAY)
An *autosomal recessive lipid* metabolism disorder characterized by lack of the *enzyme* necessary for fat processing. This creates an excessive amount of fat in body tissue. Gaucher disease can be fatal.

Gavage Feeding (guh-VAZH)
Liquid feedings given via a tube passed through the nose or mouth and into the stomach.

GDS
The abbreviation for Gesell Developmental Schedules.

GE
The abbreviation for gastroesophageal.

Gene
The basic unit of inheritance that carries individual traits from parent to child. The gene is capable of reproducing itself at each cell division. Each gene is located at a specific point on a particular *chromosome* and consists primarily of *DNA* and *protein*.
Refer to **Dominant Gene** *and* **Recessive Gene.**

General Anesthesia
Refer to **Anesthesia.**

Generalization
1. The ability to make inferences about the properties of an object based on awareness of the properties of a similar object.
2. The ability to transfer a skill learned in one environment to new environments.
3. Becoming widespread, as when a local process or disease becomes *systemic*.

Generalized Seizure
A *seizure* that affects the whole brain, causing loss of consciousness. Types of generalized seizure include *absence seizures, myoclonic seizures, atonic seizures,* and *tonic/clonic seizures.*
Compare **Partial Seizure.**
Refer to **Epilepsy.**

General Practitioner (GP)
A family physician. General practitioners are trained to take care of most non-surgical diseases.

-genesis
A suffix meaning origination or production.

Genetic (gen-ET-ik)
Inherited or pertaining to *heredity*.

Genetic Counselor
A specialist who provides information about *hereditary* disorders, including confirming a suspected genetic diagnosis, determining which other family members might be affected, and assisting with comprehension of the diagnosis.

Genetic Disorder
An inherited disorder caused by defective *genetic* material. Types of genetic disorders include chromosomal abnormalities, *unifactorial* defects, or *multifactorial* defects.

Genetic Evaluation
An evaluation done to determine the presence of a genetic disorder. The evaluation usually includes obtaining the family health history (covering several generations) and determining the family's racial and ethnic background, the parents' ages, the mother's health during her pregnancy, labor, and delivery, and the baby's health as a newborn. The infant's growth and development are also reviewed. Finally, the infant is given a physical examination and tests (such as *chromosome analysis*) may be performed.

Geneticist
A specialist who evaluates individuals for genetic disorders.

Genitalia (jen-i-TAYL-ee-uh)
The reproductive organs.

Genitals
Refer to **Genitalia**.

Genitourinary (GU) (jen-i-toe-YOOR-i-nayr-ee)
Pertaining to the genitalia and the urinary system.

Genotype (JEN-oe-tipe)
The individual's complete set of inherited characteristics (as determined by the combination and location of the *genes* on the *chromosomes*).
Compare **Phenotype**.

Gentamicin (jen-tuh-MIE-sin)
An *antibiotic drug* used to treat infections.

Genu Recurvatum (JEE-nyoo)
Abnormal *hyperextension* of the knee joints.
Also known as **Backknee**.

Genu Valgum
A deformity in which the legs are curved inward so that the knees are close together.
Also known as **Knock Knee**.

Genu Varum
A deformity in which one or both of the legs curve outward at the knee.
Also known as **Bowleg**.

GE Reflux
The abbreviation for gastroesophageal reflux.

Germ
Any *microorganism* that causes disease. Viruses and bacteria are examples of germs.

German Measles
Refer to **Rubella**.
Compare **Measles** *(Rubeola)*.

Gesell Developmental Schedules (GDS)
An evaluation tool used to measure the communication, adaptive, gross motor, fine motor, and personal/social development of the newborn- to six-year-old.

Gestation
The length of time between the first day of the mother's last menstrual period before conception and the delivery of the baby. The gestational period is usually approximately 284 days (270 days plus the 14 days prior to conception).
Refer to **Trimester**.

Gestational Age
The age of a fetus or infant stated in weeks from the first day of the mother's last menstrual period before conception until the baby reaches term (40 weeks).

Gesturing
A form of non-verbal communication involving body movements. Examples include waving "hi," motioning with the hand "come here," and patting the seat to invite someone to "sit down."

GI
The abbreviation for gastrointestinal.

Gingiva (JIN-ji-vuh)
Refer to **Gum**.

Gingival Hyperplasia (JIN-ji-vuhl-hie per-PLAY-zee-uh)
Gingiva (gum) overgrowth, or enlargement. It is usually a plaque-induced or medication-induced (such as by Dilantin) *gingivitis*.
Refer to **Hyperplasia**.

Gingivitis (jin-ji-VIE-tis)
Inflammation and swelling of the gums.

gingivo-
A prefix meaning gums.

Gland

An organ formed by a clumping of cells that secrete (release cell products for use in the body) or excrete (eliminate or discharge waste product from the body) fluid and material. The pituitary gland is an example of a gland that secretes hormones and a sweat gland is an example of a gland that excretes waste product.

Glaucoma (glaw-KOE-muh)

A condition in which there is increased pressure inside the eye which can damage the optic nerve and cause blindness. Glaucoma in children is usually the result of a birth defect in which there is a structural abnormality in the eye.

Glide Consonants

The consonant speech sounds /w/ and /y/.

Gliding Movement

A smooth, continuous joint movement that allows one bone surface to glide over another. Gliding is one of the four basic kinds of movement by the joints of the body.
  Compare **Angular**, **Circumduction**, *and* **Rotation**.

Global Developmental Delay

Delay in the child's acquisition of skills in most areas of development. A child with global developmental delay may not have an identified diagnosis, but is functioning similarly to a child who has *mental retardation*.
  Refer to **Developmental Delay**.

Glossa (GLOS-uh)

The tongue.
  Also known as **Lingua**.

glosso-

A prefix meaning tongue.

Glossoptosis (glos-op-TOE-sis)

Downward displacement or retraction of the tongue.

Glottal Fricative

The /h/ speech sound.

Glottis (GLOT-is)

The two vocal cords and the space between them.

Glucose (GLOO-kose)

A type of sugar that is found in foods and also produced as a product of digestion. It circulates in the blood and is used by the body for energy.

Gluteal Muscle (GLOO-tee-uhl or gloo-TEE-uhl)
One of the three muscles on each side of the buttocks.

Gluten (wheat) Enteropathy
Refer to **Celiac Syndrome**.

Gluten (wheat) Intolerance
Refer to **Celiac Syndrome**.

glyc-
A prefix meaning sugar or sweet.

Glycerin Suppository
A suppository used to treat children with constipation.

gm
The abbreviation for gram.

Gnashing (NASH-ing)
Grinding of the teeth.

-gnosis
A suffix meaning knowledge.

Goiter
An enlarged thyroid gland, usually seen as a swelling in the neck. Goiter may be a result of a lack of iodine in the diet.

Goldenhar's Syndrome
A sporadically occurring disorder characterized by poor development of facial structures, a lateral cleftlike extension of the corner of the mouth, *skin tags* in front of the ears, outer and inner ear defects with near normal hearing to severe *conductive hearing impairment*, *cleft palate* or other oral defects, visual impairment, spinal column abnormalities, *clubfoot*, *congenital heart defect*, and occasional *mental retardation*.
   Also known as **Oculoauriculovertebral Dysplasia**.

Gonads
The ovaries and the testes. The gonads are responsible for producing male or female reproductive cells.

Goniometer (goe-nee-OM-uh-ter)
A device that measures the *range of motion* of a joint.

Goniotomy (goe-nee-OT-oe-mee)
A surgical procedure for treating *glaucoma* in which an opening is made so the increased fluid in the eye can drain to relieve the pressure.

GP

The abbreviation for general practitioner.

Grade I, II, III, or IV Bleed

*Refer to **Intraventricular Hemorrhage.***

Gram (GM, gm, g)

The basic unit of weight in the metric system. There are 28 grams in one ounce.

Grammar

All the rules that govern how a given language is spoken and written, including the rules specifying how words are formed, pronounced, and arranged into meaningful phrases and sentences. An example of a rule of language is the need for the subject and the verb within a sentence to agree in person and number: "He is tall" (a singular noun and a singular verb) compared to "They are tall" (a plural noun and a plural verb).

Grand Mal Seizure (grahn MAHL)

*Refer to **Tonic/Clonic Seizure** and to **Epilepsy**.*

Grasp

The manner in which an object is held. There are several types of grasp that an infant uses as his fine motor skills develop. A newborn demonstrates a *grasp reflex* that is present for the first four months of life. The first voluntary grasp to develop is the *ulnar palmar* grasp which emerges around four months and is grasp of an object with the ring finger and little finger against the palm of the hand. The second grasp to develop is the *palmar grasp*, which emerges around five months and is grasp of an object with all four fingers pressing the palm of the hand; the thumb is not involved. The third type of grasp to develop is the *radial palmar grasp*, which emerges around six months and is grasp of an object with the thumb, index, and middle fingers against the palm of the hand. The fourth type of grasp to develop is the *radial digital grasp*, which emerges between seven and nine months and is grasp of an object with the thumb, index, and middle fingers without the involvement of the palm of the hand. The fifth grasp to develop is the *inferior pincer grasp,* which emerges between eight and ten months and is grasp of a small object with the index finger and thumb, the thumb to the side of the bent index finger. The final grasp to develop is the *neat pincer grasp,* which emerges between ten and twelve months and is grasp of a tiny object with precise thumb and index finger opposition (i.e., tip to tip).

Grasp Reflex

An involuntary fisting of the hand triggered by placement of a cylindrical object (such as an adult's finger) in the middle part of an infant's palm. The grasp reflex is a normal reflex in infants up to four months of age.

Also known as a **Palmar Reflex.**
Refer to **Primitive Reflex.**

Gravida (GRAHV-i-duh)

A Latin word meaning a pregnant woman. She is referred to as gravida one during the first pregnancy, gravida two during the second, etc. Primigravida is used interchangeably with gravida one.

Compare **Para.**

Grieving Process

The normal emotional response to a loss. The five stages of grieving, according to Elisabeth Kubler-Ross, psychiatrist and authority and counselor on death, include denial, anger, bargaining, depression, and acceptance. Some authorities include shock with denial and understanding with acceptance.

Gross Motor

The developmental area that involves skills which require the coordination of large muscle groups, such as those in the arms, legs, and trunk. Examples of gross motor skills include walking, jumping, and throwing a ball.

G-Tube

The abbreviation for gastrostomy tube.
Refer to **Gastrostomy.**

GU

The abbreviation for genitourinary.

Guard

An arm position used to maintain balance. When the arms are held low, closer to the body, it is considered low guard. When the arms are held high (as seen in a newly-walking toddler), it is considered high guard.

Gum

The soft tissue that surrounds the base of the teeth.
Also known as **Gingiva.**

Guthrie Test (GUTH-ree)

A blood test to detect *PKU.*

gyn-

A prefix meaning woman.

gyr-

A prefix meaning ring or circle.

H

h
The abbreviation for height.

HA
The abbreviation for hyperalimentation.

Habituation
1. A gradual adaptation (and thus decreased response) to a *stimulus* or to the environment, based upon repeated exposure to the stimulus or the environment. This is an indicator of the infant's increasing cognition. For example, the infant's interest in and attention to a picture will decrease when she becomes "bored" with it after seeing it many times; she requires a more complex picture to hold her interest. The ability to habituate is observed, too, in the newborn who is able to ignore irritating stimulation (such as noise), and to sleep or remain in a calm, alert state.
2. The process of forming a habit.

Haemophilus Influenza
Refer to **Hemophilus Influenza Type b**.

Hair Whorl (hwurl)
A spiral or twist of hair.

Half-Kneeling Position
Bearing weight on one knee and the other foot (placed forward of the knee).

Halitosis (hal-i-TOE-sis)
Foul mouth odor.

Hallucal (HAL-yoo-kuhl)
Pertaining to the hallux, or the great toe.

Hallux (HAL-uks)
The great toe.

Hammer
Refer to **Malleus**.

Hammock
An adaptive device used to encourage proper body alignment and to decrease abnormal postures. A hammock can help the child with *hypertonicity* to maintain a more flexed position while on her back, and can keep the child with *hypotonicity* from sleeping with her legs in a frog-like position. Gently swinging the hammock may be used to help the child who is

sensitive to movement in space and to help relax the child with tight muscles.

Handedness
*Refer to **Hand Preference**.*

Handling
Referring to the correct methods for lifting and carrying the infant or child with special needs. By properly holding the infant or child who has *muscle tone* problems, the adult can inhibit abnormal postures and help the child feel secure while being held.

Hand-Over-Hand Guidance
Physically guiding a child through the movements involved in a fine motor task. Helping the child to grasp a spoon and bring it to her mouth is an example of hand-over-hand guidance.

Hand Preference
The natural tendency to use the preferred hand (either the right or left hand) for most voluntary motor (manipulative) activities. For activities that require two-hand involvement, the preferred hand does the manipulating while the other hand assists. The dominant (preferred) hand may not be apparent until the child is between three and four years of age, although it frequently appears by age three. Hand preference is related to which side of the brain is dominant. For example, if the left hemisphere of the brain is dominant, the child usually will be right handed.
*Also known as **Handedness** or **Dominant Hand**.*

Hands-Feet Position
Bearing weight on the hands and feet with the abdomen off the floor.

Haploid (HAP-loid)
Referring to a single complete set of *chromosomes* (one half of the usual paired set; that is, 23 single chromosomes, rather than 23 pairs of chromosomes). Sperm and eggs (ova) are haploid because they only have one chromosome of each kind.
*Also known as **Monoploid**.*
*Compare **Diploid**.*

Hard Palate
The bony front part of the roof of the mouth. Certain speech sounds (such as the /t/ and /d/ sounds) are produced when the tongue touches or approximates the ridge of the hard palate (the alveolar ridge), which is slightly back of the upper teeth.
*Compare **Soft Palate**.*
*Refer to **Palate**.*

Harelip
Refer to **Cleft Lip**.

Harrington Rods™
Metal rods that are surgically placed along the spine during the *spinal fusion* procedure to maintain proper alignment in children with severe *scoliosis*.

Hawaii Early Learning Profile (HELP)
A criterion-referenced assessment used to evaluate the cognitive, language, gross motor, fine motor, social, and self-help development of the newborn to 36–month-old. The Hawaii may be administered by a professional or para-professional. It also includes an activity guide.

HBV
The abbreviation for hepatitis B virus.

hct
The abbreviation for hematocrit.

Head Banging
A form of *self-stimulation* in which the child repetitively bangs her head on the floor or another surface.
Refer to **Self-Stimulation** *and* **Self-Injurious Behavior**.

Head Circumference
An important body measurement that doctors use to estimate the rate at which the infant's brain is growing. Head circumference is measured just above the eyebrows and around the occiput (the back part of the base of the head).
Refer to **Body Measurements**.

Head Control
The ability to lift and keep the head up, holding it in line with the body. In a typically developing infant, head control is attained around four months of age. Head control is required for sitting.

Head Lag
The backward lag of the head when an infant without head control is pulled to a sitting position.
Refer to **Head Control**.

Head Righting
An automatic response to hold the head in an upright, midline position, even if the body is tilted to the side, downward, or backward.
Refer to **Automatic Reflex**.

Head Start
A federal program started in 1965 aimed at providing a comprehensive pre-school program for children of low-income families. Planned activities are designed to address individual needs and to help children attain their potential in growth and mental and physical development before starting school. Ten percent or more of enrollment opportunities are for children with disabilities.

Hearing
Hearing is a process involving both the ears, the auditory nerve, and the brain. For hearing to occur, sound waves in the air must pass through the pinna (the part of the ear seen on the outside of the head) and enter the auditory canal (the ear canal leading from outside the ear inward to the eardrum). The sound waves then hit the eardrum causing the eardrum to vibrate. (For the eardrum to vibrate properly, the air pressure on each side of the eardrum must be equal. Equalizing the air pressure is the job of the eustachian tube.) The vibrations then pass through the middle ear by moving along a tiny chain of bones (the malleus, incus, and stapes), and into the inner ear via the last bone, the stapes, which extends into the cochlea, located in the inner ear. As the stapes vibrates, it causes the fluid within the cochlea to ripple, stimulating the cochlea's nerve cells and begin-ning the motion of the cilia (the microscopic hairlike projections on the cells). The motion transmits sound impulses along the auditory nerve to the brain. Finally, when the impulses reach the brain, the cerebral cortex of the brain receives and analyzes the impulses, recognizing them as meaningful sound.
Refer to **Ear** *and* **Auditory Impairment.**

Hearing Aid
A device for amplifying sound (but not for making the sound clearer). For the child to benefit from hearing aids, she must have some degree of hear-ing.
Compare **Vibrotactile Hearing Aid.**

Hearing Impairment/Loss
Refer to **Auditory Impairment.**

Heart
The organ located in the center of the chest that pumps blood throughout the body. The heart is divided into four chambers. The upper two chambers are the *atria* and the lower two chambers are the *ventricles*. The openings be-tween the atria and the ventricles are the *valves*.
Refer to **Circulation.**

Heart Defect
Any structural abnormality of the heart that obstructs or creates abnormal blood flow through the heart. Examples of heart defects include *patent duc-*

tus arteriosus, atrial septal defects, and *tetralogy of Fallot.* Heart defects are often treated with drugs or surgery.

Heart Disease
*Refer to **Congenital Heart Disease**.*

Heart Failure
*Refer to **Congestive Heart Failure**.*

Heart Massage
*Refer to **Cardiac Massage**.*

Heart Murmur
A heart sound made by blood flow or by the heart valves which may be normal or abnormal depending on the cause. Many murmurs that occur when the heart contracts are benign; murmurs that occur when the heart is at rest are more likely dangerous, possibly indicating that one or more valves are not functioning properly.

Heart Rate
The rate at which the heart beats. The heart rate is expressed in beats per minute. There are normal ranges for each age group. Normally, the newborn heart rate is over 100 beats per minute and the heart rate of one- to three-year-olds is in the 100 to 160 range.

Heel Cord
*Refer to **Achilles Tendon**.*

Heel Cord Lengthening
*Refer to **Achilles Tendon Lengthening**.*

Heel Stick
Pricking the baby's heel to obtain a small blood sample.

Heel Strike
The part of walking with a normal heel-toe gait pattern when the heel comes in contact with the floor.

HEENT
The abbreviation for head, eyes, ears, nose, and throat.

Heimlich Maneuver (HIME-lik)
A life-saving procedure used when someone is choking. The rescuer puts pressure on the victim's diaphragm by thrusting inward and upward on the abdomen between the hips and the lower edge of the ribs. This pressure forces some of the air that was in the lungs upward, expelling the lodged object out of the trachea.
*Also known as the **Manual Thrust**.*

Helix (HEE-liks)
1. A coiled formation found in DNA (*deoxyribonucleic acid*) and other organic molecules.
2. The rounded rim portion of the external ear.

HELP
The abbreviation for Hawaii Early Learning Profile.

hem-
A prefix meaning blood.

Hemangioma (hee-man-jee-OE-muh)
A usually harmless tumor caused by an abnormal distribution of blood vessels. Hemangiomas can occur as birthmarks or develop later in life. They can either be flat, such as a *port wine stain*, or raised, such as a *strawberry mark*. Hemangiomas can occur anywhere in the body but are usually found in the skin.

Hemapoiesis (hem-uh-poi-EE-sis)
Refer to Hematopoiesis.

Hemapoietic (hem-uh-poi-ET-ik)
Refer to Hematopoietic.

hemato-
A prefix meaning blood.

Hematocrit (hct) (hee-MAT-oe-krit)
A measure of the number of red blood cells found in the blood. It is expressed as a percentage of the total blood volume and it yields an estimate of the amount of hemoglobin in the blood.

Hematology (hee-muh-TOL-oe-jee or hem-uh-TOL-oe-jee)
The study of blood and blood disorders.

Hematoma (hee-muh-TOE-muh)
A swelling, or collection, of blood (usually clotted) that develops in a localized area of an organ, tissue, or body space. A hematoma is caused by bleeding from a broken blood vessel. Hematomas range in severity from minor to potentially fatal conditions.

Hematopoiesis (hee-muh-toe-poi-EE-sis)
The formation and development of blood cells in the bone marrow.

Hematopoietic (hee-muh-toe-poi-ET-ik or hem-uh-toe-poi-ET-ik)
Referring to the formation of blood cells in the bone marrow.

hemi-
A prefix meaning half.

Hemianopia/Hemianopsia (hem-ee-uh-NOE-pee-uh/hem-ee-uh-NOP-see-uh)

Blindness or visual impairment in one half of the *visual field* in one or both eyes.

Hemiplegia (hem-ee-PLEE-jee-uh)

Weakness or *paralysis* of one side of the body caused by disease or injury to the nerves of the brain or spinal cord that stimulate the muscles, or by disease to the muscles themselves. Nerve damage to the left *pyramidal tract* of the brain results in hemiplegia on the right side of the body, and nerve damage to the right pyramidal tract of the brain results in hemiplegia on the left side of the body. Sometimes the word hemiplegia is used to describe *cerebral palsy* in which the arm, leg, trunk, or face on one side of the body is affected. The arm is usually more affected than the leg, trunk, or face.

Refer to **Paralysis** *and* **Pyramidal Cerebral Palsy***.*

Hemisphere

Refer to **Cerebral Hemisphere***.*

hemo-

A prefix meaning blood.

Hemoglobin (hgb) (hee-moe-GLOE-bin or hem-oe-GLOE-bin)

The oxygen-carrying, iron-containing pigment in red blood cells.

Hemoglobinopathy (hee-moe-gloe-bi-NOP-uh-thee)

Any of a group of *genetic* disorders in which there are changes (errors) in the structure of the hemoglobin molecule. An example of a hemoglobinopathy is *sickle cell anemia.*

Hemolysis (hee-MOL-i-sis)

The destruction of red blood cells. This is a normal body process, except when the breakdown occurs prematurely or in great amounts, which may cause *anemia* and *jaundice.* Abnormal hemolysis in the newborn (hemolytic disease of the newborn) is usually caused by *Rh incompatibility* between the mother and fetus.

Hemolytic Disease of the Newborn

Refer to **Erythroblastosis Fetalis***.*

Hemophilia (hee-moe-FIL-ee-uh or hem-oe-FIL-ee-uh)

A hereditary X-linked disorder caused by deficiency in one of the proteins necessary for blood clotting. Children with hemophilia have varying degrees and sites (internal and external) of spontaneous bleeding (most often bleeding is into the muscles and joints), and should avoid play activities that pose the risk of injury. Hemophilia is treated by giving infusions (slowly introducing the deficient blood protein into the bloodstream by means of *IV*) either at the time of bleeding or on a regular, preventive basis.

Hemophilus Influenza Type b (HIb) (hee-MOF-il-us in-floo-EN-zuh)

A bacterium spread by nose and mouth secretions that can cause serious illness in infants and young children, including *meningitis, pneumonia, sepsis,* and other infections. Children can carry the bacteria without actually having the infection or any of the diseases it causes. A vaccine is available.

Also known as **Haemophilus Influenzae** *and as* **H.flu**.

Hemopoiesis

Refer to **Hematopoiesis**.

Hemopoietic

Refer to **Hematopoietic**.

Hemorrhage (HEM-or-ij)

Bleeding.

hepat-

A prefix meaning liver.

Hepatitis (hep-uh-TIE-tis)

An inflammation of the liver, usually due to an infection, and sometimes due to toxic agents.

Hepatitis B Virus (HBV)

A virus transmitted most commonly through exposure to the blood of an infected person. It can be passed from mother to fetus during pregnancy. Symptoms include decreased appetite, nausea, and fatigue followed by *jaundice*. Blood for transfusion is screened for HBV infection.

Also known as **Serum Hepatitis**.

hepato-

A prefix meaning liver.

Hepatomegaly (hep-uh-toe-MEG-uh-lee)

An enlarged liver that can result from many liver disorders.

Hereditary

Referring to a trait (such as eye color) or defect or disease (such as *cystic fibrosis*) that is genetically determined (inherited). Not all hereditary disorders are apparent at birth and not all birth defects are hereditary.

Also known as **Inherited** *and* **Genetic**.

Hernia
A protrusion of an organ through an opening in the muscle wall that surrounds it. Hernias can occur *congenitally* or be *acquired* as the result of injury or muscle weakness. Examples include *hiatal hernia* and *inguinal hernia*.

Herpes Simplex Virus 1 (HSV1) (HER-peez)
A virus typically associated with infectious lesions of the mouth and face (but sometimes found in the genital area). The virus is transmitted by direct contact with the lesions (cold sores).

Herpes Simplex Virus 2 (HSV2)
A virus typically associated with infectious lesions of the genital area (but sometimes found in the mouth). The virus is usually sexually transmitted. Herpes Simplex 2 can be passed on to a baby at the time of birth (*congenital* herpes) and can cause severe illness in the baby. The effects can range from disease of the skin and mucous membranes to neurological damage and death.

hetero-
A prefix meaning varied or different.

H.flu
*Refer to **Hemophilus Influenza Type b**.*

HG, hgb
Abbreviations for hemoglobin.

Hiatal Hernia (hie-AY-tuhl)
A condition in which part of the stomach pushes upward through an opening (hiatus) in the diaphragm. Hiatal hernia in children is usually a *congenital* condition. The child with hiatal hernia usually suffers from *gastroesophageal reflux*.

HIb
The abbreviation for Hemophilus Influenza Type b.

HIb-Immune Vaccine
A vaccine that protects children against the type of *meningitis* caused by *HIb*.

Hickman Catheter™
A type of *catheter* that is used as a long-term *central line*.
*Refer to **Total Parenteral Nutrition**.*

High Guard
An early standing position in which the infant keeps her arms flexed so that the hands are at shoulder level, in order to keep her balance.
*Refer to **Guard**.*

High Risk
Refer to **At-Risk***.*

High Tone
Refer to **Hypertonia***.*

Hip Adduction Release
A surgical procedure in which the muscles and/or tendons that *adduct* the thighs are cut to lengthen them.

Hip-Knee-Ankle-Foot Orthosis (HKAFO)
A long leg brace with a pelvic band which is used to passively stretch muscles and to stabilize the joints.
Also known as an **Orthotic***.*

Hirschsprung Disease (HIRSH-sprung)
A *congenital* disorder characterized by absence or marked decrease in the number of nerve endings that cause the bowel to move feces. This causes a segment of the intestines to become dilated, resulting in constipation and poor appetite. The treatment for Hirschsprung Disease is removal of the abnormal section of bowel.
Also known as **Congenital Megacolon***.*

Hirsutism (HUR-syoot-izm)
Excessive body hair. Hirsutism is frequently used to describe coarse hair on females that grows in patterns which are typically male, such as facial hair and hair growth on the trunk of the body. It can be caused by a high level of male hormones, be associated with certain disorders such as *Scheie Syndrome*, or be a normal occurrence in some women.

histo-
A prefix meaning tissue.

History (Hx)
The circumstances preceding an event, which may be relevant to the current condition or status. For example, the factors of a woman's health history while she was pregnant may be relevant to the newborn's health status.

HIV
The abbreviation for human immunodeficiency virus.

Hives
Refer to **Urticaria***.*

HKAFO
The abbreviation for hip-knee-ankle-foot orthosis.

HMD
The abbreviation for hyaline membrane disease.

Hole in the Heart
A *septal defect*, or hole in the septum (wall) that divides the right and left atria or the right and left ventricles of the heart.
   Refer to **Atrial Septal Defect** *and* **Ventricular Septal Defect**.

Holoprosencephaly (hol-oe-pros-en-SEF-uh-lee)
A birth defect in which the forebrain (the anterior portion of the brain in the embryo) does not divide into two cerebral hemispheres or form lobes. This results in facial defects, including *cleft lip and palate*, ear *anomalies* and deafness, and eye anomalies (ranging from an abnormally decreased space between the eyes to a single, fused eye); *microcephaly*; *seizures*; heart defect; motor deficiency; *mental retardation*; and infant mortality.

homeo-
A prefix meaning alike.

Homeostasis (hoe-mee-oe-STAY-sis)
The bodily process of maintaining a balanced internal state. Steady breathing and heartbeat are indicators of homeostasis.
   Also known as **Body Homeostasis**.

homo-
A prefix meaning same.

Homonymous Hemianopia/Hemianopsia (hoe-MON-i-mus hem-ee-uh-NOE-pee-uh/ hem-ee-uh-NOP-see-uh)
A *visual field defect* on the right or left visual field of both eyes. The child is blind or visually impaired in these visual fields and should be taught to turn her head to see. This disorder may occur with children affected by *hemiplegia*.

Hospice Care (HOS-pis)
A hospital that provides *palliative* and supportive care for terminally ill patients and their families, either on an out-patient or in-patient basis.

HPI
The abbreviation for history of present illness.

HR
The abbreviation for heart rate.

hs
The abbreviation for the Latin words meaning at bedtime.

HSV1
The abbreviation for herpes simplex virus 1.

HSV2
The abbreviation for herpes simplex virus 2.

Human Immunodeficiency Virus (HIV)
A serious virus that damages the immune system and attacks the brain, resulting in *developmental delay* and increased susceptibility to infection. HIV is transmitted when the virus enters the bloodstream, and can be passed to a fetus by her mother. HIV causes AIDS (*Acquired Immune Deficiency Syndrome*).

Humerus (HYOO-muhr-uhs)
The long bone of the upper arm that extends from the shoulder to the elbow.

Hunter Syndrome
An *X-linked recessive* mucopolysaccharidosis (a metabolic disease in which complex sugars or carbohydrates accumulate in the urine) characterized by skeletal deformity (partial *contracture* of joints and *short stature*), coarse facial features, *macrocephaly*, progressive hearing loss, and mild to severe *mental retardation*. Males only are affected. Death may occur by 20 years of age, but some patients live longer.
    Also known as **mucopolysaccharidosis II.**

Hurler Syndrome
An *autosomal recessive* mucopolysaccharidosis (a metabolic disease in which complex sugars or carbohydrates accumulate in the urine) characterized by coarse facial features, clouding of the cornea, *macrocephaly*, short misshapen bones, *short stature*, excessive body hair, and severe *mental retardation*. Death usually occurs by around ten years of age.
    Also known as **mucopolysaccharidosis I.**

Hx
The abbreviation for history.

Hyaline Membrane Disease (HMD) (HIE-uh-lien)
Refer to **Respiratory Distress Syndrome.**

Hydantoin (hie-DAN-toe-in)
A class of drugs used to treat epileptic *seizures*.

Hydramnios (hie-DRAM-nee-uhs)
Excessive amniotic fluid during pregnancy. It is sometimes associated with fetal abnormality, maternal illness such as *diabetes mellitus*, or with multiple pregnancy. Hydramnios may cause premature labor.
    Also known as **Polyhydramnios.**
    Compare **Oligohydramnios.**

Hydranencephaly (hie-dran-en-SEF-uh-lee)
A *congenital* condition characterized by the absence of cerebral hemispheres (the space is instead filled with fluid). Affected infants rarely survive beyond one year of age.

hydro-
A prefix meaning water.

Hydrocephalus (hie-droe-SEF-uh-luhs)
An abnormal accumulation of *cerebrospinal fluid* in the ventricles of the brain. Hydrocephalus occurs when too much cerebrospinal fluid is produced, when the circulation of the fluid is blocked, or when both conditions are present. Hydrocephalus can occur as a *congenital anomaly* (as in *spina bifida*) or as a result of brain injury, infection, bleeding, or tumor. Children with hydrocephalus are treated by draining away the excess fluid via a *shunt* that channels the fluid to another part of the body, where it is absorbed. The fluid must be removed so that *brain damage* does not occur.
Refer to Shunt.

Hydrops (HIE-drops)
The abnormal accumulation of serous fluid (a thin, watery liquid) in body tissues or a body cavity, such as the middle ear.

Hyoid (HIE-oid)
The U-shaped bone located in the front of the neck beneath the chin and above the larynx (the voice box).

hyper-
A prefix meaning above, elevated, or excessive.
Compare hypo-.

Hyperactivity
Abnormally increased motor activity, resulting in difficulty with concentrating on one task or sitting still. Due to their overactivity and impulsivity, children who are hyperactive often have difficulty with learning, even if they score in the normal range on IQ tests. Hyperactivity can occur with *attention deficit disorder*, *mental retardation*, *seizure disorder*, sensory deficit disorders (such as hearing impairment), or other central nervous system damage.
Also known as Hyperkinetic.

Hyperalimentation (HA) (hie-per-al-i-men-TAY-shuhn)
An *intravenous* solution that is given through an intravenous line to provide nutrition to the baby who cannot take any or enough food by mouth.
Also known as Intravenous Feeding or Total Parenteral Nutrition (TPN).

Hyperbilirubinemia (hie-per-bil-i-roo-bin-EE-mee-uh)
Excess *bilirubin* in the blood caused by poor functioning of the liver. *Jaundice* occurs with increased bilirubin levels.

Hypercalcemia (hie-per-kal-SEE-mee-uh)
An excessive amount of calcium in the blood.
Compare Hypocalcemia.

Hypercapnia (hie-per-KAP-nee-uh)
An excessive amount of carbon dioxide in the blood stream.
Also known as **Hypercarbia**.

Hypercarbia (hie-per-KAR-bee-uh)
Refer to **Hypercapnia**.

Hyperextensible
Refer to **Hyperextension**.

Hyperextension
A position in which a body part is straightened out (extended) past the normal limit.

Hyperglycemia (hie-per-glie-SEE-mee-uh)
Abnormally high sugar levels in the blood. Hyperglycemia can occur as a complication of other conditions, such as *diabetes mellitus*, and can result in increased susceptibility to infection.
Compare **Hypoglycemia**.

Hyperkalemia (hie-per-kuh-LEE-mee-uh)
Excessive amounts of potassium in the blood. Hyperkalemia can be caused by kidney dysfunction or adrenal insufficiency, or occur in response to certain types of serious injury or infection. It can produce weakness and *paralysis*, and heart *arrhythmias*.
Compare **Hypokalemia**.

Hyperkinetic
Refer to **Hyperactivity**.
Compare **Hypokinetic**.

Hypermobility
Excessive movement within a joint.

Hypernasality
A voice disorder that occurs when too much air passes through the nose during speech due to failure of the soft palate to close the nasal passages.
Compare **Hyponasality**.

Hypernatremia (hie-per-nuh-TREE-mee-uh)
Excessive amounts of sodium in the blood.
Compare **Hyponatremia**.

Hyperopia (hie-per-OE-pee-uh)
A *refractive error* that causes blurred vision of close objects. Hyperopia occurs when the eye is too short, which makes the lens focus close objects be-

hind the retina rather than on it. Prescription lenses can increase the vision in a child with hyperopia.

Also known as **Far-Sightedness**.
Compare **Myopia**.
Refer to **Refraction**.

Hyperplasia (hie-per-PLAY-zee-uh)
An increased number of normal cells resulting in an enlarged organ or tissue. *Gingival hyperplasia* is an example.

Compare **Hypoplasia**.

Hyperreflexia (hie-per-ree-FLEK-see-uh)
An increased response of the *deep tendon reflexes*.

Hypertelorism (hie-per-TEL-or-izm)
A birth defect in which there is an abnormally wide space between two paired organs or body parts, such as the eyes.

Compare **Hypotelorism**.

Hypertension
High blood pressure. Either a high systolic or high diastolic pressure reading may indicate hypertension.

Compare **Hypotension**.
Refer to **Blood Pressure**.

Hyperthermia
Abnormally high body temperature. It may be caused by heatstroke (a condition characterized by high fever, cessation of sweating, headache, rapid pulse and respiration rates, and sometimes high blood pressure and *coma*), burn, sweat gland disorder, or as a reaction to certain general anesthetics in individuals who have *inherited* this genetic trait.

Compare **Hypothermia**.

Hyperthyroidism
Increased activity of the thyroid gland, resulting in increased appetite, weight loss, enlarged thyroid, rapid heart rate, intolerance to heat, increased sweating, and sometimes *exophthalmos* (an abnormal protrusion of the eyeball).

Compare **Hypothyroidism**.

Hypertonia (hie-per-TOE-nee-uh)
Increased tone (stiffness) in the muscles.

Also known as **Hypertonicity** *and* **High Tone**.
Compare **Hypotonia**.
Refer to **Muscle Tone**.

Hypertonic (hie-per-TON-ik)
Refer to **Hypertonia**.

Hypertonicity (hie-per-toe-NI-si-tee)
Refer to **Hypertonia**.

Hyperventilation (hie-per-ven-ti-LAY-shuhn)
An abnormally rapid breathing rate or increased volume of air exchanged.
Compare **Hypoventilation**.

hypo-
A prefix meaning under, below, or less than normal.
Compare **hyper-**.

Hypoactivity
1. Abnormally diminished activity. It is usually used to describe diminished peristalic activity (the progressive wave of contraction of certain muscle fibers of tubular organs that propels its contents through the tube, such as with the intestine).
2. The opposite of *hyperactivity*.

Hypocalcemia (hie-poe-kal-SEE-mee-uh)
Abnormally low levels of calcium in the blood.
Compare **Hypercalcemia**.

Hypoglycemia (hie-poe-glie-SEE-mee-uh)
Abnormally low blood sugar levels. Hypoglycemia may be caused by pancreatic dysfunction, intestinal malabsorption, injection of an excessive quantity of insulin, or liver or endocrine disease.
Compare **Hyperglycemia**.

Hypogonadism (hie-poe-GOE-nad-izm)
Abnormally low activity of the gonads (testes or ovaries) caused by a disorder of the gonads or pituitary gland. This condition usually results in retarded growth and sexual development.

Hypokalemia (hie-poe-kuh-LEE-mee-uh)
Too little potassium in the blood.
Compare **Hyperkalemia**.

Hypokinetic (hie-poe-ki-NET-ik)
Slow moving or lethargic.
Compare **Hyperkinetic**.

Hyponasality
A voice disorder that occurs when too little or no air passes through the nose during speech. It can be caused by blockage of the nasal passages, allergies, and colds.
Compare **Hypernasality**.

Hyponatremia (hie-poe-nuh-TREE-mee-uh)
Too little sodium in the blood.
  Compare **Hypernatremia.**

Hypoplasia (hie-poe-PLAY-zee-uh)
An underdeveloped or incomplete organ or tissue, usually due to a decrease in the number of cells.
  Compare **Hyperplasia.**

Hypoplastic
Underdeveloped.

Hypoplastic Left Heart
A nearly always fatal group of heart malformations in which the entire left side of the heart is underdeveloped. This causes severe *cyanosis* (a lack of oxygen in the bloodstream that results in a blue color to the skin and mucous membranes), and heart failure. A heart transplant may save the affected infant's life.

Hypoproteinemia (hie-poe-proe-tee-in-EE-mee-uh)
An abnormally low level of protein in the blood.

Hypospadias (hie-poe-SPAY-dee-uhs)
A *congenital* defect in which the urethral canal opens on the undersurface of the penis, before it reaches the tip of the penis. Similarly, the urethra may open into the vagina in a female.

Hypotelorism (hie-poe-TEL-oe-rizm)
A birth defect in which there is an abnormally decreased space between two paired organs or body parts, such as the eyes.
  Compare **Hypertelorism.**

Hypotension
Abnormally low blood pressure.
  Compare **Hypertension.**
  Refer to **Blood Pressure.**

Hypothalamus
A part of the *diencephalon* of the brain that activates and controls the part of the nervous system that regulates internal body functioning (such as appetite, temperature, sleep, and emotions) and endocrine activity, including indirectly regulating the pituitary gland (which, in turn, controls many body functions including growth, sexual development, and fertility).

Hypothermia
Abnormally low body temperature. Hypothermia can lead to death.
  Compare **Hyperthermia.**

Hypothyroidism

A condition in which the thyroid gland is underactive, resulting in insufficient or no thyroid hormone. It is characterized by a lowered basal metabolic rate, low blood pressure, and lethargy.

Compare **Hyperthyroidism.**

Compare **Congenital Hypothyroidism.**

Hypotonia (hie-poe-TOE-nee-uh)

Decreased tone, or floppiness, in the muscles, characterized by excessive *range of motion* of the joints and little muscle resistance when parts of the body are being moved. Hypotonia is often observed in babies who are ill due to a heart defect, babies with *Down syndrome* or other *chromosomal* abnormalities, babies with certain types of *cerebral palsy*, and premature infants. A baby with hypotonia may be referred to as a *floppy infant*.

Also known as **Hypotonicity** *and* **Low Tone.**

Compare **Hypertonia.**

Refer to **Muscle Tone.**

Hypotonic (hie-poe-TON-ik)

Refer to **Hypotonia.**

Hypotonicity (hie-poe-toe-NI-si-tee)

Refer to **Hypotonia.**

Hypoventilation

Underventilation of the *alveoli* of the lungs, resulting in a lower than normal rate of breathing and volume of air exchanged.

Compare **Hyperventilation.**

Hypovolemia (hie-poe-voe-LEE-mee-uh)

An abnormally low volume of blood in the body.

Hypoxemia (hie-poks-EE-mee-uh)

A condition in which there is too little oxygen in the *arterial* blood. Untreated, this leads to *hypoxia.*

Hypoxia (hie-POKS-ee-uh)

A lack of sufficient oxygen in the body cells or blood. Hypoxia can lead to *brain damage.*

hystero-

A prefix meaning uterus.

I

IAC
The abbreviation for indwelling arterial catheter.

IAL
The abbreviation for indwelling arterial line.

I and O
The abbreviation for input and outflow (the amount of fluids entering and leaving the body). This includes feedings, IV fluid, drawn blood samples, and urine and stool elimination.

-iasis
A suffix meaning condition.

iatr-
A prefix meaning medicine.

Iatrogenic (ie-at-ruh-JEN-ik)
Referring to an injury, disease, or condition induced by medical treatment. An example of an iatrogenic disease is *bronchopulmonary dysplasia*, which is caused by use of a *ventilator*.

ICF
The abbreviation for intermediate care facility.

ICH
The abbreviation for intracranial hemorrhage.

ICN
The abbreviation for Intensive Care Nursery.

ICSN
The abbreviation for Intensive Special Care Nursery.

Icterus
Refer to Jaundice.

id
1. The abbreviation for the same.
2. The abbreviation for during the day.

IDEA
The abbreviation for Individuals with Disabilities Education Act.

Identical Twins

Twins that develop when a single, fertilized ovum divides at an early stage of development giving rise to two individuals with the same *genes*. Identical twins are always of the same sex.

Also known as **Monozygotic Twins**.

Identification

The determination that a child should be evaluated as a possible candidate for *early intervention* or *special education* services.

idio-

A prefix meaning peculiar or distinctive.

Idioglossia (id-ee-oe-GLOS-ee-uh)

An inability to articulate sounds correctly, resulting in speech that sounds like an invented or foreign language and is unintelligible. Idioglossia may include sound omissions, substitutions, distortions, and transpositions. It is often associated with mental retardation.

Idiolalia (id-ee-oe-LAY-lee-uh)

Refer to **Idioglossia**.

Idiopathic (id-ee-oe-PATH-ik)

Referring to a disease without an identified cause.

Idiopathic Epilepsy

Epilepsy that does not have an identified cause.

Also known as **Primary Epilepsy**.

Refer to **Epilepsy**.

IDM

The abbreviation for infant of a diabetic mother.

IEP

The abbreviation for Individualized Education Program.

IFSP

The abbreviation for Individualized Family Service Plan.

Ig

The abbreviation for immunoglobulin.

IL

The abbreviation for intralipid.

Ileal Conduit (IL-ee-uhl)

Refer to **Ileal Loop**.

Ileal Loop
A surgical procedure in which a segment of ileum (the third section of the small intestine) is used to replace another hollow organ (usually the bladder).

ileo-
A prefix meaning ileum.

Ileostomy (il-ee-OS-toe-mee)
An *ostomy* in the ileum (the third section of the small intestine). A surgical procedure is performed to create an opening in the abdominal wall so fecal matter can be eliminated from the body.

Ileum (IL-ee-uhm)
The third section of the small intestine. It opens into the large intestine. (The duodenum is the first section and the jejunum is the middle section of the small intestine.)

Ilium (IL-ee-uhm)
The superior part of the coxae, or hip bone.

IM
The abbreviation for intramuscular (such as an intramuscular injection).

Imipramine (i-MIP-ruh-meen)
A drug used to treat depression, as well as nocturnal *enuresis*.

Imitative Play
Copying the actions of another child or an adult. Pretending or attempting to comb one's hair and helping to wipe a table are examples of imitative play. (The imitative play of young children frequently involves copying the actions of daily routines.)

Immune System
A collection of cells and proteins within body organs and tissues and the physiological processes used by the body to identify potentially harmful *microorganisms*, such as bacteria, fungi, and viruses, and prevent them from harming the body.

Immunity (i-MYOO-ni-tee)
Protection from, or resistance to, certain diseases or conditions that is either natural (*inherited*) or *acquired* by having the disease, or by injection, inoculation, or vaccination with an *antigen*.
   Refer to **Vaccine.**

Immunization
The process by which protection from an infectious disease is induced. A *vaccine* may be used.
  Refer to **Inoculate.**

Immunoglobulin (Ig) (im-yoo-noe-GLOB-yoo-lin)
  Refer to **Antibody.**

Impedance Audiometry (im-PEE-dans aw-dee-OM-uh-tree)
An auditory test that is used to determine the approximate threshold of hearing and to measure eardrum mobility (which may reflect possible *otitis media*).
  Also known as **Tympanometry** *or* **Impedance Tympanometry.**

Impedance Tympanometry (im-PEE-dans tim-puh-NOM-uh-tree)
  Refer to **Impedance Audiometry.**

Imperforate Anus (im-PER-foe-rayt AY-nuhs)
A *congenital* defect in which the anal opening is absent or obstructed, making elimination of stools impossible.
  Also known as an **Anal Atresia.**

Impetigo (im-puh-TIE-goe or im-puh-TEE-goe)
A bacterial, inflammatory skin infection characterized by reddened skin that blisters. When the lesions burst, the fluid may dry on the skin creating a characteristic honey-colored crust. Impetigo often initially appears around the nose and mouth but can be spread (usually by the hands), to other parts of the body. Impetigo is highly contagious and is common in children.

Impulsivity
Behavior characterized by acting on impulse, or without thought or conscious judgment.

in-
A prefix meaning into or not.

Inborn
Referring to a condition obtained while in the uterus (prenatally). An inborn condition may be, but is not necessarily, *inherited*.
  Also known as **Innate.**

Inborn Error of Metabolism
A *genetic* disorder caused by an *inherited* deficiency in an important *enzyme*. Many inborn errors of metabolism can be diagnosed prenatally in mothers who are known to be at risk. If not detected and treated early, some of these disorders will lead to *mental retardation* and death. Examples of inborn errors of metabolism include *PKU* and *Tay-Sachs Disease*.

Incidence
Frequency of occurrence, such as the number of new cases of a disease occurring in a given period of time.

Incompetent Cervix
A condition in which the mother's uterus opens at the cervix in mid to late pregnancy, risking a miscarriage or premature birth.

Incontinence
The inability to control urination or defecation.

Incubator
An enclosed bed that provides an ill or premature infant with the benefits of an environment with controlled temperature, humidity, and oxygen.

Incus (ING-kuhs)
The middle of the three small bones of the middle ear. (The other two bones are the malleus and the stapes.)
*Also known as the **Anvil**.*
*Refer to **Ear**.*

Individualized Education Program (IEP)
A written statement of a child's current level of development (abilities and impairments) and an individualized plan of instruction, including the goals, the specific services to be received, the people who will carry out the services, the standards and time lines for evaluating progress made, and the amount and degree to which the child will participate with non-handicapped peers at school. The IEP is developed by the child's parents and the professionals who evaluated the child. It is required by the *Individuals with Disabilities Education Act* (IDEA) for all children in *special education,* ages three years and up.

Individualized Family Service Plan (IFSP)
A written plan describing the infant's current level of development; the family's strengths and needs related to enhancement of the infant's or toddler's development; goals for the infant and the other family members (as applicable), including the criteria, procedures, and time lines used to evaluate progress (the IFSP should be evaluated and adjusted at least once a year and reviewed at least every six months); and the specific early intervention services needed to meet the goals (including the frequency and intensity and method of delivering services, the projected date of initiating services, and the anticipated duration of services). The IFSP is developed and implemented by the child's parents and a multidisciplinary early intervention team (for example, the case manager, infant educator, physical therapist, occupational therapist, or speech and language therapist). The name of the person responsible for implementation of the IFSP (the case manager) should be listed on the IFSP. If it is likely, at age three, that the

child will require special education services, a *transition* plan should also be
stated in the IFSP. The Individualized Family Service Plan is required by
the *Individuals with Disabilities Education Act* (IDEA) for all infants receiving
early intervention services.
Refer to **Early Intervention**.

Individuals with Disabilities Education Act (PL 101–476)
A federal law passed in 1991 that reauthorizes and amends the *Education for
All Handicapped Children Act* (PL 94–142). Part H of the law focuses on ser-
vices to infants and toddlers who are at-risk or have developmental dis-
abilities.
Also known as **IDEA**.

Indomethacin (in-doe-METH-uh-sin)
A drug that is sometimes used to close the *ductus arteriosus*. Indomethacin is
also used to reduce pain and inflammation.

Indwelling Arterial Catheter (IAC)
Refer to **Arterial Catheter** *and* **Catheter**.

Indwelling Arterial Line (IAL)
Refer to **Arterial Catheter** *and* **Catheter**.

Indwelling Catheter
Refer to **Catheter**.

Indwelling Thumb
Abnormal fisting of the hand with the thumb next to the palm and the
fingers over the thumb holding it tucked in.
Also known as **Cortical Thumbing**.

Indwelling Venous Catheter (IVC)
Refer to **Venous Catheter** *and* **Catheter**.

Indwelling Venous Line (IVL)
Refer to **Venous Catheter** *and* **Catheter**.

Infant
A child up to 12 months of age.

Infant Development Program
A program of activities designed to promote the development of the
infant's basic skills. An *Infant Educator* or the child's parent/primary
caregiver may implement the developmental activities (often in the form of
play activities), which are chosen for and adapted to the individual child
based on his areas of strength and deficit. The activities may be natural and
as simple as an adult describing the actions and sensations of an activity the
baby is experiencing. For example, as the baby is being dressed, the adult

might say, "Now I am putting your arm through the sleeve of your shirt. Where is your hand? There it is! Your blue shirt is so soft and warm! . . ." Infant development activities also include planned experiences. For example, offering the child a sticky ball of brightly-colored masking tape (too large to fit in the mouth) is a planned play activity that incorporates many areas of development. The child experiences transferring an object hand-to-hand (the sticky quality encourages the child to pull the ball of tape from one hand to the other); the sensations of stickiness, texture, and color; descriptive language associated with the activity; and the social aspects of cooperative ball play (rolling, tossing, or chasing the ball). The child's infant development program should focus on the child's *developmental age* (the level at which the child is functioning) rather than his *chronological age*. This makes it possible to set appropriate and realistic goals (and implementations designed to help minimize the child's *developmental delays*). The child's health, his family and home environment, his style of learning, and his likes/dislikes are all important considerations for planning the infant development program. Addressing the parents' questions and concerns is also a critical infant program component. The individualization of the components of the infant development program is usually reflected in the *Individualized Family Service Plan*.

*Also known as **Infant Stimulation Program**.*
*Refer to **Individualized Family Service Plan**.*

Infant Development Specialist
*Refer to **Infant Educator**.*

Infant Educator
A specialist trained to assess infants and young children in the six main areas of development: cognitive, communication (language), gross motor, fine motor (perceptual), social/emotional, and self-help (adaptive), and to plan and implement a program which addresses the infant or young child's developmental needs. The infant educator should have knowledge of how infants and young children develop on a typical basis so appropriate and realistic goals, objectives, and implementations (often in the form of play activities) can be planned. The role of the infant educator varies from one early intervention program to the next, but the infant educator should be part of a multidisciplinary team that includes other specialists who address specific developmental concerns (such as the pediatrician; the speech, occupational, physical, or vision therapist; and the case manager).

*Also known as an **Infant Specialist**, **Infant Development Specialist**, **Infant Teacher**, **Early Interventionist**, and **Early Educator**.*
*Refer to **Infant Development Program**.*

Infantile
Referring to an infant or infancy.

Infantile Autism
Refer to **Autism**.

Infantile Cerebral Sphingolipidosis
Refer to **Tay Sach's Disease**.

Infantile Muscular Atrophy
Refer to **Werdnig-Hoffmann Disease**.

Infantile Myoclonic Seizure
Refer to **Infantile Spasms**.

Infantile Scoliosis
Curvature of the spine that develops in children under three years of age.
Refer to **Scoliosis**.

Infantile Spasms
A form of *epilepsy* with onset usually within the first year of life that usually involves flexion of the head and trunk (dropping of the head) and flexion of the arms and legs. (Most children have a mixture of *flexor* and *extensor* spasms.) These *seizures* may occur hundreds of times a day, frequently in clusters. The prognosis for the child who has infantile spasms varies greatly, depending on whether the seizures are idiopathic (there is no known cause) or symptomatic (there is an identifiable cause).
Also known as **Infantile Myoclonic Seizures**.

Infantile Spinal Muscular Atrophy
Refer to **Werdnig-Hoffmann Disease**.

Infant of a Substance-Abusing Mother (ISAM)
Refer to **Prenatally Exposed to Drugs**.

Infant Specialist
Refer to **Infant Educator**.

Infant Stimulation Program
Refer to **Infant Development Program**.

Infant Teacher
Refer to **Infant Educator**.

Infarction
Death of small amounts of body tissue. Infarction is usually caused by an interruption in the blood supply to the organ or tissue.

Infection
Invasion of the body or a body part by *microorganisms* (germs) that multiply and cause disease.

Inferior Pincer Grasp

Grasp of a small object using the thumb and the index finger with the thumb positioned at the side of the bent index finger. The inferior pincer grasp usually develops between eight and ten months of age.

Compare Neat Pincer Grasp.
Refer to Grasp.

Inferior Vena Cava

Refer to Vena Cava.

Infiltrate

The passing of fluid or cells into surrounding tissues, such as when an IV (*intravenous*) *catheter* slips out of a vein or when fluid collects in the lungs.

Influenza (in-floo-EN-zuh)

A highly contagious viral infection, transmitted by airborne particles through direct person-to-person contact and contact with secretions. Symptoms include inflammation of the respiratory tract, sore throat, cough, chills, fever, muscular pains, irritation in the intestinal tract, and weakness.

Also known as the Flu.

infra-

A prefix meaning beneath.

Infusion Pump

A device attached to an *intravenous catheter* through which fluids or medications are injected in measured amounts.

Ingestion

The process of taking food, drink, or medication by mouth.

Refer to Nutrition.

Inguinal Hernia (ING-gwi-nuhl)

A *hernia* that occurs when part of the intestine protrudes through the abdominal wall or into the inguinal canal (the passageway in the groin area that leads to the scrotum in the male, and transmits a ligament in the female). Inguinal hernias are usually repaired surgically.

Refer to Hernia.

Inherited

Referring to the transmission of traits, via the *genes*, from parents to their baby.

Also known as Hereditary or Genetic.
Compare Acquired and Congenital.

Inhibitive Casting

Use of a cast that holds the foot in normal alignment (a neutral position with toes forward, foot flexed) and helps to reduce increased *muscle tone* or unwanted reflexes.

Innate

Existing from birth. An innate condition may also be a *congenital* condition, an *inborn* condition, or a *hereditary* condition.

Inner Ear

Refer to **Ear.**

Inoculate (i-NOK-yuh-layt)

To introduce into the body *immune serums, vaccines,* or other foreign materials that are capable of causing the production of an antibody to prevent or cure disease. Immunity is achieved when the body produces *antibodies* that defend the body from the bacteria, virus, or other *microorganism* which causes the disease. A *vaccine* may be used.

Refer to **Immunization** *and* **Vaccine.**

Insulin (IN-soo-lin or IN-syuh-lin)

A hormone produced by the pancreas to regulate the metabolism of blood sugar and to maintain proper blood sugar levels. Insulin can also be prepared synthetically or obtained from animals for the treatment of *diabetes.*

Integration

Including children with special needs in classroom or school activities with their typically developing peers. There are degrees of integration. Some children with special needs may be integrated only into nonacademic activities such as recess, physical education, and lunch, while others may be integrated into all school activities.

Refer to **Full Inclusion.**

Integrity

1. The quality of being unbroken or unimpaired.
2. Honesty.

Intelligence

The ability to understand and apply knowledge. Intelligence is measured using a standardized intelligence test, and the results are expressed numerically. (This is the *intelligence quotient,* or IQ). 100 is considered to be the average IQ. Based on IQ test scores, the following levels have commonly been used to describe a child's intelligence

Normal Intelligence—*An IQ score between 85 and 116. (Above 130 is considered gifted.)*

Borderline Intelligence—An IQ score between 70 and 84. Scoring in this range does not mean the child has mental retardation; skills may be acquired at a slower rate, but the child is able to learn independent living skills.

Mild Mental Retardation—An IQ score between 50 and 69. The child learns more slowly but, as an adult, is typically able to work and/or live independently or with some assistance. Many adults with mild mental retardation marry.

Moderate Mental Retardation—An IQ score between 35 and 49. The child is able to learn basic skills for coping with daily living. As an adult, he usually needs living assistance and may be able to work in a supervised setting.

Severe Mental Retardation—An IQ score between 20 and 34. The child also often has other disabilities such as seizures, cerebral palsy, or speech problems. As an adult, he usually needs to live in a supervised setting and may be able to participate in a supervised workshop or activity center.

Profound Mental Retardation—An IQ score below 20. The child also often has other disabilities such as seizures, cerebral palsy, or speech problems. As an adult, he will need to live in a supervised setting and may learn skills to care for some of his basic needs.

The terminology describing the five levels of mental retardation is being phased out in favor of new terminology to describe intellectual functioning. The new levels, as defined by the American Association on Mental Retardation, identify the level of support a person needs. The level of support can be identified once an individual receives a diagnosis of mental retardation and his need for support is classified. (The diagnosis of mental retardation is made if the individual is 18 years or younger with an IQ score below 70–75 and has significant disability in two or more adaptive skill areas. Classification of an individual's need for support is based on intellectual functioning and adaptive skills, psychological and emotional considerations, health and physical considerations, and environmental considerations.) The four levels of support include :

Intermittent—The individual only requires support on a short-term basis for special circumstances, such as help in finding a new job.

Limited—The individual has a consistent need for certain supports, such as handling finances or job training.

Extensive—The individual requires consistent support in certain aspects of daily living, such as long-term job support.

Pervasive—The individual requires constant support for all aspects of life.

Intelligence Quotient (IQ)

A numerical test score that describes the relationship between a child's *mental age* and chronological age. The average IQ is considered to be 100. On several scales, the IQ is determined by dividing the child's mental age (based on the results of standardized test scores) by the chronological age and multiplying the result by 100.

Intelligence Test
A standardized test that measures the child's *mental age*.
Refer to **Intelligence Quotient**.

Intensive Care Nursery (ICN)
Refer to **Neonatal Intensive Care Unit**.

Intensive Special Care Nursery (ISCN)
Refer to **Neonatal Intensive Care Unit**.

Intensive Special Care Unit (ISCU)
Refer to **Neonatal Intensive Care Unit**.

inter-
A prefix meaning between.

Intercostal (in-tuhr-KOS-tuhl)
Pertaining to the space between two ribs.

Interdisciplinary Team
Refer to **Multidisciplinary Team**.

Intermediate Care Facility (ICF)
A residential institution for people who have disabilities and are unable to live independently.

Intermittent Positive Pressure Breathing (IPPB) Machine
A type of *ventilator* used to help a baby breathe by intermittently forcing pressurized air into the lungs. The baby then relieves the pressure by exhaling.
Refer to **Ventilator**.

Intern
A doctor in the first postgraduate year from medical school who is in supervised training.

Internalization
A cognitive process in which the child is able to remember an action or experience (internalize it) and repeat it at a later time, in a new situation. He doesn't have to experiment all over again, but can draw on past experience. For example, if the child is playing with nesting cups, he will be able to immediately place the small cup in the large cup rather than need to experiment to see how they fit together.
Also known as **Internal Representation**.

Internal Representation
Refer to **Internalization**.

Internist
A medical doctor who specializes in the diagnosis and treatment of adult diseases of the internal organs.

Intervention
Treatment to repair or help relieve an abnormality or deficit in mental, emotional, or physical function.

Intestinal Disorder
Refer to Gastrointestinal Disorder.

Intestinal Ostomy
Refer to Ostomy.

intra-
A prefix meaning inside or within.

Intracerebral (in-truh-SER-uh-bruhl)
Referring to within the cerebrum.

Intracranial (in-truh-KRAY-nee-uhl)
Referring to within the skull.

Intracranial Hemorrhage (ICH)
Bleeding in or around the brain caused by a *stroke,* loss of integrity of the blood vessels, injury to the head, or a lack of oxygen. A small amount of bleeding may resolve without serious complications, but a large bleed can result in brain damage or death.
   Compare **Intraventricular Hemorrhage**, **Periventricular Hemorrhage**, *and* **Subarachnoid Hemorrhage**.

Intralipid (IL)™ (in-truh-LIP-id)
An *intravenous,* calorie-rich fat solution that may be used during *total parenteral nutrition* to help the infant gain weight.

Intramuscular Injection (IM)
An injection into the muscle.

Intraocular (in-truh-OK-yuh-luhr)
Referring to within the eye.

Intraocular Pressure (IOP)
The pressure of the fluid within the eye.

Intrauterine Growth Retardation (IUGR) (in-truh-YOO-tuhr-in)
Insufficient fetal growth that results in a baby who is *small for gestational age* (SGA). IUGR can be *symmetric* or *asymmetric,* depending on whether the infant's height, weight, and head circumference are all involved. (The head circumference will be the last to be affected; head circumference involve-

ment occurs when IUGR is most severe.) IUGR may be caused by *genetic* factors, a fetal defect, fetal malnutrition, maternal disease, or maternal cigarette smoking or alcohol consumption. The impact of the IUGR depends on the severity of the factors causing the IUGR as well as the time during prenatal life that the factors were present. For example, an infant affected later in gestational life will be born at a lower weight, but not necessarily smaller in length or head circumference.

*Refer to **Birth Weight**, **Birth Length**, **Head Circumference**, and to the* **Growth Charts** *in the Appendix.*

Intravenous (IV) (in-truh-VEE-nuhs)
1. Referring to within a vein.
2. Referring to a tube or needle placed into a vein for injecting drugs or fluids into the blood stream.

Intravenous Feeding
*Refer to **Hyperalimentation**.*

Intravenous Pyelogram (IVP)
A procedure in which contrast material is injected into a vein and followed via X-ray as it passes through the kidneys, ureters, and bladder to determine whether there are any problems within or damage to these organs.

Intraventricular Hemorrhage (IVH) (in-truh-ven-TRIK-yuh-luhr)
Bleeding into the fluid-filled chambers (*ventricles*) of the brain. IVH may be caused by rupture of blood vessels due to oxygen deprivation, abrupt fluctuations in blood pressure, improper blood flow, or trauma to the head. The IVH is graded by severity, from Grade I (also known as a *Subependymal Hemorrhage*), which refers to slight leaking of blood within brain tissue (but not so severe that the blood enters the ventricles of the brain) to Grade IV, which indicates such severe bleeding into the ventricles that it pushes blood back into surrounding brain tissue. Intraventricular hemorrhage does not always have a serious or fatal outcome. The location, amount, and cause of bleeding determine whether disability or death will result. Some problems that can occur due to IVH include *hydrocephalus*, *mental retardation*, visual or hearing impairment, and *cerebral palsy*. Neurological damage usually results with a Grade IV hemorrhage.

*Also known as a **Brain Bleed**.*

*Compare **Periventricular Hemorrhage**, **Intracranial Hemorrhage**, and **Subarachnoid Hemorrhage**.*

Intubation (in-tyoo-BAY-shuhn)
The insertion of a tube into the trachea to deliver air, oxygen, or *anesthetic* gas to the lungs. The tube may be inserted through the nose or mouth, or through a *tracheostomy*.

*Compare **Extubation**.*

In Utero (in-YOO-tuhr-oe)
Referring to within the womb, or uterus.

Inversion
1. A turning of a body part toward midline, such as turning the foot inward.
2. An abnormal condition in which an organ is turned inside out.
   Compare **Eversion.**

Involuntary Movements
Movements made without conscious control or direction, such as *automatic reflexes* or *athetosis.*

Iodine
An essential trace element primarily found in the thyroid gland.

IOP
The abbreviation for intraocular pressure.

Ipecac Syrup (IP-uh-kak)
A drug taken orally to induce vomiting.

IPPB
The abbreviation for intermittent positive pressure breathing.

IQ Score
   Refer to **Intelligence Quotient.**

Iris
The clear tissue of the eye under which are pigment cells that give the eye its color. The iris sits between the cornea and the lens. The iris is made up of circular muscular fibers surrounding the pupil which function to dilate the pupil. (This is how the amount of light entering the eye is regulated.)
   Refer to **Eye.**

Iron
1. A common mineral component of hemoglobin and certain *enzymes.*
2. A medication used to treat iron-deficiency *anemia.*

is-
A prefix meaning equal.

ISAM
The abbreviation for infant of a substance-abusing mother.

Ischemia (is-KEE-mee-uh)
Poor blood supply to an organ or part. It results from disease or damage which causes obstruction (usually a narrowing) of a blood vessel supplying the organ or part. Pain and organ disease may result.

Ischium (IS-kee-uhm)
The inferior back part of the hip bone.

ISCN
The abbreviation for Intensive Special Care Nursery.

ISCU
The abbreviation for Intensive Special Care Unit.

iso-
A prefix meaning equal or like.

Isochromatic (ie-soe-kroe-MAT-ik)
Of the same color throughout (for example, the eyes).

Isolette™
A brand of *incubator*.

Isomil™
A milk-free formula made with soy protein used with infants sensitive to milk.

Isoxsuprine (ie-SOK-syoo-preen)
A drug used to suppress uterine contractions of premature labor.

-itis
A suffix meaning inflammation.

IUGR
The abbreviation for intrauterine growth retardation.

IV
The abbreviation for intravenous.

IVC
The abbreviation for indwelling venous catheter.

IVH
The abbreviation for intraventricular hemorrhage.

IVL
The abbreviation for indwelling venous line.

IVP
The abbreviation for intravenous pyelogram.

Jabbering
Referring to the talk of the toddler as she plays or experiments with words and the sound of her own voice. Around 18 months of age, the child begins to "practice" talking and to expand on the ways she can control her environment with speech.

*Compare **Cooing**, **Babbling**, and **Jargon**.*

Jargon
The vocal play that emerges in the child between 18 and 22 months of age in which she "talks" to herself (or to someone else) using a string of repetitive consonant sounds (and occasional actual words). Jargon sounds similar to adult speech because of the inflection and rate used.

*Compare **Cooing**, **Babbling**, and **Jabbering**.*

Jaundice (JAWN-dis)
A yellowing of the skin, the mucous membranes, and the whites of the eyes (and deeper eye tissues) caused by too much *bilirubin* (a pigment by-product of the breakdown of red blood cells) in the blood. Jaundice is common in newborns, but untreated jaundice (an extremely high level of bilirubin) can result in a form of *brain damage* known as *kernicterus*.

*Also known as **Icterus**.*
*Refer to **Hyperbilirubinemia**.*

Jaw Deviation
Pulling of the jaw to one side or the other. For example, the child with *athetosis* may experience jaw deviation because of the involuntary movements of her face.

jejuno-
A prefix meaning jejunum.

Jejunostomy (jee-joo-NOS-toe-mee)
An *ostomy* in the jejunum (the middle section of the small intestine).

Jejunum (juh-JOO-nuhm or jee-JOO-nuhm)
The middle section of the small intestine. (The duodenum is the first section and the ileum is the third section of the small intestine.)

Jervell and Lange-Nielsen Syndrome
A *congenital* disorder characterized by *bilateral conductive hearing loss*, *seizures* that cause loss of consciousness, heart *anomalies*, and *syncopal* attacks (periods of brief unconsciousness) that may result in sudden infant

death. If the infant survives these attacks, they become less frequent as the child grows older.

Joint
An *articulation,* or point of connection between two bones.

Joint Compression
Refer to **Compression.**

Joint Contracture
An abnormal condition in which the joint is bent with decreased *range of motion* due to permanent shortening of muscle fibers.
Refer to **Contracture.**

Joint Fusion
Refer to **Arthrodesis.**

Joint Stability
Referring to the support of a joint provided by the surrounding muscles and ligaments which enable the joint to successfully perform motor responses.

Jugular Shunt
Refer to **Ventriculojugular Shunt** *and to* **Shunt.**

Jugular Vein
One of three veins on each side of the neck that returns deoxygenated blood to the heart from the head and neck.

Jumping
Movement in which both feet propel the child's body into the air and then land at the same time.

juxta-
A prefix meaning next to.

K

k
The abbreviation for constant.

K
The chemical symbol for potassium.

KABC
The abbreviation for Kaufman Assessment Battery for Children.

KAFO
The abbreviation for knee-ankle-foot orthosis.

Kanamycin (kan-uh-MIE-sin)
A type of *antibiotic drug* used for treating some severe infections.

Kanner's Syndrome
  Refer to **Autism**.

Karyotyping (KER-ee-oe-tie-ping)
A type of *genetic* test in which cells are photographed through a microscope lens in order to examine the *chromosomes'* size, shape, and number. A normal karyotype shows 23 pairs of chromosomes. *Chromosomal abnormalities* can be detected both before and after birth using this procedure.

Kaufman Assessment Battery for Children (KABC)
A *norm-referenced* intelligence test used to evaluate the intelligence and academic achievement of the 2.5– to 12.5–year-old. The KABC is useful in detecting *learning disabilities*. Typically, the Kaufman is administered by a professional with a minimum of a bachelor's degree.

Keflex™ (KEF-leks)
  Refer to **Cephalexin**.

kerato-
A prefix meaning cornea or horny tissue.

Kernicterus (ker-NIK-tuhr-uhs)
A disorder that is caused by an abnormally high level of *bilirubin* in the central nervous system. It can result in *brain damage, choreoathetoid cerebral palsy,* hearing loss, and *mental retardation* if it is not caught in time. Without treatment, kernicterus is fatal.

kg
The abbreviation for kilogram.

Kidney
One of two organs located on each side of the spine, in back below the ribs. The kidneys filter waste products from the blood (in the form of urine) so it can be eliminated from the body.

Kidney Failure
Refer to **Renal Failure**.

Kilogram (kg)
The unit of weight of the metric system that equals 1000 grams or 2.2 pounds.

Kindling
The "learned" response of the cells in the brain to have more *seizures*.

Kinesthesia (kin-is-THEE-zee-uh)
The muscle sense by which the child is aware of his body position and his movements in relation to the environment.

Kinesthetic (kin-is-THET-ik)
Related to *kinesthesia*.

Kinesthetic Learner
A child who learns best through movement and touch. For example, playing a game of "follow the leader" that involves climbing in a box and crawling under a table might be an activity that would help the kinesthetic learner understand what the prepositions "in" and "under" mean.
Also known as an **Active Learner**.

Kinney Sticks™
Crutches that include bands around the forearms.

Klinefelter Syndrome
A *genetic* disorder in which a boy is born with at least one extra X *chromosome*. The disorder is characterized by low to normal intelligence, small penis and testes, sterility, female-like breasts, usually minimal tendency toward obesity, and long limbs with relatively tall stature.
Also known as **XXY Syndrome**.

Klonopin™ (KLON-oe-pin)
Refer to **Clonazepam**.

Knee-Ankle-Foot Orthosis (KAFO)
A long leg brace used to passively stretch muscles and to stabilize joints. Also known as an **Orthotic**.

Knee Jerk Reflex

A *deep tendon reflex* which can indicate neurological system function. A normal reflex is noted when there is a quick upward jerk of the leg at the knee after the tendon below the kneecap has been stretched by a tap.

Also known as the **Patellar Reflex**.

Knee Joint Hyperextensibility

Refer to **Genu Recurvatum**.

Kneel-Stand Position

To stand on the knees.

Knock Knees

Refer to **Genu Valgum**.

Kugelberg-Welander Disease

The mildest form of *spinal muscular atrophy* (a disorder characterized by weakness and wasting of muscle caused by spinal cord nerve defect). This hereditary (usually *autosomal recessive*) disorder progresses slowly, and usually the patient is still able to walk 20 years after onset. Onset is typically late childhood or adolescence. Intervention such as physical therapy and orthopedic care can help the child develop or maintain motor skills.

Also known as **Juvenile Spinal Muscular Atrophy**.
Refer to **Spinal Muscular Atrophy**.

Kwashiorkor (kwah-shee-OR-kor)

Severe protein malnutrition that primarily affects children between one and three years of age who are suddenly weaned onto a nutritionally insufficient diet. It results in stunted growth, *edema* (fluid retention that causes swelling), weakness, lethargy, skin disorder, enlargement of the liver, dehydration, and loss of resistance against serious infection. The condition may lead to death.

Kyphosis (kie-FOE-sis)

An exaggerated curve of the upper part of the spine, creating a rounded back. Kyphosis can be caused by a disorder of the spine, a tumor, a fracture, or poor posture.

Compare **Scoliosis** *and* **Lordosis**.

L

L
The abbreviation for left.

Labeling
1. Naming objects or actions the child encounters, such as by saying to the child, "Here comes the red ball! You caught it!"
2. Identifying someone by her disability, such as by describing a child as a "mentally retarded baby." Identifying a child's at-risk factors or disability is a necessary step in determining her eligibility for early intervention or special education services.

labi-, labio-
A prefix meaning lip.

Labile (LAY-bile)
Unstable or changing.

Labiodental Speech Sound
Sound that is produced by the contact of the lower lip and the upper teeth, such as the /v/ sound.

Labor
The process of childbirth from dilation of the cervix to delivery of the infant and afterbirth (placenta).

Labyrinth (LAB-uh-rinth)
The inner ear, which contains the three ring-shaped structures called the vestibular apparatus (which function to provide the sense of balance), and the cochlea (which makes hearing possible).
   Refer to **Ear**.

Labyrinthitis (lab-uh-rin-THIE-tis)
Inflammation of the inner ear which causes *vertigo* (a feeling that one's surroundings or one's own body is spinning) and loss of balance. Labyrinthitis is usually caused by a bacterial or viral infection.

Laceration
A wound resulting from the tearing of the skin.

Lacrimal Bone (LAK-rim-uhl)
A small bone of the skull located in the front and medial part of the orbit (the bony socket that contains the eye) near the tear duct opening.

Lactation
The production of milk by the breasts.

Lactose
Sugar found in milk.

Lactose Intolerance
Inability to digest milk and some dairy products, which may be a *congenital* condition or develop in later years due to a deficiency in the enzyme lactase, which is necessary for absorption of *lactose*. Treatment is by dietary restrictions.

Landau Reflex (LAN-dou)
A normal response in infants six months to two and one-half years of straightening out the spine and legs when held prone, in mid-air, with support around the trunk, and the head raised. This reflex is normally not present in children younger than six months and older than two and one-half years.
  Refer to **Primitive Reflex**.

Language
  Refer to **Communication, Expressive Language**, *and* **Receptive Language**.

Language Disorder
An inability or difficulty with expressing, understanding, or processing language (oral or written information). Language disorders often occur in children who have other disorders, including *cerebral palsy*, a *chromosomal* or other *genetic* disorder, or a structural *anomaly* of the speech or hearing systems. A child can have a language disorder without any other apparent condition. *Aphasia* is an example of a language disorder.
  Compare **Speech Disorder**.

Lanugo (la-NOO-goe)
Fine, downy hair that covers the body of the fetus. It is almost all shed by the ninth month of gestation.

Large for Gestational Age (LGA)
A newborn infant who is above the 90th percentile in weight for her *gestational age*.
  Compare **Small for Gestational Age** *and* **Appropriate for Gestational Age**.

Large Intestine
The portion of the digestive tract made up of the cecum (the chamber at the beginning of the large intestine); the appendix; the ascending, transverse, descending, and sigmoid colons; and the rectum.

laryngo-
A prefix meaning larynx.

Laryngologist (ler-in-GOL-oe-jist)
A medical doctor who specializes in the care of the larynx (voice box).

Laryngomalacia (ler-ing-goe-muh-LAY-shee-uh)
Softening of the tissues of the larynx that may result in *stridor* (an abnormal high-pitched breath sound). It may be *congenital* and, if so, is usually outgrown in two years.

Laryngopharynx (ler-in-goe-FER-ingks)
The lowest portion of the pharynx, or throat. It lies below the hyoid bone.

Laryngoscope (ler-IN-goe-skope)
A long, lighted tube that allows the doctor to see the vocal cords during the process of *intubation,* and to perform diagnostic and surgical procedures such as removal of a tumor on the *larynx.*

Laryngotracheobronchitis (le-ring-goe-tray-kee-oe-brong-KIE-tis)
Refer to **Croup**.

Larynx (LER-ingks)
The voice box. The larynx is located in the throat and functions to produce voice.

Lasix™ (LAY-siks)
Refer to **Furosemide**.

later-, latero-
A prefix meaning side.

Lateral
Relating to the side.
Compare **Bilateral**.

Laterality
1. Internal awareness of the right and left sides of the body and their differences.
2. The tendency to use preferentially the organs on one side of the body (having a sidedness), especially when engaging in voluntary movement.
3. This is determined by dominance of one cerebral hemisphere over the other. Preferring to use the right hand to catch a ball and the right foot to kick a ball is an example of laterality.

Lateralization
Affecting one side of the body, such as one hemisphere of the brain.

Lateral Rotation
A turning away from the midline of the body, such as when twisting the arm outward.
Compare **Medial Rotation**.

Laurence-Moon-Biedl Syndrome (LAW-rens moon BEE-duhl)

An *autosomal recessive disorder* characterized by *retinitis pigmentosa*, obesity beginning in infancy, extra or fused fingers or toes, underdeveloped genitals, abnormally decreased functional activity of the gonads, and mild to moderate *mental retardation*.

Also known as **Bardet–Biedl Syndrome**.

Laxative

A substance that is used to treat constipation by increasing the bulk of the feces, by softening the stool, or by lubricating the intestinal wall.

Lazy Eye

Refer to Amblyopia.

LBW

The abbreviation for low birth weight.

LD

The abbreviation for learning disability.

LE

The abbreviation for lower extremity.

LEA

The abbreviation for Local Education Agency.

Lead Agency

The state agency responsible for the provision of early intervention services. The lead agency (or an agency with which it contracts) provides intake, assessment, referral to services needed by the child and/or family, and case management.

Lead Poisoning

Illness caused by ingesting or inhaling lead that can result in *anemia* and damage to many organs, including the brain, kidneys, liver, and *gastrointestinal* system. *Seizures, brain damage, paralysis,* and death can also result.

Lead Wires

Wires that lead from *electrodes* placed on the body to a monitoring device (such as an *electrocardiograph,* or EKG, machine) that records the body's electrical activity.

Learning Disability (LD)

As defined in the *Individuals with Disabilities Education Act* (IDEA) [formerly Education for All Handicapped Children Act, PL 94–142]: ". . . a disorder in one or more of the basic psychological processes involved in understanding or in using language, spoken or written, which may manifest itself in an imperfect ability to listen, speak, read, write, spell, or do mathematical calculations." Children with learning disabilities may have problems with learning for a variety of reasons, including *hyperactivity* and *dyslexia*. These children have normal or above-average intelligence and learning potential.

Learning Style
The way in which a child best acquires knowledge or processes information. For example, some children learn best by listening (*auditory learners*), and others by doing (*kinesthetic learners*).

Least Restrictive Environment (LRE)
The educational setting that permits a child with disabilities to derive the most educational benefit while participating in a regular educational environment to the maximum extent appropriate. LRE is a requirement under the *IDEA*.

Lecithin (LES-ith-in)
A group of fats, rich in phosphorus, found in plants and animals. Lecithin is also one of the components of *surfactant*.

Legally Blind
Refer to **Blindness**.

Lens
The part of the eye that functions to focus an image on the retina. The lens is located between the iris of the eye and the vitreous humor (the gel-like substance of the eye).
Also known as the **Crystalline Lens**.
Refer to **Eye**.

Lesion
Any wound or injury.

leuk-, leuko-
Prefixes meaning white.

Leukemia (loo-KEE-mee-uh)
Any of several types of cancer in which there is proliferation (rapid reproduction) of white blood cells in the bone marrow. This leads to an excessive number of leukemic cells accumulating in the blood and in body organs, such as the brain, liver, spleen, and lymph nodes, and to dysfunction of these organs. In addition, the production of leukemic cells causes the production of red blood cells, platelets, and normal white blood cells to be impaired. Leukemias are classified as either acute or chronic types. Chronic leukemia rarely develops in children. A type of acute leukemia called acute lymphoblastic leukemia is the most common type in children. It appears to result from *mutation* of a single white blood cell. Treatment is by anticancer drugs, blood and platelet transfusion, and, sometimes, radiation therapy.

Bone marrow transplantation may also be considered. Treatment may provide a cure.

Leukocyte (LOO-koe-site)
Refer to **White Blood Cell**.

Levothyroxine (lee-voe-thie-ROK-seen)
A thyroid replacement hormone used to treat *hypothyroidism*.

LGA
The abbreviation for large for gestational age.

Lice
1. Parasitic insects that can be found in the hair or on the body of humans. Secretions from the bites can result in a rash which, if scratched, can become infected with bacteria. (Infestation with lice commonly causes itching.) Lice are transmitted via direct contact with infected persons and indirect contact with the infected person's belongings, such as a hair brush or hat.
2. Plural of louse.

Licensed Practical Nurse (LPN)
A *nurse* who is trained in basic nursing techniques and who provides care to patients under the supervision of *registered nurses* and doctors.
Compare **Licensed Vocational Nurse** *and* **Registered Nurse**.

Licensed Vocational Nurse (LVN)
A *licensed practical nurse* who is permitted by license to practice in certain states.
Compare **Registered Nurse**.

Life-Support Machine
Refer to **Ventilator**.

Ligation (lie-GAY-shuhn)
A surgical procedure to close, or tie off, a duct or blood vessel. Ligation is sometimes required to close a *patent ductus arteriosus*.

Light Perception (LP)
The ability to distinguish light from dark.

Limb Girdle Muscular Dystrophy
An *autosomal recessive* form of *muscular dystrophy* characterized by weakness in the muscles of the hips and shoulders.

Linear Growth
Height gain.

Lingua (LING-gwuh)
The tongue.
Also known as the **Glossa**.

Lingual
Pertaining to the tongue.

Linguistics
The study of the origin and structure of language.

Lioresal™ (lie-OR-uh-sahl)
Refer to **Baclofen**.

lip-
A prefix meaning fat (as in lipid).

Lip Closure
Bringing the lips together. Lip closure is necessary for many functions, including production of certain speech sounds (/m/, /b/, and /p/) and drinking from a cup.

Lipid (LIP-id)
Fatty substances in tissue.

lipo-
A prefix meaning fat.

Lipodystrophy (lip-oe-DIS-troe-fee)
A condition caused by abnormal metabolism of fats in the body, in which the fat deposits under the skin disappear in patches and sometimes build up in other areas.

Lipreading
Refer to **Speechreading**.

lith, litho-
A prefix meaning stone.

Liver
The largest internal organ, located on the right beneath the diaphragm. The liver has many functions, including producing proteins and metabolizing proteins, sugars, and fats; producing *bile* and purifying the blood; and storing sugars and fats.

LLE
The abbreviation for left lower extremity.

Local Anesthesia
Refer to **Anesthesia**.

Local Education Agency (LEA)
The agency responsible for providing special educational services on the local (school district, city, and county) level.

Localization
Limitation to one place or part.

Localize
The ability to "find" a sensation one is experiencing, such as touching or looking at the foot when it is touched, or turning the head and eyes to the source of a voice or sound.

Local Seizure
A *simple partial seizure*.
   Refer to **Partial Seizure** *and* **Epilepsy**.

Lockjaw
   Refer to **Tetanus**.

Locomotion
The educational term for movement from one place to another.

Locomotor
Referring to locomotion.

Lofstrand Crutches™
Crutches that have a band around the forearm and a handle.

Longitudinal
Referring to a study in which the same group of children are tested repeatedly on the same items as they get older.

Long Leg Sitting
Sitting with the legs extended to the front and slightly apart.

Lordosis (lor-DOE-sis)
An exaggerated curvature of the spine. Lordosis is most often noted in the lower spine, creating a swayback appearance. Weak abdominal muscles and poor posture contribute to excessive lordosis, as can *neuromuscular* disease.
   Also known as **Swayback**.
   Compare **Kyphosis** *and* **Scoliosis**.

Lorenz Night Splint™
A splint that is usually worn when the child sleeps to separate the legs to stretch the *adductors* and prevent *hip dislocation*.

Louse
Singular of lice.

Low Birth Weight Infant (LBW)

A baby who weighs less than 5.5 pounds (2500 grams) at birth. Low birth weight can result from prematurity (and may be average for the baby's gestational age) or from *intrauterine growth retardation* (and be small for gestational age).

Compare **Birth Weight**.

Refer to **Premature Infant** *and* **Intrauterine Growth Retardation**.

Low Blood Sugar

Refer to **Hypoglycemia**.

Lower Respiratory Infection (LRI)

An infection affecting the trachea, bronchi, or the lungs.

Compare **Upper Respiratory Infection**.

Lowe Syndrome

An *X-linked recessive disorder* characterized by *failure to thrive*, *hypotonia*, eye abnormalities including *cataracts* and blindness, kidney abnormalities, *cryptorchidism* (undescended testes), diminished or absent *deep tendon reflexes*, *hyperactivity*, and *mental retardation*.

Also known as **Oculocerebrorenal Syndrome**.

Low Tone/Low Muscle Tone

Refer to **Hypotonia**.

Low Vision

A label used by many school systems to describe children with *visual acuity* of less than 20/70 in the better eye. Low vision may be enhanced by optical aids, such as magnifying devices and special lenses.

Low-Vision Aid

A device that helps people to see. These optical aids are used when prescription lenses do not help, or in addition to prescription lenses to magnify things such as words on a page.

LP

1. The abbreviation for lumbar puncture.
2. The abbreviation for light perception.

LPN

The abbreviation for licensed practical nurse.

LRE

The abbreviation for least restrictive environment.

LRI

The abbreviation for lower respiratory tract infection.

LSO
The abbreviation for lumbar-sacral orthosis.

L/S Ratio
The relative proportions between *l*ecithin and *s*phingomyelin (components of *surfactant*) in the amniotic fluid. A higher amount of L in relation to S indicates the maturity of the unborn baby's lungs. This is because lecithin levels increase after 35 weeks gestation.

LUE
The abbreviation for left upper extremity.

Lumbar
Referring to the lower back.

Lumbar Puncture (LP)
A procedure involving the insertion of a hollow needle in between the vertebrae of the lower back to withdraw *cerebrospinal fluid* or to inject drugs, contrast (to perform an X-ray study), or an anesthetic.
   *Also known as a **Spinal Tap**.*

Lumbar-Sacral Orthosis (LSO)
A brace that counteracts spinal deformities such as *scoliosis*, *kyphosis*, and *lordosis*.

Luminal™ (LOO-mi-nahl)
   *Refer to **Phenobarbital**.*

Lungs
The organs located in both sides of the chest which function to supply the body with oxygen from air that is inhaled, and to rid the body of carbon dioxide with the air that is exhaled.

LVN
The abbreviation for licensed vocational nurse.

Lymph
A body fluid that plays an important role in the *immune system* and in absorbing fats from the intestine. Lymph provides a defense against local infection.

Lymph Node
One of many small glands clustered throughout the body that fight infection by housing the white blood cells which produce antibodies and filter out and destroy bacteria.

Lymphocyte (LIM-foe-site)
One of two principal kinds of white blood cells: B cells and T cells. B cells primarily function to produce *antibodies*. T cells are principally responsible for initiating and regulating the immune system.

-lysis
A suffix meaning breakdown, separation, or destruction.

Lysis
Destruction of a cell by damage to its outer membrane.

Lysosomal Storage Diseases
Diseases in which a lysosomal *enzyme* is defective and, as a result, the *lysosome* stores rather than metabolizes biochemicals in the body. An example of a lysosomal storage disease is *Hurler's syndrome*.

Lysosome (LIE-soe-soem)
A small structure within a cell that contains *enzymes* that break down large molecules and are capable of metabolizing certain chemicals in the body.

M
The abbreviation for male.

MA
The abbreviation for mental age.

macro-
A prefix meaning long or large.

Macrocephaly (mak-roe-SEF-uh-lee)
An abnormally large head size in relation to the body. Macrocephaly may be *congenital* or *acquired*. *Mental retardation* is sometimes associated with this birth defect.

Macroglossia (mak-roe-GLOS-ee-uh)
An abnormally large tongue.

Macrognathia (mak-roe-NAY-thee-uh)
An abnormally large jaw.

Macro-orchidism (MAK-roe OR-kid-izm)
Abnormally large testes. This condition is common in males with *Fragile X syndrome*.

Macrophage (MAK-roe-fayj)
A type of large white blood cell found in tissue that destroys foreign substances which have entered the body.

Magnesium Sulfate
A drug used in the treatment of *toxemia* and in stopping pre-term labor. It is also used to stimulate the production of bowel movements.

Magnetic Resonance Imaging (MRI)
A diagnostic procedure that involves creating cross-sectional images of body organs and structures. MRI is done by exposing the patient to a magnetic field while lying inside a large magnet structure. Images or "maps" are created when the body's hydrogen ions move (the movement is caused by exposure to radio waves), producing a radio signal that is detected and changed by computer to an image. Body tissue that contains a large amount of hydrogen will produce a bright image. Body tissue that contains little or no hydrogen is dark. No radiation is used in MRI.

Mainstreaming
Placing a child with disabilities in the educational setting that is as close to normal as possible. Mainstreaming may allow the child with disabilities to

be a member of a regular classroom, even though supplemental resource services may be needed and provided.

mal-
A prefix meaning abnormal.

malac-, malaco-
Prefixes meaning soft.

Malacia (muh-LAY-shee-uh)
An abnormal softening in an organ due to degeneration of its tissues.

Malar (MAY-lar)
Pertaining to the cheek or cheekbone.
Refer to **Zygomatic Bone**.

Malecot Tube™
A *gastrostomy tube*.

Malignancy
A condition (often a tumor) that becomes progressively worse and will likely result in death. Malignancy frequently refers to cancer that is invasive or spreading to other organs.
Compare **Benign**.

Malleable
Referring to something that is soft or easily molded.

Malleolus (muhl-EE-oe-luhs)
A rounded bone, such as those on each side of the ankle.

Malleus (MAL-ee-uhs)
One of the three small bones of the middle ear. (The other two bones are the incus and the stapes.)
Also known as the **Hammer**.
Refer to **Ear**.

Malnutrition
Nutritional disorders that develop for a variety of reasons, including an unbalanced diet (usually lacking in carbohydrate or protein), a diet consisting of too little food or too much food, or the improper body utilization of foods.

Malocclusion (mal-uh-KLOO-zhuhn)
An abnormal relationship of the teeth of the upper jaw with the teeth of the lower jaw based on their contact, or the bite. (For example, teeth may meet improperly, overlap too much, or not overlap at all). Malocclusion is usually the result of heredity. It may also result from thumb-sucking.

mammo-
A prefix meaning breast.

Mandated Reporter
Any professional who is required by law to report cases of child abuse or neglect. The professional needs only to have reasonable suspicion of abuse or neglect. Individuals who are considered to be mandated reporters include child care custodians (such as teachers, administrative officers, social workers, foster parents, and certificated pupil personnel employees) and health practitioners (such as physicians, nurses, psychologists, dentists, and counselors).
Refer to **Child Abuse and Neglect** *and* **Emotional Abuse**.

Mandible (MAN-di-buhl)
The lower jaw bone.

Manual Alphabet
An alphabet of hand-signs which are used to spell out words. Each letter of the alphabet has its own sign.
Also known as **Fingerspelling**.

Manual English
A form of sign language in which each word expressed is represented with a hand sign. Two types of Manual English are *Signed English* and *Signed Exact English*. For words that do not have a sign, *fingerspelling* is used.

Manual Thrust
Refer to **Heimlich Maneuver**.

Maple Syrup Urine Disease
Refer to **Branched Chain Ketoaciduria**.

Marasmus (muhr-AZ-muhs)
Severe protein calorie malnutrition that is primarily seen in young children with failure to thrive and in starving people.

Marking Time Pattern
Refer to **Non-reciprocal Gait**.

Maroteaux-Lamy Syndrome I
An *autosomal recessive disorder* of carbohydrate metabolism (it is a *mucopolysaccharidosis*) characterized by coarse facies, irregular dentition, visual impairment, *small stature*, *kyphosis* (a form of spinal curvature), *genu valgum* ("knock knees"), tendency toward bone fractures, finger abnormalities, and normal intelligence.
Also known as **Mucopolysaccharidosis VI**.

Maroteaux-Lamy Syndrome II

An *autosomal recessive disorder* with onset in early infancy that is characterized by *small stature, scoliosis,* tendency toward bone fractures, finger and toe abnormalities, a small lower jaw, irregular dentition, delayed closure of *fontanelles,* and occasional *mental retardation.*

Also known as **Pyknodysostosis.**

masto-

A prefix meaning breast.

Mastoiditis (mas-toid-IE-tis)

A serious inflammation of the air cells of the mastoid bone behind the ear. Mastoiditis may result when middle ear infection spreads to the mastoid bone. It can cause *conductive hearing loss.*

Maturation

Referring to the process of becoming an adult or fully developed.

Maxilla (mak-SIL-uh)

One of a pair of bones that forms the upper jaw.

Maxillary

Pertaining to the upper jaw.

MBD

The abbreviation for minimal brain dysfunction.

McCarthy Scales of Children's Abilities

A *norm-referenced* evaluation tool used to assess the verbal, perceptual, quantitative, memory, motor, and cognitive abilities of the child between two and one-half and eight years of age. Typically, the McCarthy is administered by a professional with a Ph.D. in psychology or education.

MD

The abbreviation for the Latin words meaning doctor of medicine.

MDI

The abbreviation for Mental Development Index (the score given on the Mental Scale of The Bayley Scales of Infant Development).

MDR

The abbreviation for minimum daily requirement.

Mean

The average of a group of values (numbers). The mean is obtained by adding all of the values given and dividing by the number of items which were added.

Measles

A highly contagious, viral illness symptomized by high fever, runny nose, cough, *conjunctivitis*, discomfort, and an itchy red rash. Measles is spread by nasal secretions. Patients with measles may be sick enough to be hospitalized and may even die.

Also known as **Rubeola**.
Compare **Rubella (German Measles)**.

Measles, Mumps, and Rubella Vaccine (MMR)

An *immunization* against measles, mumps, and rubella made from live, weakened strains of the three viruses. Usually a single injection of this vaccine is given to children at 12 months of age. Recommendations for a booster at four and one-half to five years of age (before starting school) depend upon the prevalence of the disease.

Meatus (mee-A-tuhs)

An opening or passageway in the body.

Mebaral™ (MEB-uh-rahl)

Refer to **Mephobarbital**.

Meconium (mee-KOE-nee-uhm or me-KOE-nee-uhm)

A greenish-black material that collects in the fetal intestinal tract before birth and is usually passed during the first day or two after birth. Meconium passed before birth into the amniotic fluid (meconium staining) can indicate fetal distress. Physicians caring for the meconium-stained newborn must do all they can to prevent the baby from inhaling the meconium while taking his first breaths (meconium aspiration), because this can result in blocked airways.

Meconium Aspiration

Refer to **Meconium**.

Meconium Plug

A solid plug of *meconium* blocking the colon of a newborn infant. A meconium plug may be identified when the newborn is unable to defecate within 48 hours after birth, or if the infant has vomiting or abdominal distention. It can be caused by a deficiency of certain necessary secretions. The meconium plug must be removed.

Meconium Staining

Refer to **Meconium**.

MED

The abbreviation for minimum effective dose.

med-, medi-

Prefixes meaning middle.

Medial
Referring to a position toward the middle of the body.

Medial Rotation
A turning toward the middle of the body, such as the arm turning inward.
   Compare **Lateral Rotation**.

Median Plane
The vertical plane which divides the body into right and left halves.

Medicaid
A federally funded program that supports individual state programs in providing medical assistance to people who qualify for *Supplemental Security Income* (SSI).

Medically Fragile
Referring to an infant or child whose health status either is unstable, or renders him *at-risk* for *developmental delay* (often due to poor health or limitations on the infant's ability to participate in normal activities). Examples of infants who may be medically fragile include those who were *premature*, have *chronic lung disease*, or were *prenatally exposed to drugs*.

Medicare
A federal health insurance program that funds medical care for adults who are over 65 years old and for children and adults who are permanently disabled.

Medulla (muh-DUL-uh)
The innermost part of a body structure or organ.

Medulla Oblongata (muh-DUL-uh ob-long-GAH-tuh)
The lower part of the brain stem through which nerve fibers from higher brain centers pass on their way to the spinal cord. The heart, blood vessel, and breathing centers of the brain are contained in the medulla, and the nerve fibers of the *pyramidal tract* cross over in the medulla.
   Refer to **Brain**.

mega-
A prefix meaning great or large.

megalo-
A prefix meaning great or large.

Megalocephaly (meg-uh-loe-SEF-uh-lee)
An enlargement of the head that is most commonly caused by increased intracranial pressure with *hydrocephalus*. It may also be caused by excessive brain growth. Megalocephaly may be present at birth or be *acquired*. People with megalocephaly usually have *mental retardation*.

-megaly
A suffix meaning enlargement.

Meiosis (mie-OE-sis)
Division of sex cells (before fertilization occurs) into *daughter cells,* each containing half of the number of *chromosomes* (23) of regular cells. When egg and sperm cells unite, a total of 46 chromosomes are again present, producing a unique child with half of his *inherited genetic* material from his mother and half from his father.
Compare **Mitosis.**

Meiotic Division
Refer to **Meiosis.**

melan-
A prefix meaning black.

Mellaril™ (MEL-uh-ril)
Refer to **Thioridazine.**

Membrane
A thin layer of tissue that covers a body surface, divides a space or organ, or lines a cavity.

mening-
A prefix meaning membrane. It usually refers to the membranes covering the brain and spinal cord.

Meninges (men-IN-jez)
The membranes surrounding the brain and spinal cord. There are three layers of meninges, the *dura mater*, the *arachnoid*, and the *pia mater*.

Meningitis (men-in-JIE-tis)
Inflammation of the *meninges*, which is usually caused by either a viral or bacterial infection. Viral meningitis is usually mild and the infected child suffers no brain damage. Bacterial meningitis requires prompt medical attention, in the form of large doses of *antibiotics*. Children with bacterial meningitis typically recover without brain damage if they receive immediate medical assistance.

Meningocele (men-IN-goe-seel)
A birth defect in which the *meninges* (the membranes surrounding the spinal cord) protrude through an opening in the spinal column under the skin. This form of *spina bifida* must be surgically repaired, but the child usually suffers no functional problems such as the *paralysis* common to *myelocele*.
Compare **Myelocele.**
Refer to **Spina Bifida.**

Meningoencephalitis (men-in-goe-en-sef-uh-LIE-tis)
An inflammation of both the brain and the *meninges* (the membranes surrounding the brain), usually caused by a bacterial infection. Meningoencephalitis can lead to serious illness, and, depending on the type of bacteria that caused the infection, can be fatal.

Meningoencephalocele (men-in-goe-en-SEF-uhl-oe-seel)
A birth defect in which brain tissue, *cerebrospinal fluid*, and the *meninges* (the membranes surrounding the brain) protrude through an opening in the skull. This condition usually results in *brain damage*.

Meningomyelocele (men-in-goe-mie-EL-oe-seel)
Refer to Myelocele.

mens-
A prefix meaning month.

Mental Age
Refer to Developmental Age.

Mental Deficiency
Refer to Mental Retardation.

Mental Development Index (MDI)
The score given on the Mental Scale section of the Bayley Scales of Infant Development.

Mental Handicap
In Canada, the term preferred for *mental retardation.*

Mental Retardation
According to the American Association on Mental Retardation (1992), "mental retardation refers to substantial limitations in present functioning. It is characterized by significantly subaverage intellectual functioning, existing concurrently with related limitations in two or more of the following applicable adaptive skill areas: communication, self-care, home living, social skills, community use, self-direction, health and safety, functional academics, leisure, and work. Mental retardation manifests before age 18." In other words, someone with mental retardation performs significantly below his age level in both intellectual functioning (*intelligence*) and *adaptive behavior*. Mental retardation is the most common developmental disorder, affecting about 2 to 3 percent of the population.
Refer to Intelligence.

Mephobarbital (mef-oe-BAR-bi-tol)
A drug used to treat *seizure* disorders.

Mesencephalon (mes-en-SEF-uh-lon)
Refer to **Midbrain**.

meso-
A prefix meaning middle.

meta-
A prefix meaning beyond or after.

Metabolic
Pertaining to metabolism.

Metabolism
All the chemical processes carried out by the cells in the body that are necessary for sustaining life.
Refer to **Inborn Errors of Metabolism**.

Metacarpals (met-uh-KAR-puhlz)
The five bones of the hand to which the finger bones are attached.

Metachromatic Leukodystrophy (met-uh-kroe-MAT-ik loo-kuh-DIS-truh-fee)
A disorder of *lipid* metabolism (a *sphingolipidosis*) in which the body does not produce enough of the enzyme cerebroside sulfatase. Deficiency of this enzyme results in an accumulation of metachromatic lipids, which leads to progressive *paralysis* and brain disease. Onset of symptoms begins by two years of age, and children usually die by ten years of age.

Metaproterenol (met-uh-proe-TER-uh-nol)
A *bronchodilator drug* used to treat bronchospasm associated with chronic bronchitis and bronchial asthma.

Metatarsals (met-uh-TAR-suhlz)
The five bones of the foot to which the toe bones are attached. This area forms the forefoot.

Metatarsus Adductus (met-uh-TAR-suhs a-DUKT-uhs)
An orthopedic condition in which the baby's forefoot turns inward (but the ankle and heel are in their normal positions), possibly due to fetal positioning in the uterus.
Refer to **Metatarsals**.

Methicillin (meth-uh-SIL-in)
An *antibiotic* given mostly in the treatment of severe penicillin-resistant *staphylococcal* infections.

Methsuximide (meth-SUK-si-mide)
An *antiepileptic drug*.

Methylphenidate (meth-il-FEN-i-dayt)
A central nervous system stimulating drug used to treat *attention deficit hyperactivity disorder* in children over six years of age.

Metoclopramide (met-oe-kloe-PRAM-ide)
A drug used to treat nausea and vomiting and to stimulate motility of the upper gastrointestinal tract. It is commonly used for treating *reflux esophagitis*.

metro-
A prefix meaning uterus.

micro-
A prefix meaning small.

Microcephaly (mie-kroe-SEF-uh-lee)
An abnormally small head size, resulting in poor brain growth. Microcephaly is nearly always due to a small brain size associated with prenatal factors such as intrauterine infection (for example, from *congenital rubella, toxoplasmosis, AIDS,* or *herpes simplex 2), PKU, fetal alcohol syndrome,* radiation exposure, and *chromosomal abnormalities,* or due to conditions occurring at or soon after birth, such as brain injury or disease (often associated with *anoxia,* or insufficient oxygen). There is also a rare form of microcephaly which is *inherited.* Babies with microcephaly usually have *mental retardation* and may have *cerebral palsy* and *seizures.*

Micrognathia (mie-kroe-NAY-thee-uh)
Small jaws, especially the lower jaw.

Microorganism (mie-kroe-OR-gan-izm)
Any minute (microscopic) plant or animal organism such as bacteria, fungi, and viruses. Some microorganisms cause disease.

Microphthalmos, Microphthalmus (mie-krof-THAL-muhs)
An abnormally small eyeball present at birth.

Microtia (mie-KROE-shee-uh)
Congenital abnormal smallness of the external ear.

Midbrain
The highest part of the brain stem, which connects the pons and the cerebellum with the hemispheres of the cerebrum.
Also known as the **Mesencephalon.**
Refer to **Brain.**

Middle Ear
Refer to **Ear.**

Midline
The vertical center line of the body.

Midsupination
A position in which the forearm is turned so that the little finger is down and the thumb is up. Normal reaching and grasping are done in midsupination.

Miller Assessment for Preschoolers
An evaluation tool used to assess the preacademic, motor coordination, language, and cognitive development of the child between two years, nine months and five years, two months. Typically, the Miller is administered by a professional with a minimum of a master's degree.

Mineral
A naturally occurring element of the earth. Minerals are necessary nutrients for the regulation of many body functions, including *electrolyte* balance and hormone production required for normal growth.

Mineral Oil
A laxative used to treat constipation. Mineral oil is also used as a skin softener.

Minimal Brain Dysfunction (MBD)
A term previously used to describe children with behavioral problems and/or *learning disabilities*. These children may exhibit many of the same characteristics as children with *hyperactivity*.

Misarticulation
Producing the sounds of speech incorrectly. Misarticulations include substituting, omitting, and adding sounds, as well as sound distortion. Young children frequently misarticulate sounds, but persistent misarticulations may be caused by hearing impairment or a structural malformation such as *cleft palate*.

Miscarriage
A spontaneous end of pregnancy before the middle of the second trimester (prior to the fetus being able to survive on its own outside of the uterus). Miscarriage often occurs for unknown reasons. Known causes of miscarriage include defects of the fetus or uterus, exposure to toxins such as X-rays or drugs, and maternal infection.
   *Also known as **Spontaneous Abortion**.*

Mist Tent
   *Refer to **Tent**.*

Mitosis (mie-TOE-sis)

The simplest type of cell division. It results in two identical cells (*daughter cells* with the same *chromosomes*, or *genetic* material) being formed. Mitosis occurs so that the body can make new cells to replace dead cells.

Compare **Meiosis**.

Mitral Valve

One of four valves in the heart that open and close with each heart beat to control the flow of blood. Blood exits each chamber of the heart through one of the valves. The mitral valve is located between the left atrium and the left ventricle. It usually has two cusps (small flaps) and may have some additional smaller cusps, which close to force blood from the left ventricle to the aorta. The mitral valve is the only valve that typically has just two cusps. (The other valves each have three cusps.)

Also known as the **Bicuspid Valve**.

Compare **Aortic Valve**, **Pulmonary Valve**, *and* **Tricuspid Valve**.

Mixed Hearing Loss

Hearing impairment that involves a combination of both *conductive hearing loss* and *sensorineural hearing loss*. Mixed hearing loss can occur *congenitally* or be *acquired*.

Compare **Conductive Hearing Loss** *and* **Sensorineural Hearing Loss**.

Mixed-Type Cerebral Palsy

A form of *cerebral palsy* in which both *spasticity* and *choreoathetoid* movements are present. Mixed-type cerebral palsy results when there is damage to both the *pyramidal* and *extrapyramidal* areas of the brain.

MMR

The abbreviation for Measles, Mumps, and Rubella Vaccine.

Mobility Aid

A piece of adaptive equipment that offers support, makes movement easier, or provides balance and stability. Mobility aids include wedges, scooter boards, wheelchairs, and walkers.

Mobility Specialist

An individual trained to teach children or adults with developmental disabilities or visual impairments how to move about independently. Initially, the child is taught how to move about within familiar environments and then, as his skills develop, he may be taught how to travel beyond familiar areas.

Mobius Syndrome (MEE-bee-uhs)

A condition characterized by *palsy* of several of the cranial nerves. Patients have facial *paralysis*, droopy eyelids that may not close completely, and inability to move the eyes away from midline. This syndrome is associated with *webbing* of the neck, fingers, and toes; extra fingers or toes; *mental retardation;* and sometimes deafness, *cleft palate,* and a small mouth and jaw. Children with Mobius syndrome may also have nutritional difficulty (which can affect body growth), due to the paralysis and deformities of the facial and oral structures.

Modality
Any sensory pathway, such as vision, taste, or touch, through which information may be received.

Model
To provide an example for imitation, such as pronouncing a word to be repeated.

Molluscum Contagiosum (muh-LUS-kuhm kuhn-tay-jee-OE-suhm)
A viral infection consisting of a skin rash (small, light-colored, waxy-appearing bumps) that is transmitted by direct contact with the lesions. Molluscum contagiosum is generally harmless and usually heals without treatment.

Mongolian Spot (mong-GOE-lee-uhn)
A harmless, blue-black spot most commonly appearing on the lower back or buttocks of some newborns. (A Mongolian spot may also be on the whole back, legs, etc.) It is caused by an accumulation of pigment-producing cells and usually disappears by three or four years of age. (The Mongolian spot should be carefully documented so it is not confused with abuse.)

Mongolism (MONG-guh-liz-uhm)
A formerly-used and less-accepted name for *Down syndrome.*

Monilia (moe-NIL-ee-uh)
Refer to **Candida Albicans**.

mono-
A prefix meaning one or single.

Mono
Referring to infectious *mononucleosis.*

Mononucleosis (mon-oe-noo-klee-OE-sis)
An infection caused by the Epstein-Barr virus or *cytomegalovirus* and symptomized by fever, sore throat, swollen lymph glands, and lethargy.

Monoplegia (mon-uh-PLEE-jee-uh)
A form of *cerebral palsy* in which only one extremity (an arm or leg) is affected. The child's movements may only be mildly impaired and his motor abilities frequently improve.
   Refer to **Pyramidal Cerebral Palsy**.

Monoploid (MON-uh-ploid)
   Refer to **Haploid**.

Monosomy (MON-uh-soe-mee)
Any *chromosome* disorder that occurs due to the lack of one chromosome. (Normally, chromosomes are paired.) Most pregnancies which produce a monosomic embryo end during the early embryonic stage.
   Compare **Trisomy**.

Monozygotic Twins (mon-oe-zie-GOT-ik)
Twins that originate from one zygote (fertilized ovum).
   Refer to **Identical Twins**.

Moro Reflex/Moro Response
A startle reaction normal in infants up to four months of age. The moro response is observed when the infant reacts to a sudden change of body or head position by opening his hands and rapidly extending and *abducting* his arms briefly, then more slowly bringing them and the legs back close to his body into a flexed and *adducted* (embrace) position. This response appears to be a protective reaction for the young infant.
   Compare **Startle Reflex**.
   Refer to **Primitive Reflex**.

morph-, morpho-
Prefixes meaning shape or form.

Morpheme (MOR-feem)
The smallest unit of meaning in language, such as a root word, prefix, or suffix. For example, both the word "cat" (which is a root word) and the ending "s" on the word "cats" (which changes the meaning of the root word) are morphemes.

Morphological (mor-foe-LOJ-i-kuhl)
Pertaining to *morphology*.

Morphology (mor-FOL-uh-jee)
The science of the shape and structure of living organisms, both plants and animals.

Morquio Syndrome (mor-KEE-oe)
A disorder of carbohydrate metabolism (a *mucopolysaccharidosis*) characterized by growth deficiency, coarse facial features, skeletal *anomalies* in-

cluding kyphoscoliosis (an exaggerated curve of the upper part of the spine creating a "humped" appearance in addition to a lateral curve of the spine), an enlarged liver, hearing loss, and occasionally *mental retardation.*

Also known as **Mucopolysaccharidosis IV**.

Mosaicism (moe-ZAY-i-sizm)

A condition in which some of a child's cells have normal *chromosomes* and some do not. Mosaicism is probably caused by faulty early cell division and is a process by which *chromosomal abnormalities,* such as *Down syndrome* and *Turner syndrome,* can occur. Because a portion of cells divided normally and continue to have the correct amount and structure of chromosomes, there will be normal cell lines and abnormal cell lines present. The percentages of normal and abnormal cells depend upon how early in development the faulty division occurred. These percentages also determine the features associated with the disorder. Frequently, the features will be less noticeable than those of the child who developed the disorder due to chromosomal abnormality in all cells.

Motor

Referring to movement produced by a muscle or nerve.

Motor Control

The ability to voluntarily engage muscles in purposeful movement.

Motor Cortex

The area within the *cerebral cortex* of the brain that controls motor activity.
  Refer to **Cerebral Cortex**.

Motor Nerve

Any nerve composed of motor fibers.
  Refer to **Peripheral Nervous System**.

Motor Pattern

A sequence of movements.

Motor Planning

The ability to organize sensory information in order to plan and carry out the appropriate sequence of movements required to complete a task (for example, climbing stairs).
  Refer to **Dyspraxia**.

Motor Skill

Referring to the learned ability to perform movements, such as holding the body in an upright position to sit, using the hands to manipulate small toys, scooping food onto a spoon and bringing the spoon to the mouth, and moving the lips and tongue to articulate different sounds.
  Refer to **Gross Motor** *and* **Fine Motor**.

Mottling
A condition of spotting or variability of coloration without a distinct pattern, such as on the skin.

Mouthing
Placing objects into the mouth for oral exploration. This behavior usually emerges between three and six months of age. The mouthing of safe objects helps the infant learn about and develop tolerance for different textures, temperatures, sizes, and shapes. Oral play can help to decrease an excessive gag reflex, and is also an important experience needed for the development of speech.
Also known as **Oral Play** *and* **Oral Exploration**.
Refer to **Oral Stimulation**.

Mouth-to-Mouth
Referring to the mouth-to-mouth respiration technique used with cardiac massage to perform *cardiopulmonary resuscitation*.

MP Finger Joint
The Metacarpal Phalangeal joint between the finger and the hand.

MPS
The abbreviation for mucopolysaccharidosis.

MR
The abbreviation for mental retardation.

MRI
The abbreviation for magnetic resonance imaging.

muco-
A prefix meaning mucus.

Mucopolysaccharidosis (MPS) (myoo-koe-pol-ee-sak-uh-rie-DOE-sis)
One of several *inherited* disorders of carbohydrate metabolism in which carbohydrate substances collect in a variety of body tissues due to an enzyme deficiency. The characteristics depend upon the exact enzyme deficiency but can include variable degrees of *mental retardation*, growth deficiency, bone abnormalities, an enlarged liver and spleen, and coarse facial features. Typically, there is also a shortened life expectancy. Examples of MPS disorders include *Hunter syndrome* and *Hurler syndrome*.

Mucopolysaccharidosis I
Refer to **Hurler Syndrome**.

Mucopolysaccharidosis II
Refer to **Hunter Syndrome**.

Mucopolysaccharidosis III
*Refer to **Sanfilippo Syndrome**.*

Mucopolysaccharidosis IV
*Refer to **Morquio Syndrome**.*

Mucopolysaccharidosis V
*Refer to **Scheie Syndrome**.*

Mucopolysaccharidosis VI
*Refer to **Maroteaux-Lamy Syndrome I**.*

Multidisciplinary Team
A group of professionals who each represent areas of expertise useful in planning and implementing the educational, therapeutic, and/or medical treatment program of the child who has special needs. The team gathers periodically to evaluate the child and, with the child's parents, determines the child's areas of strength and deficit. Based on the evaluation, a plan for addressing the child's needs is developed, as well as a determination of the professionals who will implement the plan. Members of the multidisciplinary team may include a physician, infant educator, psychologist, physical or occupational therapist, speech pathologist, social worker, and the parents.
*Also known as **Interdisciplinary Team**.*

Multifactorial Disorder
A disorder caused by the interaction between *genetic* and environmental factors. Sometimes the environmental factors can be identified, such as maternal drug use during pregnancy, but often they are unknown, as with *spina bifida* or *cleft palate*.
*Compare **Chromosomal Abnormalities** and **Unifactorial Disorder**.*

Multi-handicapped
Referring to a child who has impairments in more than one area of development, such as a child who has orthopedic and visual disabilities.

Multipara (mul-TIP-uh-ruh)
Referring to a woman who has had two or more pregnancies which resulted in viable fetuses.

Multiple Birth
Referring to carrying and delivering more than one infant per single pregnancy.

Mumps
A viral infection resulting in swelling of the salivary, and sometimes other, glands. Many children show no symptoms or just mild symptoms of discomfort. Swelling under the jaw line, fever, and headache are the usual

symptoms in more severe cases. Mumps infection of mature males can affect the testes, causing inflammation, pain, and swelling.

Murmur

Refer to **Heart Murmur**.

Muscle

A type of tissue, or body structure, composed of bundles of cells capable of contraction and relaxation. Muscles function to effect movement of a part of the body or an organ. There are three types of muscle: skeletal muscle (also called striated muscle because of the stripes marking the muscle fibers), smooth muscle (non-striated muscle), and cardiac muscle. The movement response of skeletal muscle is voluntary; the movement of smooth muscle and cardiac muscle is not under conscious control. Skeletal muscles move body parts up and down, and toward and away from the body, and extend and flex at the joints. Another type of skeletal muscle is sphincter, or constrictor muscle, which closes off certain body openings, such as the anal sphincter. Smooth muscle is found in the internal organs, such as in the digestive tract, the respiratory passages, and the urinary bladder. Cardiac muscle (also called *myocardium*) enables the heart to contract.

Muscle Biopsy

A diagnostic procedure in which a small amount of muscle tissue is surgically removed and examined under the microscope. Muscle biopsy is done using a local *anesthetic*.

Muscle Enzyme Test

A diagnostic procedure to determine the existence of muscle disease or muscle abnormality. The test involves obtaining and studying a blood sample for its level of specific muscle *enzymes*.

Muscle Lengthening

A surgical procedure that lengthens a muscle and releases muscle *contractures*.

Muscle Relaxant

A drug given to relax *hypertonic* muscles. Sometimes muscle relaxants are referred to as *antispastic medications*.

Muscle Tone

A muscle's level of tension while at rest, or its resistance to passive movement. Muscle tone reflects the condition of the muscle and the nerves which supply it. Abnormal muscle tone may be described as *hypertonic* (stiff) or *hypotonic* (floppy).

Refer to **Tonus**.

Muscular Dystrophy (DIS-troe-fee)
A group of *inherited*, degenerative muscle disorders characterized by progressive weakness and wasting. There are several forms of muscular dystrophy, each of which varies in age of onset, the pattern of inheritance, the speed of disease progression, and the level of resulting disability. The most common form of muscular dystrophy is *Duchenne muscular dystrophy*.

Mutation
An alteration in *genetic* information. A *gene* can be affected by a mutation, as can a piece of or a whole *chromosome*. A mutation can occur due to outside influence (such as X-rays, which could modify the genetic material), or spontaneously, without outside influence. A mutation can be passed from parent to child. *Achondroplasia* is an example of a disorder that usually occurs due to a mutation.

Mutism
A condition of being unable to speak due to organic disability (such as *paralysis*), structural disability (such as deafness), or emotional disability (such as certain types of *schizophrenia*).

-myces
A suffix meaning fungus.

myco-
A prefix meaning fungal.

Mycostatin™ (MIE-koe-stat-in)
*Refer to **Nystatin**.*

myelo-
A prefix meaning bone marrow or spinal cord.

Myelocele (MIE-uh-loe-seel)
A birth defect in which the *meninges* (the membranes surrounding the brain and spinal cord) and the spinal cord protrude through an opening in the spinal column, exposing the nerves. With this form of *spina bifida*, the child has some (partial to total) degree of loss of sensation and *paralysis* below the area of the spinal cord protrusion, and often other symptoms/conditions such as *hydrocephalus*, *cerebral palsy*, visual impairment, *mental retardation*, and/or *seizures*.
*Also known as **Meningomyelocele** and **Myelomeningocele**.*
*Compare **Meningocele**.*
*Refer to **Spina Bifida**.*

Myelomeningocele (mie-uh-loe-muh-NING-goe-seel)
*Refer to **Myelocele**.*

myo-
A prefix meaning muscle.

Myocardium (mie-oe-KAR-dee-uhm)
The layer of muscle cells that forms most of the heart wall (heart muscle).

Myoclonic Seizure (mie-oe-KLON-ik)
A form of *generalized seizure* characterized by brief, involuntary jerking of muscles. Myoclonic seizures can affect a limited area, such as an arm or leg, or they can involve jerking of the entire body. Loss of consciousness often, but not always, occurs.
Refer to **Epilepsy**.

Myoclonus (mie-OK-luh-nuhs)
A muscle jerk.

Myofascial Release (mie-oe-FASH-ee-uhl)
Refer to **Soft Tissue Release**.

Myopia (mie-OE-pee-uh)
Blurred vision of distant objects. Myopia occurs when the eyeball is too long (which makes the lens focus distant objects in front of the retina rather than on it), or due to a problem with the lens or cornea. Prescription lenses can improve the vision in a child with myopia.
Also known as **Nearsightedness**.
Compare **Hyperopia**.
Refer to **Refraction**.

Myotomy (mie-OT-oe-mee)
A surgical procedure in which muscle is cut to release muscle *contractures*.

Myotonia (mie-oe-TOE-nee-uh)
A condition in which muscles do not relax promptly after contracting.

Myotonic Dystrophy (mie-oe-TON-ik DIS-troe-fee)
An *autosomal dominant* form of *muscular dystrophy* characterized by strong muscle contraction with poor muscle relaxation, and *floppy muscle tone*. Myotonic dystrophy begins in infancy and affects the muscles of the hands, feet, neck, and face. The affected person has a great deal of difficulty using the facial muscles for speech and for expressing emotion. Associated features that develop over the years include *mental retardation*, *cataracts*, and *endocrine* problems.
Refer to **Muscular Dystrophy**.

Myringotomy (mir-in-GOT-oe-mee)
A surgically created opening in the eardrum to allow drainage from the middle ear and to relieve pressure. Sometimes a tube (an *ear tube*) will be placed in the opening to keep fluid draining. The tube usually falls out on

its own when the hole closes up. Myringotomy can prevent hearing loss that can occur due to persistent fluid accumulation in the middle ear.

Mysoline™ (MIE-soe-leen)
Refer to **Primidone**.

myx-
A prefix meaning mucus.

N
The abbreviation for normal.

Na
The chemical symbol for sodium.

NA
The abbreviation for not applicable.

NaHCO$_3$
The chemical symbol for sodium bicarbonate.

Narcotic Drug
A very potent type of prescribed controlled drug that relieves pain. Morphine and Demerol™ are examples of prescribed narcotic drugs.

Nasal Bones
The bones of the nose.

Nasal Consonants
The /m/, /n/, and /ing/ speech sounds.

Nasal CPAP
The delivery of oxygen and air pressure via Continuous Positive Airway Pressure through a small tube inserted in the nose to help keep the patient's airways and alveoli (the tiny air sacs in the lungs) from collapsing. CPAP oxygen delivery can also be administered through a tube inserted in the mouth.
Refer to Continuous Positive Airway Pressure.

Nasal Regurgitation
The passing of swallowed food back out through the nose.
Refer to Gastroesophageal Reflux.

naso-
A prefix meaning nose.

Nasogastric Tube (NG Tube) (nay-zoe-GAS-trik)
A small, flexible tube inserted through the nose and esophagus, and into the stomach. It is used to remove digestive juices and gas and to *gavage* feed (feed liquids through a tube). Feeding through an NG tube can be done by allowing formula to flow down the tube over a period of approximately fifteen to twenty minutes or it can be administered with a syringe. For infants who cannot tolerate a large volume of food all at once, a continuous drip

method is used to deliver formula over a few hours (or continuously), with the use of a machine called an *infusion pump*.

Nasojejunal Tube (NJ Tube) (nay-zoe-juh-JOO-nuhl)
A small, flexible feeding tube inserted through the nose, esophagus, and stomach, and into the jejunum (the middle section of the small intestine). Placing the tube in the intestine allows for feeding that bypasses the stomach.

Nasopharynx (nay-zoe-FER-ingks)
The part of the throat behind the nose. It lies above the *soft palate* and extends to the oropharynx (the central portion of the pharynx, or throat) below.
   Refer to **Pharynx**.

Natal (NAY-tuhl)
Pertaining to birth.

Navel
   Refer to **Umbilicus**.

Navicular Bone (nuh-VIK-yuh-luhr)
A small bone of the wrists and ankles.

NBIC
The abbreviation for Newborn Intensive Care.

NBICU
The abbreviation for Newborn Intensive Care Unit.

NDT
The abbreviation for neurodevelopmental treatment.

Nearsightedness
   Refer to **Myopia**.

Near Vision
The ability to perceive objects distinctly at normal reading distance (usually about 14 inches from the eye).

Neat Pincer Grasp
Grasp of a tiny object using the tip of the thumb and the tip of the index finger. A neat pincer grasp typically develops between 10 and 12 months of age.
   Also known as **Precise Finger Opposition**.
   Compare **Inferior Pincer Grasp**.
   Refer to **Grasp**.

Nebulizer (NEB-yoo-lie-zer)

A device used to administer medications in mist form for inhalation. A nebulizer may use humidified oxygen and/or air, creating a mist that is delivered through a mask over the nose and mouth or in a *mist tent* (a tent erected over the patient's bed).

NEC

The abbreviation for necrotizing enterocolitis.

Neck Righting Reflex

A normal response in infants between two and ten months of age. When the infant is supine (on her back) and her head is turned to one side, this reflex causes her shoulders and trunk to turn to the same side as the head.
   *Refer to **Primitive Reflex**.*

necro-

A prefix meaning dead.

Necrosis (ne-KROE-sis)

The death of tissue cells in a small, localized area. Causes may include an inadequate blood supply to the tissue (which can result in gangrene, or tissue death that may spread), infection, or damage to tissue cells caused by exposure to certain harmful chemicals, excessive X-rays, or extreme heat or cold.

Necrotizing Enterocolitis (NEC) (NEK-roe-tie-zing en-tuh-roe-koe-LIE-tis)

An inflammation of the bowels of premature or *low birth weight* infants that can result in a gangrene-like condition (*necrosis*) in the walls of the intestinal tract. The inflammatory disease causes decreased blood flow to the intestines, which results in tissue death. The exact cause is not known, but is probably related to other medical problems of the premature or low birth weight infant. Treatment may include cessation of feedings, antibiotics, and, if the condition is advanced, surgical removal of the segment of dead bowel tissue.

Negative Reinforcement

   *Refer to **Reinforcement**.*

Neglect

As defined by the Child Abuse Prevention and Treatment Act, Public Law 93–247: "The physical or mental injury, sexual abuse or exploitation, negligent treatment or maltreatment of a child under the age of 18 . . . by a person who is responsible for the child's welfare. . . ."

Neonatal (nee-oe-NAY-tuhl)

   *Refer to **Neonatal Period**.*

Neonatal Abstinence Syndrome
A constellation of symptoms seen in an infant during the first six weeks of life caused by a sudden withdrawal of drugs she experienced as a fetus. Symptoms may include irritability, tremors or *seizures*, tonal problems (muscle stiffness and jerkiness), difficulty with eating and sleeping, and incessant crying/inconsolability. Drug withdrawal can be fatal to newborns. (Some of the symptoms of drug withdrawal, such as seizure disorders and muscle tone abnormalities, may remain after infancy.)
Refer to **Prenatally Exposed to Drugs**.

Neonatal Intensive Care Unit (NICU)
The hospital unit staffed with specially trained medical practitioners who care for critically ill newborns, both premature babies and sick full-term babies. The NICU is supplied with special equipment, including *isolettes* that help the baby regulate her temperature; monitors to track and record the baby's vital signs; respiration aids such as an *oxygen hood* and *ventilator*; *bililights* to treat *jaundice*; and *catheters* (tubes) to provide food and medication, and to withdraw blood.
Also known as **Newborn Intensive Care Unit**, **Intensive Special Care Nursery**, *and* **Intensive Care Nursery**.

Neonatal Period
The first four weeks of life.

Neonate
A baby during the first four weeks of life.
Also known as a **Newborn**.

Neonatologist (nee-oe-nay-TOL-uh-jist)
A pediatrician who has received extra training in the care of premature and/or sick *neonates*.

nephr-, nephro-
Prefixes meaning kidney.

Nephrectomy (nuh-FREK-toe-mee)
Surgical removal of a kidney.

Nephrologist (nef-ROL-uh-jist)
A physician who specializes in treating diseases of the kidney.

Nerve
A bundle of fibers consisting of many neurons (nerve cells) that carry signals between the brain and the spinal cord (the *central nervous system*) and other parts of the body (by way of the *peripheral nervous system*).
Compare **Nerve Tract**.
Refer to **Central Nervous System** *and* **Peripheral Nervous System**.

Nerve Block
An injection of a local *anesthetic* into a specific nerve to inhibit pain in the areas supplied by the nerve. Nerve blocks are also done on some children who have *cerebral palsy* to reduce *spasticity*.

Nerve Conduction Study
A procedure that records the speed and patterns of electrical conductivity of a nerve. It is used as a diagnostic measure to determine whether a child's condition is caused by muscle disease or nerve damage, and if nerve damage, the type.

Nerve Tract
A collection of nerve fibers within the central nervous system (the brain and the spinal cord).
Compare **Nerve**.
Refer to **Central Nervous System** *and* **Peripheral Nervous System**.

Neural Tube (NOOR-uhl)
A tube of nerve-like tissue that develops along the back of the embryo. As the fetus develops, the neural tube differentiates into the brain, spinal cord, and other parts of the nervous system.

Neural Tube Defect
Any *congenital* defect of the brain and spinal cord caused by failure of the neural tube to close during embryonic growth. Examples of neural tube defects include *spina bifida* and *anencephaly*.

Neurectomy (noo-REK-toe-mee)
A surgical procedure involving cutting out a part of a nerve, usually done to reduce *spasticity* of the muscle group that the nerve is supplying.

neuro-
A prefix meaning nerve.

Neurocutaneous Disorder (noo-roe-kyoo-TAY-nee-uhs)
One of several *inherited* disorders of the central nervous system that is also characterized by skin abnormalities. Examples of neurocutaneous disorders include *neurofibromatosis* and *tuberous sclerosis*.
Also known as **Phakomatosis**.

Neurodevelopmental Treatment (NDT)
An approach to therapy, used by some physical, occupational, and speech therapists, that focuses on the development of normal movement patterns and function while inhibiting abnormal reflexes, postures, and movements.
Also known as **Bobath Therapy**.

Neurofibromatosis (noo-roe-fie-broe-muh-TOE-sis)

An *autosomal dominant disorder* characterized by many fibrous growths (neurofibromas, or tumors) of the central nervous system, nerves, and skin; *cafe au lait spots* on the skin; curvature of the spine; drooping of the eyelids; occasional *seizures*; and varying degrees of *mental retardation* and growth abnormality. When a neurofibroma grows along the optic nerve or auditory nerve, visual or hearing impairment may result. Neurofibromas are usually benign but may need to be removed if they press on adjacent body structures and cause pain.

*Also known as **von Recklinghausen Disease**.*

Neurogenic Bladder (noo-roe-JEN-ik)

A disorder characterized by loss of voluntary control of the urinary bladder. This can result in either incontinence or retention. It is caused by nerve damage or a nervous system tumor.

Neurogenic Bowels

A disorder characterized by loss of voluntary control of the bowel. This can result in either incontinence or retention. It is caused by nerve damage or a nervous system tumor.

Neurological Disorder (noo-roe-LOJ-i-kuhl)

A disorder of the nervous system. Examples include *epilepsy, spina bifida,* and *neurofibromatosis.*

Neurologist

A physician who specializes in diagnosing and treating disorders of the brain and nervous system.

Neuromotor

*Refer to **Neuromuscular**.*

Neuromuscular (noo-roe-MUS-kyoo-luhr)

Referring to the nerves and the muscles and their relationship.

Neuromuscular Disorder

Disease that affects the nerves and/or muscles. Examples of neuromuscular disorders include *Werdnig-Hoffmann disease* and *muscular dystrophy.*

Neuron (NOOR-on)

A nerve cell. Neurons transmit electrical impulses which signal other neurons and organs of the body to function. Neurons that receive stimuli and transmit them to the brain are called *afferent*, or sensory, neurons. Neurons that carry impulses away from the brain and other nerve centers to muscles are called *efferent*, or motor, neurons.

Neurosurgeon
A medical doctor who specializes in performing surgery on the brain, spinal cord, or nerves.

Neurotransmitter
A chemical substance that is released from one nerve cell and either stimulates or inhibits a response from the next nerve cell. Examples of neurotransmitters include *norepinephrine* and *acetylcholine*.

Neutral Position
1. Referring to the normal arm position when the child is standing (arms down, relaxed at the sides of the body with the palms facing the body).
2. Referring to the normal position of the legs when the child is standing (knees and toes are pointing forward and the feet are flat).

Neutral Rotation
Moving a leg or arm to the *neutral position* (so that it is turned neither toward or away from the midline of the body).

Nevus Flammeus (NEE-vuhs FLAM-ee-uhs)
Refer to **Port Wine Stain**.

Newborn
Refer to **Neonate**.

Newborn Intensive Care Unit (NBICU)
Refer to **Neonatal Intensive Care Unit**.

NG Tube
Refer to **Nasogastric Tube**.

NICU
The abbreviation for Neonatal Intensive Care Unit.

Niemann-Pick Disease (NEE-muhn pik)
An *inherited* disorder of *lipid* metabolism (a *sphingolipidosis*) in which "Niemann-Pick" cells, or cells filled with *sphingomyelin* (a substance found in nervous system tissue and in the lipids, or fatty substances, in the blood), collect in the bone marrow, spleen, liver, lungs, and lymph nodes. It is characterized by failure to thrive, *mental retardation*, and an enlarged liver and spleen. The disease is usually fatal before the third year.

Night Splint
A *splint* worn while sleeping. Night splints are most commonly used to prevent *contractures* and to stretch tight muscles.

Nipple Flow Rate
The rate liquid flows or drips out of a baby bottle nipple. Nipples that allow fluids to flow out quickly do not require the infant to suck to obtain the food.

Nippling
Sucking on a baby bottle.

Nissen Fundoplication
Refer to **Fundoplication**.

Nits
The eggs of *lice*.

NJ Tube
Refer to **Nasojejunal Tube**.

NL
The abbreviation for normal.

NLP
The abbreviation for no light perception.

Node
A small rounded tissue mass.
Refer to **Lymph Node**.

Nonambulatory
Referring to the child who has not yet learned to walk or is unable to walk.

Noncategorical Placement
Placement of a child who is at-risk or has developmental delays in a class setting of children with a variety of special needs. This type of environment is useful for observing and testing the individual child until a determination can be made regarding the type of program that would best meet the child's needs, such as a class for children who are primarily delayed in the language and cognitive areas versus a class for children who have visual impairments. A noncategorical class setting may provide an opportunity for the child with disabilities to be placed with nondisabled children.
Compare **Categorical Placement**.

Nonconvulsive Seizure
A *seizure* without *convulsions*. An *absence seizure* is an example of a nonconvulsive seizure.

Nondisjunction
Refer to **Chromosomal Nondisjunction**.

Nondisjunction Trisomy 21
*Refer to **Down Syndrome**.*

Non-immune
Not protected from a particular disease.

Non-Reciprocal Gait
A marking time pattern of walking. This is accomplished by stepping forward on one foot, then placing the second foot next to it, followed by moving the second foot forward, then placing the other foot next to it. (Typically, walking is accomplished in a reciprocal manner: stepping forward on one foot, then stepping forward on the second foot, placing it ahead of the first foot.) A non-reciprocal gait is most commonly seen on ascending and descending stairs and is usually used until two and one-half to three years of age (or later) when the ability to alternate feet while climbing up and down stairs develops.
*Refer to **Gait**.*

Nonsteroidal Anti-inflammatory Drug (NSAID)
A drug that is used to alleviate pain and reduce inflammation in joints and soft tissues. Indomethacin is an example of a NSAID.

Nonverbal Communication
Information expressed without the use of words. Gestures, facial expressions, and *sign language* are examples of nonverbal communication.

Noonan Syndrome
A *congenital* disorder with a *multifactorial* pattern of inheritance characterized by congenital heart disease, *mental retardation* or *learning disabilities, short stature, epicanthal folds* (a vertical skin fold at the inner corner of the eyes), *ptosis* (drooping down) of the eyelids, *myopia*, low-set ears, small lower jaw, *webbing* of the neck, *cryptorchidism* (undescended testes), *anomalies* of the fingers and vertebrae, *hirsutism* (excessive body hair), and skeletal problems.

Norepinephrine (nor-ep-i-NEF-rin)
A hormone released by the adrenal glands, along with *epinephrine*, to help the heart maintain a constant blood pressure.

Normocephalic (nor-moe-se-FAL-ik)
Referring to normalcy of the head.

Norm-Referenced Test
A standardized test that compares a child's test score (performance) to the average score of a group of children who are representative of that child. The Bayley Scales of Infant Development-II is an example of a norm-referenced test.
*Compare **Criterion-Referenced Test** and **Screening Test**.*

nos-, noso-
Prefixes meaning disease.

NPO/npo
The abbreviation for the Latin words meaning nothing by mouth. This means the child will be fed intravenously.

NSA
The abbreviation for no significant abnormality.

NSAID
The abbreviation for nonsteroidal anti-inflammatory drug.

Nurse
A health care professional whose duties may vary from simple patient-care tasks (such as administering medications) to expert techniques (such as assisting with surgical procedures, responding to acute life-threatening situations, or managing a nursing staff and overseeing the care provided to the patients of a particular hospital unit), depending on the type of health care setting and the particular staff position.

Nutramigen™
A hypoallergenic formula for infants sensitive to milk and lactose (milk sugar). It contains hydrolyzed protein and is used for easy digestibility.

Nutrition
The sum of the processes involved in taking in nutrients and assimilating and utilizing them. The body requires nutrients for maintenance, growth, and energy. Nutrition involves ingestion, digestion, absorption, assimilation, and excretion.

Nutritionist
A specialist who studies nutrition and assists patients with issues regarding food intake.

Nystagmus (nis-TAG-muhs)
A disorder involving involuntary, rapid, rhythmic movement of the eyes. The eye movement is usually horizontal, but can be vertical or rotary. The cause of nystagmus is variable but, when *congenital*, the cause is usually unknown.

Nystatin (NIS-tuh-tin)
An *antifungal drug* for treatment of skin, intestinal, and mucous membrane fungal infections.

o̅

The abbreviation for no.

O₂

The chemical symbol for oxygen.

OB

The abbreviation for obstetrician.

Objective

*Refer to **Annual Goal**.*

Object Permanence (Constancy)

The understanding that an object still exists even when it is not in sight. Children typically grasp this concept between eight and twelve months of age.

Obstetrician (OB) (ob-stuh-TRISH-uhn)

A medical doctor who specializes in obstetrics.

Obstetrics (ob-STET-riks)

The branch of medicine dealing with pregnancy and childbirth.

Obstructive Malformation

Any defect characterized by blockage. *Imperforate anus* is an example of an obstructive malformation.

Occipital (ok-SIP-i-tuhl)

Referring to the back part of the base of the head.

Occiput (OK-si-puht)

The back part of the base of the head.

Occupational Therapy (OT)

Therapeutic treatment aimed at helping the injured, ill, or disabled child develop and improve self-help skills and adaptive behavior and play. The occupational therapist also addresses the young child's motor, sensory, and postural development with the overall goals of preventing or minimizing the impact of impairment and developmental delay, and promoting the acquisition of new skills to increase the child's ability to function independently.

ocul-, oculo-

Prefixes meaning eye.

Ocular (OK-yoo-luhr)
Referring to the eyes or vision.

Oculoauriculovertebral Dysplasia (ok-yoo-loe-or-ik-yoo-loe-VER-tuh-bruhl dis-PLAY-zee-uh)
Refer to Goldenhar's Syndrome.

Oculocerebrorenal Syndrome (ok-yoo-loe-ser-uh-broe-REE-nuhl)
Refer to Lowe Syndrome.

Oculomotor (ok-yoo-loe-MOE-tuhr)
Related to eye movements.

Oculus Dexter (OD)
The Latin words meaning right eye.

Oculus Sinister (OS)
The Latin words meaning left eye.

Oculus Unitas (OU)
The Latin words meaning both eyes together.

Oculus Uterque (OU) (yoo-TUR-kwee)
The Latin words meaning each eye.

OD
The abbreviation for oculus dexter.

odyn-, odyno-
Prefixes meaning pain.

-odynia
A suffix meaning pain.

OG Tube
Refer to Oral Gastric Tube.

-oid
A suffix meaning resembling.

-ole
A suffix meaning small.

Olfactory
Referring to the sense of smell.

oligo-
A prefix meaning few or little.

Oligohydramnios (ol-ig-oe-hie-DRAM-nee-oes)
Too little amniotic fluid.
  Compare **Hydramnios**.

Oligophrenia
A clinical term for *mental retardation*.

-ology
A suffix meaning study of.

-oma
A suffix meaning tumor or swelling.

omphal-, omphalo-
Prefixes meaning navel.

Omphalocele (om-FAL-oe-seel)
A *congenital* defect in which a segment of the intestines protrudes through an opening in the abdominal wall into the base of the umbilical cord.
  Also known as **Exomphalos**. *(This is a lesser-used term.)*

onych-, onycho-
Prefixes meaning nail.

oophor-, oophoro-
Prefixes meaning ovary.

-opathy
A suffix meaning disease or disorder.

Operant Level
  Refer to **Baseline**.

ophth-, ophthal-, ophthalmo-
Prefixes meaning eye.

Ophthalmologist (of-thuhl-MOL-oe-jist)
A medical doctor who specializes in diagnosing and treating disorders of the eye. The ophthalmologist also prescribes corrective lenses and medications and performs surgery.
  Compare **Optometrist** *and* **Optician**.

-opia
A suffix meaning vision.

Opponens Splint (oe-POE-nens or o-POE-nens)
A *splint* that holds the thumb in correct alignment.

Opposition Movement
The ability to touch the tip of the thumb to the tip of any finger on the same hand.
Also known as **Finger Opposition**.

optic-
A prefix meaning eye or vision.

Optic (OP-tik)
Pertaining to the eye or to vision.

Optic Atrophy (OP-tik AT-roe-fee)
A condition characterized by wasting away of the optic nerve fibers due to heredity, disease, or injury of the optic nerve. Visual impairment results.

Optic Glioma (OP-tik glie-OE-muh)
A malignant tumor of the optic nerve.

Optic Hypoplasia (OP-tik hie-poe-PLAY-zee-uh)
A *congenital* defect in which the optic nerve fibers are underdeveloped, causing visual impairment ranging from very slight to severe.

Optician
A technician who fits and makes corrective lenses.
Compare **Ophthalmologist** *and* **Optometrist**.

Optic Nerve
The bundle of nerve fibers leading from the retina at the back of each eye to the brain. Visual impulses are transmitted along the two optic nerves for *binocular vision*.
Refer to **Eye**.

Optometrist
A nonmedical specialist who tests vision and prescribes corrective lenses. Optometrists are not physicians and thus do not treat eye disease or prescribe medication, although they may diagnose eye disease and then refer patients to an ophthalmologist for further care.
Compare **Ophthalmologist** *and* **Optician**.

OPV
The abbreviation for oral polio vaccine.

OR
The abbreviation for operating room.

Oral Defensiveness
Refer to **Oral Tactile Defensiveness**.

Oral Exploration
Refer to **Mouthing***.*

Oral Gastric Tube (OG Tube)
A small flexible feeding tube inserted through the mouth and esophagus, and into the stomach.
Refer to **Nasogastric Tube***.*

Oral Motor
Referring to the movements of the mouth.

Oral Play
Refer to **Mouthing***.*

Oral Polio Vaccine (OPV)
An *immunization* against *poliomyelitis* made from a live, weakened polio virus. The child receives two doses during infancy (at two and four months of age) and boosters at 18 months and at four and one-half to five years of age (before beginning school). It is administered orally.
Also known as the **Sabin Vaccine***.*
Refer to **Poliomyelitis***.*

Oral Reflex
Refer to **Rooting Reflex***,* **Suck Reflex***,* **Bite Reflex***, and* **Gag Reflex***.*

Oral Stimulation
Referring to the natural *mouthing* of toys that emerges in the infant between three and six months of age, or to the specific activities (such as massaging the gums or lips) designed to help the child with *oral tactile defensiveness* tolerate having things placed in his mouth. The child fed through a tube often needs oral stimulation so he does not develop an aversion to food taken orally.
Refer to **Oral Tactile Defensiveness***.*

Oral Tactile Defensiveness
An increased sensitivity, and often intolerance, to touch around the mouth. The child may also have intolerance for having things placed in the mouth.
Refer to **Oral Stimulation***.*

Orbit (OR-bit)
One of a pair of bony sockets in the skull that contains the eye and related structures.

orchi-
A prefix meaning testicle.

Ordinal Scales of Intellectual Development
Refer to **Assessment in Infancy Ordinal Scales of Psychological Development.**

Organ
A somewhat independent part of an organism (such as the human body) that performs one or more special functions. For example, the heart and lungs are organs.

Organic
Relating to an organ or body structure.
Denoting any impairment, such as an illness or *genetic* disorder, that results from a structural alteration or weakness of the organism.

Organomegaly (or-ga-noe-MEG-uh-lee)
Enlargement of an internal organ, usually one of the abdominal organs.

Orientation
The process by which a child with visual impairments develops awareness and knowledge about his environment (i.e., a "mental map"), in order to relate effectively to the environment. For example, the child can orient himself to the playground by using all of his senses (especially his auditory and tactile sensations) to help him move from place to place. Specifically, he may learn that the path to the sand box is a gradually-sloping grassy area, and that when he hears the leaves on the tree above him rustle and feels the cool shade of the tree, he is almost to the sandbox.

Oropharynx (or-oe-FER-ingks)
The central portion of the pharynx, or throat (the part behind the mouth). It lies between the soft palate and the hyoid bone (the bone lying at the base of the tongue).
Refer to **Pharynx.**

Orphan Drug
A drug that is effective for treating certain (usually rare) diseases, but has little commercial value for pharmaceutical companies. For example, the drug Pimozide, which is used to treat Tourette syndrome, was considered an orphan drug until it had a commercial sponsor to help cover the costs of needed research and development.

orth-, ortho-
Prefixes meaning straight, normal, or correct.

Orthodontist
A dentist who specializes in correcting irregular tooth placement (such as teeth that are crooked, crowded, or unevenly spaced), through the use of braces or other appliances.

Orthopedic
Concerning the prevention or correction of disorders involving the skeleton, joints, muscles, ligaments, tendons, and fascia.

Orthopedically Handicapped (or-thoe-PEE-dik-lee)
Referring to a child who has an impairment involving *locomotor* structures of his body (such as the bones, joints, muscles, and fascia, or fibrous membrane), which affects his ability to perform in other developmental areas. *Cerebral palsy* and *clubfoot* are examples of conditions that may be classified as orthopedic handicaps.

Orthopedic Appliance
Adaptive equipment used to correct abnormal or maintain normal body positioning, to inhibit unwanted postures or reflexes, and to maintain *range of motion*. Examples of orthopedic appliances include *braces, splints,* casts, traction, shoe inserts, and custom seating and standing devices.

Orthopedics
The branch of medicine concerned with the form and function of the bones, joints, muscles, tendons, ligaments, and cartilage.

Orthopedist
A medical doctor who specializes in *orthopedics*.

Orthoptic (or-THOP-tik)
Referring to normal *binocular vision*.

Orthosis (or-THOE-sis)
Refer to **Orthotic**.

Orthotic (or-THOT-ik)
A custom-made orthopedic appliance (such as a *brace, splint,* or cast) used to promote proper body alignment, to stabilize joints, or to passively stretch muscle or other soft tissue.
Also known as an **Orthosis**.

OS
The abbreviation for oculus sinister.

-osis
A suffix meaning condition or process (usually abnormal).

oss-, osseo-, ossi-
Prefixes meaning bone or bony.

Ossicles (OS-i-kuhlz)
The tiny bones of the ear (the malleus, incus, and stapes).
Refer to **Ear**.

ost-, oste-, osteo-
Prefixes meaning bone or bony.

Osteogenesis Imperfecta (os-tee-oe-JEN-uh-sis im-pur-FEK-tuh)
A (usually) *autosomal dominant disorder* characterized by fragile bones that break easily, bluish sclerae (the white membrane covering most of the back of the eyeball), and possible hearing loss. With one *congenital* form of the disease, the newborn has many bone defects and, if not stillborn, dies in early infancy. If the first fractures occur later in infancy, the disease is usually not as severe. With all types of osteogenesis imperfecta, the risk of broken bones decreases as the child gets older.

Osteopathic Medicine (os-tee-oe-PATH-ik)
A form of medical practice that focuses on the importance of treating the body as an integrated whole, the effects of the body systems on each other, and the role of the musculoskeletal system in revealing and influencing health and disease. Osteopathy utilizes physical, medicinal, and surgical techniques as well as manipulative therapy for diagnosing and treating medical disorders and for maintenance of good health. The physician practicing osteopathic medicine is called a Doctor of Osteopathy, or D.O.

Osteotomy (os-tee-OT-uh-mee)
A surgical procedure in which a bone is cut for any purpose, including realigning, shortening, or lengthening it.

Ostium Primum Defect (OS-tee-uhm PRIE-muhm)
An *atrial septal defect* (a type of heart defect) in which there is a hole low in the septum (the wall separating the right and left atria of the heart).
   Compare **Ostium Secundum Defect**.
   Refer to **Atrial Septal Defect**.

Ostium Secundum Defect (OS-tee-uhm se-KUN-duhm)
An *atrial septal defect* (a type of heart defect) in which there is a hole in the central portion of the septum (the wall separating the right and left atria of the heart).
   Compare **Ostium Primum Defect**.
   Refer to **Atrial Septal Defect**.

-ostomy
A suffix meaning new opening.

Ostomy (OS-tuh-mee)
A surgically created opening in an organ. *Colostomy* is an example of an ostomy.

ot-, oto-
Prefixes meaning ear.

OT
The abbreviation for occupational therapy or occupational therapist.

Otitis Media (oe-TIE-tis MEE-dee-uh)
An inflammation of the middle ear usually caused by an upper respiratory tract infection that affects the eustachian tube. Chronic inflammation results in a collection of fluid that does not drain and becomes infected. Chronic otitis media can cause hearing loss.

Otolaryngologist (oe-toe-ler-in-GOL-uh-jist)
A medical doctor who specializes in the diagnosis and treatment of disorders of the ears, nose, and throat.
   *Also known as an **Ear, Nose, and Throat (ENT) Specialist**.*

Otologist (oe-TOL-uh-jist)
A medical doctor who specializes in diagnosing and treating disorders of the ear and related structures.

-otomy
A suffix meaning incision.

Otoscope (OE-toe-skope)
An instrument used to examine the ear canal and eardrum.

Ototoxicity (oe-toe-toks-IS-i-tee)
Having the property of causing damage to the ear. For example, certain drugs, such as the antibiotics gentamicin and streptomycin, can have a toxic effect on the ear when taken in high doses.

OU
The abbreviation for oculus unitas or oculus uterque.

Outer Ear
   *Refer to **Ear**.*

ov-
A prefix meaning egg.

Ova
Plural of ovum.

ovari-, ovario-
Prefixes meaning ovary.

Ovary
One of a pair of the female gonads, or sex glands, which forms ova (egg) cells, necessary for reproduction. The ovaries are attached to the uterus on either side of the pelvic cavity.
   *Compare **Testis**.*

Overstimulated
*Refer to **Sensory Overload**.*

Ovum
The egg cell (female cell) of reproduction. If the ovum is fertilized by a sperm and implants in the uterus, the ovum develops into an embryo.

Oxygen (O_2)
A gas that is essential for life. Oxygen makes up 21 percent of the earth's atmosphere.

Oxygen Hood
A plastic dome that is placed over the infant's head to provide him with a constant flow of warm, moist, oxygenated air as he lies in his incubator.

Oxygen Tent
*Refer to **Tent**.*

Oxygen Therapy
Treatment in which oxygen-enriched air is supplied to the child who has *hypoxia* (a lack of sufficient oxygen in the body cells or blood) or breathing difficulties. Oxygen can be given through a mask worn over the nose and mouth, through a small tube inserted in the nose, through an *oxygen hood* or tent, through an *endotracheal tube*, or through a *tracheostomy* tube.

Oxytocin (ok-see-TOE-sin)
A hormone produced by the pituitary gland that causes uterine contractions and stimulates the flow of milk (the "let down" response) in nursing mothers. Oxytocin is also made synthetically and is given to induce uterine contractions.

P

P̄
The abbreviation for after.

P
1. The abbreviation for pulse.
2. Referring to the short arm of a *chromosome*.

P
The abbreviation for probability.

p-
Referring to the partial deletion of the short arm of a *chromosome*. For example, 5p- syndrome (*cri du chat syndrome*) is a chromosomal disorder that occurs when part of the short arm of chromosome number 5 is deleted.

Palate (PAL-it)
The roof of the mouth. It separates the mouth from the nasal passages.
  Refer to **Hard Palate** *and* **Soft Palate**.

Palatine (PAL-uh-tine)
Relating to the palate or the palate bone.

Palliative (PAL-ee-uh-tiv)
Descriptive of treatment that provides relief from some of the symptoms of an illness or condition, but not a cure.

Palmar Grasp (PAHL-mer)
Grasp of an object with all four fingers pressing against the palm of the hand (the thumb is not involved). The palmar grasp usually develops around four to five months of age.
  Refer to **Grasp**.

Palmar Reflex
  Refer to **Grasp Reflex**.

Palpebral Fissure (PAL-puh-bruhl)
The opening between the upper and lower eyelids.

Palsy (POL-zee)
A temporary or permanent condition characterized by partial *paralysis*. *Cerebral palsy* is an example.

Pancreas (PAN-kree-uhs)
A gland located behind the stomach in the abdomen. The pancreas secretes digestive *enzymes* and the hormones insulin and glucagon.

Pancreatic (pan-kree-AT-ik)
Referring to the pancreas.

pancreato-
A prefix meaning pancreas.

Pancuronium (pan-kyoo-ROE-nee-uhm)
A neuromuscular blocking agent that works as a skeletal muscle relaxant and causes temporary *paralysis*.

P and PD
The abbreviation for percussion and postural drainage.

Panhypopituitarism (pan-hie-poe-pi-TOO-i-ter-izm)
Poor or absent functioning of the anterior pituitary gland, which, when it occurs in young children, can result in *short stature* and low levels of hormone functions. In the young child, this condition may be caused by a brain tumor or the cause may be unknown.

par, para-
Prefixes meaning beside, closely related to, or abnormal.

Para (PAR-uh)
A Latin word meaning a woman who has given birth. It applies to a delivery after the stage of viability has been reached whether or not the infant is born alive or dead. A numeral is placed after para to indicate the number of times she has given birth to an infant. For example, gravida 2, para 1 describes a woman in her second pregnancy who previously gave birth. (Note: a multiple delivery is considered to be a single parous event.)
Compare **Gravida**.

Parachute Reflex/Reaction
A protective reaction to a sudden movement of the body. The arms and legs extend in response to the movement to protect the body from falling.
Also known as **Protective Extension**.
Refer to **Automatic Reflex**.

Parallel Bars
An ambulation aid that supports the child so she can practice walking. The child uses the bars to support her weight on her arms, allowing her legs to move forward.

Parallel Play
The typical play of the 18– to 24–month-old in which the child plays beside other children, rather than actually interacting with them.

Parallel Speech
Describing the child's experiences for her as they occur. For example, "I am changing your diaper now. A dry diaper sure feels nice!" or "You are bouncing the ball. Oh-oh—it got away! Now you are getting it out of the sand box. No, the ball won't bounce in the sand."

Paralysis (puh-RAL-uh-sis)
Complete or partial loss of muscle movement caused by brain injury, disease, or injury to the nerves that stimulate the muscles. Paralysis can be a temporary or a permanent condition. Paralysis can make the affected body parts floppy or stiff (and may cause loss of feeling in those body parts) and can result from many conditions, including a *stroke*, *cerebral palsy*, and *meningitis*. Paralysis is often described by the areas of the body that are affected, such as *diplegia*, *hemiplegia*, *paraplegia*, and *quadriplegia*.
   *Compare **Paresis**.*

Paraplegia (per-uh-PLEE-jee-uh)
Weakness or *paralysis* of the legs and generally the lower trunk as the result of disease or injury to the nerves of the brain or spinal cord that stimulate the muscles or by disease of the muscles themselves. Sometimes the word paraplegia is used to describe *cerebral palsy* in which only the legs are affected.
   *Refer to **Paralysis** and **Pyramidal Cerebral Palsy**.*

Parapodium (per-uh-POE-dee-uhm)
A body brace that supports the child's trunk and legs in a standing position. Crutches or a walker can be used with a parapodium to help the child walk.

Paraprofessional
An individual who is trained to assist a professional.

Parasite
An organism living in or on another organism. The parasite obtains nourishment from the host organism (the organism in which it is living), which is either detrimental to the host or does not contribute to the survival of the host.

Parathyroid Glands
Two pairs of glands in the region of the thyroid gland that secrete parathyroid hormone and are involved with the metabolism of calcium and phosphorus.

Parenteral Nutrition (puh-REN-tuhr-uhl)
   *Refer to **Total Parenteral Nutrition**.*

Parent-Professional Partnership
The teaming of parents and teachers (or doctors, nurses, therapists, or other professionals) to work together to facilitate the development of infants and children with special needs.

Paresis (puh-REE-sis or PER-uh-sis)
Muscle weakness or partial *paralysis* caused by disease or injury to the nerves that stimulate the muscles.
*Refer to **Paralysis**.*

Parietal Bone (puh-RIE-uh-tuhl)
One of two paired bones that make up part of the side and top of the skull.

Partially Sighted
Referring to the child whose *visual acuity* measures better than 20/200 (20/200 is considered legally blind), but not more than 20/70 in the corrected, better eye. (20/70 means that the child can only see at 20 feet what can ordinarily be seen at 70 feet.)
*Compare **Blindness**.*

Partial Seizure
A *seizure* that begins locally or focally, affecting a specific part of the brain. There are three classes of partial seizures: *simple partial, complex partial*, and partial seizures which become secondarily generalized. When the child remains conscious during a partial seizure, this is referred to as a simple partial seizure. When consciousness is impaired, it is referred to as a complex partial seizure. When a partial seizure progresses to a *generalized seizure* (a seizure affecting the brain as a whole), it is referred to as a partial seizure which has become secondarily generalized.
*Also known as **Focal Seizures** and **Local Seizures**.*
*Compare **Generalized Seizure**.*

Parturition
The process of giving birth.

Passive Range of Motion
Guiding the child's movement (such as at an arm or leg joint) through the normal *range of motion* without the child's help or effort.
*Refer to **Range of Motion**.*

Patau Syndrome
*Refer to **Trisomy 13**.*

Patella (pu-TEL-uh)
The kneecap.

Patellar Reflex
*Refer to **Knee Jerk Reflex**.*

Patent (PAT-ent or PAYT-ent)
Open.

Patent Ductus Arteriosus (PDA)
A condition in which the *ductus arteriosus* (the fetal blood vessel connecting the aorta and the pulmonary artery so that blood can bypass the fetal lungs) fails to close at or soon after birth. The patent (open) vessel allows oxygenated blood to backflow to the lungs rather than to circulate to the rest of the body, which makes the heart overwork. This defect is common in *premature infants* and in newborns with heart defects. The ductus often closes on its own, or the drug *indomethacin* may be prescribed. If this treatment is not successful, surgery is done to close the ductus.
   Refer to Ductus Arteriosus.

path-, patho-
Prefixes meaning disease.

Pathological (path-uh-LOJ-i-kuhl)
Involving or caused by disease.

-pathy
A suffix meaning disease.

Patterning
Guiding the child's arm or leg through a series of movements without the child's help or effort. Patterning is done to stimulate normal movement patterns. This form of treatment is considered controversial with regard to its benefits.

Pavlik Harness™
A device used to keep the infant's legs apart and the hips back, to treat *dislocated hips*. It consists of a firm roll positioned between the child's thighs and a cloth harness worn over the chest.

Pavulon™ (PAYV-yoo-lon)
   Refer to Pancuronium.

pc
The abbreviation for the Latin words meaning after a meal.

PD
The abbreviation for postural drainage.

PDA
The abbreviation for patent ductus arteriosus.

PD and P
The abbreviation for postural drainage and percussion.

PDD
Refer to **Pervasive Developmental Disorder.**

PDI
The abbreviation for Psychomotor Development Index (the score given on the Motor Scale section of The Bayley Scales of Infant Development-II).

PE
The abbreviation for physical examination.

Peabody Picture Vocabulary Test-Revised (PPVT-R)
A norm-referenced evaluation tool used to assess the language ability (specifically, the recognition of single words) of people two and one-half years or older. Typically, the PPVT-R is administered by a professional with a minimum of a bachelor's degree.

Pectus Excavatum (PEK-tuhs eks-KAYV-uh-tuhm)
A *congenital* malformation in which the sternum (breast bone) is abnormally depressed (sunken). This condition may decrease the child's ability to engage in sustained active play and delay recovery from upper respiratory infections. It can usually be corrected surgically.

ped-
A prefix meaning foot.

PED
The abbreviation for prenatally exposed to drugs.

Pedaling
A normal movement in the four- to six-month-old infant in which the baby, while lying on her back with both hips flexed, extends one leg and then the other, and then flexes both hips again.

Pediatric
Pertaining to children.

Pediatrician
A medical doctor who specializes in the growth and care of infants, children, and adolescents.

Pediculosis (pee-dik-yoo-LOE-sis)
Infestation with *lice.*

PEEP
The abbreviation for positive end expiratory pressure.

Pellagra
A nutritional disorder caused by a deficiency of niacin (one of the B-complex vitamins). It is characterized by skin, digestive tract, and nervous system dysfunction and can lead to death.

Pelvic Band
A band worn around the waist or pelvis to provide extra control for the child using *bilateral* long-legged *braces*.

Pelvis
The bony structure made up of the hipbones, sacrum (the fused vertebrae that form the back of the pelvis), and the coccyx (tailbone). It rests on the legs and supports the spinal column.

Pemoline (PEM-oe-len)
A drug used to treat children with *attention deficit disorder*.

Pendred Syndrome
A *congenital* disorder characterized by *bilateral sensorineural hearing loss* associated with *goiter* (enlargement of the thyroid gland) in middle childhood. The child usually has normal intelligence and physical development.

Penicillin (pen-i-SIL-in)
Any of a group of *antibiotic drugs* extracted from cultures of the mold penicillium or prepared semi-synthetically.

pep-
A prefix meaning to digest.

-pepsia
A suffix meaning digestion.

Perception
The process of receiving and interpreting sensory information to be aware of or recognize objects.

Perceptual Skill
The ability to interpret information gained through the senses.

Percussion (puhr-KUSH-uhn)
A method for examining the organs of the chest and abdomen by tapping with the fingers to estimate the condition and size of the organs. (The examiner does not actually tap the patient's body, but instead taps her own—the examiner's—finger, which is placed firmly over the area to be percussed.) The sound made when the organ is tapped as well as the size

and borders of the organ that can be felt are all part of the physical examination.

Compare **Chest Percussion**.

Perforated Eardrum
Refer to **Eardrum Perforation**.

Perfusion (puhr-FYOO-zhuhn)
The movement of blood or fluid through an artery to supply an organ or a part of the body with nutrients and oxygen. Perfusion also refers to the process of delivering local medication to an organ or part of the body via the blood.

peri-
A prefix meaning around or surrounding.

Perilymph (PER-uh-limf)
A clear fluid in the inner ear.

Perilymphatic Fistula (per-uh-lim-FAT-ik FIS-chuh-luh)
A defect within the ear resulting in a leak of inner ear fluid that can cause *sensorineural hearing loss*. Hearing may improve if treatment is received before permanent damage occurs.

Perinatal (per-uh-NAY-tuhl)
Describing the period from 28 weeks *gestation* to one week following delivery.

Perinatologist (per-uh-nay-TOL-uh-jist)
A medical doctor who specializes in fetal and *neonatal* care. The doctor has training in obstetrics and neonatology.

Perineal (per-uh-NEE-uhl)
Referring to the area between the thighs from the genital organs to the anus.

Perineum (per-uh-NEE-uhm)
The part of the body between the thighs from the genital organs to the anus.

Periodic Breathing
A pattern of breathing in which the baby stops breathing (has a respiratory pause) for at least three seconds and not more than 20 seconds. This is followed by a breathing period of 20 seconds or less. Periodic breathing is seen in most *premature infants* and many full-term newborns during their first few days of life. No treatment is necessary unless periodic breathing is associated with recurrent periods of *apnea*.

Compare **Apnea**.

Periodontal Disease (per-ee-oe-DON-tuhl)
Disease of the gums and bones that surround the teeth.

Periodontist (per-ee-oe-DON-tist)
A dentist who specializes in treating disease of the tissues surrounding the teeth.

Peripheral
Referring to the parts of an organ distant from the center, such as the peripheral nervous system (the nerves that branch out from the central nervous system).

Peripheral Nervous System (PNS)
The nerves that branch out from the *central nervous system* and connect the brain and the spinal cord to the rest of the body.
Compare **Central Nervous System**.

Peripheral Vision
The ability to see objects which are to the sides of straight-ahead vision.

Peritoneal (per-i-tuh-NEE-uhl)
Referring to the peritoneum, or membrane lining the abdominal cavity and covering the organs in it.

Peritoneum (per-i-tuh-NEE-uhm)
The membrane lining the abdominal cavity and covering the organs in it.

Periventricular Encephalomalacia (PVL) (per-uh-ven-TRIK-yuh-luhr en-sef-uh-loe-muh-LAY-shuh)
A condition in which tissue around the *ventricles* of the brain is damaged due to insufficient blood flow or a lack of oxygen. It can cause neurological damage, such as *cerebral palsy*.

Periventricular Hemorrhage
Bleeding in the areas that surround the fluid-filled chambers (*ventricles*) of the brain.
Refer to **Intracranial Hemorrhage**.
Compare **Intraventricular Hemorrhage** *and* **Subarachnoid Hemorrhage**.

Permanent Teeth
Refer to **Secondary Teeth**.

Peroneal Muscular Atrophy (per-uh-NEE-uhl)
Refer to **Charcot-Marie-Tooth Disease**.

PERRLA
The abbreviation for pupils equal, round, react to light, and accommodate. It describes a normal condition of the eyes.

Perseveration (pur-sev-ur-AY-shun)
Continuing to repeat a behavior or response after it is no longer appropriate. An example of perseveration is noted when a child of preschool

age or older says the same words over and over, even though her words were intelligible the first time uttered and she received acknowledgement that she was understood. (The repetition of sounds, words, or motor actions by infants and toddlers younger than preschool age is not considered perseveration.)

Persistent Fetal Circulation (PFC)
A condition in which the newborn's blood continues to circulate as it did before birth. In the fetus, blood bypasses the lungs through an open *ductus arteriosus*, but at or soon after birth the ductus arteriosus should close, allowing blood to circulate through the infant's lungs to become oxygenated. With persistent fetal circulation, the blood continues to bypass the lungs, sending poorly oxygenated blood to the rest of the body.

*Also known as **Persistent Pulmonary Hypertension**.*
*Compare **Circulation** and **Fetal Circulation**.*

Persistent Pulmonary Hypertension
*Refer to **Persistent Fetal Circulation**.*

Pertussis (per-TUS-is)
An infectious bacterial disease that primarily affects children, causing coughing fits. It is spread by airborne droplets and can result in serious illness and lead to death. A *vaccine* for pertussis is given to immunize against the disease. (This is the "P" part of the DPT vaccine.)

*Also known as **Whooping Cough**.*

Pervasive Developmental Disorder (PDD)
A diagnosis sometimes given to a child who has some, but not all, of the symptoms of *autism*.

pes-
A prefix meaning foot.

Pes (peez or pays or pes)
The foot or a foot-like structure.

Pes Cavus (pes KAY-vuhs)
A foot defect in which the arch is excessively high and the tips of the toes turn downward. Pes cavus can occur as a *congenital* defect or result from nerve or muscle disease.

*Also known as **Clawfoot**.*

Pes Planus (pes PLAY-nuhs)
A condition in which a child has little or no arch in the foot. Babies are typically born with flat feet, but develop arches in the soles of the feet usually by age six. A flatfoot which persists may be flexible (assumes a normal arch when not weight-bearing), for which nothing needs to be done if the child

has no symptoms of disease. When the flatfoot is not flexible, treatment depends on the cause and the symptoms.

Also known as **Flatfoot**.

PET
The abbreviation for Positron Emission Tomography.

Petechiae (pee-TEE-kee-ee)
A pin-point rash caused by tiny areas of bleeding under the skin.

Petit Mal Seizure (pet-EE mahl)
Refer to **Absence Seizure**.

Pezzer Catheter
Refer to **de Pezzer Catheter**.

Pezzer Tube™
A type of *gastrostomy* tube (a feeding tube inserted directly into the stomach through a surgically created opening in the abdominal wall).

PFC
The abbreviation for persistent fetal circulation.

pH
The degree to which a solution is acidic or alkaline. The lower the pH rating, the more acidic the solution. The pH scale expresses values from zero to fourteen, with zero to six describing an acidic solution, seven neutrality, and eight to fourteen an alkaline solution.

phag-, phago-
Prefixes meaning eat.

Phakomatosis (fak-oe-muh-TOE-sis)
Refer to **Neurocutaneous Disorder**.

Phalanges (fay-LAN-jeez)
Plural of phalanx.

Phalanx (FAY-langks)
Any one of the small bones of the fingers or toes. There are three phalanges in each finger and toe, except in the thumb and big toe, which each have two.

pharyngo-
A prefix meaning throat.

Pharynx (FER-ingks)
The throat. The pharynx is made up of the *nasopharynx*, the *oropharynx*, and the *laryngopharynx*.

Phenobarbital (fee-noe-BAR-buh-tol)
An *antiepileptic drug*.

Phenotype (FEE-noe-tipe)
The observable characteristics (the expression of the *genes*) of an individual, determined by the interactions of *heredity* and the environment.
   Compare **Genotype**.

Phenylalanine (fen-uhl-AL-uh-neen)
An *amino acid* (the basic building block of proteins) required by infants and children for normal growth. It is also a dietary requirement for normal protein use.

Phenylketonuria (PKU) (fen-uhl-kee-toe-NOOR-ee-uh)
A *genetic* disorder in which the inability to break down *phenylalanine* (an *amino acid*) causes a build-up of the amino acid in the body. If the condition is not diagnosed soon after birth, the build-up leads to *mental retardation*. With early diagnosis, mental retardation can be prevented by restricting the infant's intake of phenylalanine (which is found in most protein food sources).

Phenytoin (FEN-i-toe-in)
An *antiepileptic drug*.

phil-
A prefix meaning affinity for.

-philia
A suffix meaning affinity for.

Philtrum (FIL-truhm)
The grooved area between the upper lip and the nose.

phlebo-
A prefix meaning vein.

Phonation (foe-NAY-shuhn)
Voice production. Vocalization is possible when a stream of air passes over the vocal cords, causing them to vibrate.

Phoneme (FOE-neem)
The smallest unit of sound found in speech. Vowel and consonant sounds are phonemes.

Phonetics (fuh-NET-iks)
The system of speech sounds of a particular language.

Phonics (FON-iks)
The study of speech sounds.

Phosphorus (FOS-fuhr-uhs)
An essential mineral element in the diet that is involved in most metabolic processes within the body.

Photic Stimulation (FOE-tik)
A technique in which a flashing strobe light is used during an EEG (*electroencephalogram*) to determine if a *seizure* can be induced.

Photophobia (foe-tuh-FOE-bee-uh)
Abnormal sensitivity to and discomfort from light. It is associated with some eye conditions, including inflammation and abrasion to parts of the eye, *congenital glaucoma*, and *albinism*. It may also be one of the symptoms of *meningitis*.

Phototherapy
Treatment for *hyperbilirubinemia* (an excess of *bilirubin*, which is the pigment by product of the breakdown of red blood cells). The infant is placed under *bililights*, which help break down the bilirubin which has accumulated in the skin so it can be excreted from the body.

Physical Therapy (PT)
Therapeutic treatment designed to prevent or alleviate movement dysfunction through a program tailored to the individual child. The goal of the individualized program may be to develop muscle strength, *range of motion*, coordination, or endurance; to alleviate pain (such as with *contractures*); or to attain new motor skills. Physical therapists use a variety of methods of treatment, including therapeutic exercise and the use of physical agents such as heat, cold, and water. Therapeutic exercise for some children may include passive exercise (in which the therapist moves and stretches the child's muscles) or the child may actively participate in learning new ways to acquire and control positions and movement.

Physician
A health care worker who has earned a degree of Doctor of Medicine (M.D.) or of Doctor of Osteopathy (D.O.). Physicians are licensed to examine and care for the sick.

PI
The abbreviation for present illness.

Piaget, Jean (pee-uh-ZHAY)
A Swiss psychologist whose research examined the stages through which infants and children progress as they develop adult patterns of thinking.
  Refer to **Sensory-Motor Stage** *and* **Preoperational Stage**.

Pia Mater (PEE-uh MAY-tuhr or PIE-uh MAY-tuhr)
The innermost layer of the *meninges* (the membranes surrounding the brain and spinal cord). The middle layer is the arachnoid and the outermost layer is the dura mater.
Refer to **Meninges**.

Pica (PIE-kuh)
A craving to eat non-food substances, such as dirt, hair, or chalk.

PIE
The abbreviation for pulmonary interstitial emphysema.

Pierre Robin Sequence (pee-YER roe-BA)
A *congenital* disorder characterized by underdevelopment of the lower jaw, *cleft palate*, downward displacement or retraction of the tongue, and absent gag reflex resulting in difficulty in breathing and feeding. Children with this condition may also have defects of the eyes and skeleton, and usually have normal intelligence.

Pigeon-Toed
Refer to **Toeing In**.

Pincer Grasp (PIN-suhr)
Grasp of a small or tiny object using the thumb and index finger of one hand.
Refer to **Inferior Pincer Grasp** *and* **Neat Pincer Grasp**.

Pineal Body (PIN-ee-uhl)
A tiny endocrine gland within the brain that secretes the hormone melatonin.

Pinna (PIN-uh)
The external ear, consisting of cartilage covered by skin. In humans, the pinna plays a very small role in the process of hearing.
Also known as the **Auricle**.
Refer to **Ear**.

Pinnae
Plural of pinna.

Pinworm
Refer to **Worms**.
Also known as **Enterobius Vermicularis**.

Pitocin™ (pi-TOE-sin)
Refer to **Oxytocin**.

Pituitary Gland (pi-TOO-i-ter-ee)

A tiny endocrine (hormone secreting) gland located at the base of the brain that is attached by a stalk to the hypothalamus. The hypothalamus stimulates the pituitary gland to secrete hormones which regulate other gland activity. The pituitary gland is important to the growth, maturation, and reproduction of the individual.

PKU

The abbreviation for phenylketonuria.

PL 94–142

Refer to **Education for All Handicapped Children Act of 1975.**

PL 99–457

Refer to **Education of the Handicapped Act Amendments of 1986.**

PL 101–336

Refer to **Americans with Disabilities Act.**

PL 101–476

Refer to **Individuals with Disabilities Education Act of 1991.**

Placement

The selection of the educational program for the child who needs special education services.

Placenta (pluh-SEN-tuh)

The organ that supplies the fetus with nourishment while in the uterus. The placenta also functions to provide the fetus with oxygen and to remove the fetus's waste products.

Placenta Abruptio (pluh-SEN-tuh uh-BRUP-shee-oe)

Refer to **Abruptio Placenta.**

Placenta Previa (pluh-SEN-tuh PREE-vee-uh)

A condition in which the placenta is implanted in the uterus near or over the cervix. This can result in bleeding during middle or late pregnancy and premature delivery may be unavoidable.

Plantar (PLAN-tuhr)

Referring to the sole of the foot.

Plantar Flexion

The position of the foot when the front part is pointing down, such as during the pushing-off action of walking.

Compare **Dorsiflexion.**

Plantar Reflex

A normal response in which a stroke or firm touch to the soles of the feet, from the heel to the base of the toes, causes the toes to flex or curl under. The toes respond in this manner during walking when the foot feels pressure against the floor.

Refer to **Primitive Reflex***.*

-plasia

A suffix meaning growth.

Plasma

The clear, fluid portion of blood, excluding the red and white blood cells and the platelets. Plasma differs from *serum* in that plasma still contains clotting factors.

Compare **Serum***.*

Plasticity

Adaptability, flexibility.

plasty-

A suffix meaning shape or repair.

Platelet

One of three types of blood cells. The platelet is the smallest cellular element of the blood and is needed for proper clotting.

Also known as a **Thrombocyte***.*

Play Therapy

A diagnostic and treatment method used in child psychotherapy to help children resolve any emotional or psychological conflicts. The child is encouraged to play freely with a selected group of toys as the therapist observes. (The role of the therapist is usually a passive one.) While at play, the child is encouraged to express his thoughts and feelings and to gain understanding of the difference between fantasy (a daydream, or imagined event) and reality.

-plegia

A suffix meaning paralysis.

Pleura (PLOO-ruh)

A thin two-layered membrane that lines the outside of the lungs and the inside of the chest cavity. There is a thin layer of fluid between the two membrane layers.

pleuro-

A prefix meaning rib or pleura, or the membrane lining the lungs and chest cavity.

Plexus
A network of blood or lymphatic vessels and nerves.

Plosives
Speech sounds produced when the outgoing breath stream is completely obstructed, such as with /g/ and /k/ (velar plosives, as in velum or soft palate) and /b/ and /p/ (*bilabial* plosives).

-pnea
A suffix meaning breathing.

pneo-
A prefix meaning breathing or lungs.

pneum-, pneumo-
Prefixes meaning breathing or lungs.

Pneumococcus (noo-moe-KOK-uhs)
The bacterium which is the most common cause of bacterial *pneumonia*.

Pneumogram (NOO-moe-gram)
A test to monitor the baby's breathing patterns while she sleeps.
   Also known as a **Sleep Study**.

Pneumonia (noo-MOE-nee-uh)
An inflammation of the lung tissue. Symptoms include shortness of breath, pain while inhaling, fever, and a sputum-producing cough. Pneumonia is usually caused by either a viral or bacterial infection, but it can also be caused by other types of microorganisms.

Pneumothorax (noo-moe-THOR-aks)
A condition in which air enters and collects between the two layers of the *pleura* (the two-layered membrane that lines the outside of the lungs and the inside of the chest cavity). It can be caused by a ruptured lung, a perforation in the chest wall, or as a complication of lung disease such as *asthma*. The *premature infant* who requires high *ventilator* pressures is vulnerable to the bursting of the *alveoli* (air sacs) in her lungs, which causes pneumothorax.

PO/po
The abbreviation for the Latin words meaning by mouth.

POE Position
The abbreviation for prone on elbows (lying on the abdomen with weight on the forearms).

PO Feeding
The abbreviation for the Latin words meaning by mouth (oral feeding).

-poiesis
A suffix meaning make or produce.

Polio
The informal word for poliomyelitis.

Poliomyelitis (poe-lee-oe-mie-uhl-IE-tuhs)
A viral infection that can affect the central nervous system, specifically the gray matter of the spinal cord, causing *paralysis*. Infants and young children are given a vaccine to immunize them against the disease.
Also known as **Polio**.
Refer to **Oral Polio Vaccine**.

poly-
A prefix meaning much or many.

Polycythemia (pol-ee-sie-THEE-mee-uh)
A condition in which there is an abnormally high number of red blood cells. It can result from another disorder such as lung or heart disease, or from *hypoxia* (a lack of sufficient oxygen in the body cells or blood), and can cause impaired blood circulation. Polycythemia most commonly occurs when a newborn receives more blood than normal from the placenta.

Polydactyly (pol-ee-DAK-ti-lee)
A birth defect that results in one or more extra fingers or toes. They may look like the other digits or they may be incompletely formed.
Compare **Adactyly**.

Polyhydramnios (pol-ee-hie-DRAM-nee-os)
Refer to **Hydramnios**.

Poly-Vi-Flor™
A multivitamin containing fluoride (a mineral used to prevent tooth decay) and iron.

Poly-Vi-Sol™
A multivitamin containing iron.

Pommel (POM-uhl)
A piece of adaptive equipment that is placed between the legs to keep them apart, such as while sitting in a wheelchair.

Pons (ponz)
The middle part of the brain stem.
Refer to **Brain**.

Pope Night Splint™
A *splint* that is typically worn while the child sleeps to help prevent heel-cord tightness and *contracture*.

Popliteal (pop-LIT-ee-uhl)
Referring to the back surface of the knee.

Porencephaly (por-en-SEF-uh-lee)
A *cyst* that develops within the brain and connects the ventricles with the subarachnoid space (the space inside the arachnoid membranes that surround the brain). It may develop either prenatally due to a *congenital anomaly*, or in early infancy as a result of poor blood supply (which may be the result of a birth trauma). Motor and/or sensory function may be impaired, depending on the size and location of the cyst, and *hydrocephalus* may result. Some children have normal intelligence.

Port Wine Stain
A flat, purple-red birthmark. It is usually found on the head or neck and usually persists throughout life.
*Also known as **Nevus Flammeus**.*
*Refer to **Hemangioma**.*

Positioning
Placing a child's body in correct alignment to facilitate optimal posture and performance. Special equipment, such as an adaptive seat, may be required for the child to maintain proper positioning.

Positive End Expiratory Pressure (PEEP)
The constant pressure provided by a *ventilator* to help keep the baby's lungs from collapsing.

Positive Reinforcement
*Refer to **Reinforcement**.*

Positive Support Reflex
A normal reflex in infants from birth to six to eight weeks of age and then again from approximately three months to ten months of age. The infant extends her legs and hips when held upright with the balls of her feet touching the floor, supporting some of her weight. It is not desirable for this reflex to continue beyond ten months of age because the increased *muscle tone* in the legs makes learning to walk difficult.
*Refer to **Primitive Reflex**.*

Positron Emission Tomography (PET) (POZ-i-tron tuh-MOG-ruh-fee)
A diagnostic imaging technique used to study the metabolic and chemical activity of tissue, especially that of the brain. PET scanning visualizes the organ, producing three-dimensional color images.

post-
A prefix meaning behind or after.

Posterior
Behind.
Also known as **Dorsal**.
Compare **Anterior**.

Posterior Rhizotomy
Refer to **Dorsal Rhizotomy**.

Postictal (poest-IK-tuhl)
Referring to the recovery period just after a *seizure* in which the child is usually sleepy.
Refer to **Epilepsy**.

Postpartum
After delivery.

Postural Drainage (PD)
A technique which allows mucus to drain from the lungs in which the baby is tilted with the head positioned below the lungs. This can be accomplished by placing the infant in different positions on a bed in which the foot of the bed is raised higher than the head of the bed, and is usually accompanied by *percussion*.

Postural Reaction/Reflex
Refer to **Automatic Reflex**.

Posture/Posturing
Positioning of the body.

Potassium
A mineral needed by the body for nerve and muscle functioning, for regulation of the body's water and acid-base balance, and to assist with maintaining the heart's normal rhythm.

Potter Syndrome
A *congenital* disorder characterized by absence of both kidneys. Other characteristics that may be present include poor lung development, a flat nose, a small lower jaw, low-set and malformed ears, *epicanthal folds* (vertical skin folds at the inner corner of the eyes), and *clubbed* hands and feet (broadening and thickening of the soft tissues of the ends of the fingers and toes). Potter Syndrome is thought to result from an insufficient amount of amniotic fluid around the fetus.

Potts Shunt™
A surgically created heart connection that enables blood to bypass the malformed pulmonary valve.

PPVT-R
The abbreviation for Peabody Picture Vocabulary Test-Revised.

PR
The abbreviation for the Latin words meaning by rectum.

Prader-Willi Syndrome
A *congenital* disorder characterized by almond-shaped eyes, *strabismus* (a condition in which the eyes do not work together), low forehead, small lower jaw, abnormalities of the hands and fingers, *hypogonadism* (abnormally low activity of the gonads), slow height growth, early *hypotonia* (decreased *muscle tone*), *mental retardation*, and *failure to thrive* in early infancy, with obesity beginning between one and three years of age.

Pragmatics
The understanding of how and why language is used. Pragmatics involves understanding the context in which language is expressed and the intent of what is expressed. Elements of pragmatics include facial expressions, the appropriate use of space and distance in interpersonal situations, and conversational skills such as taking turns, knowing how to make requests, and clarifying misunderstandings. Usually, infants develop an early understanding of pragmatics even before they are able to speak. For example, an infant who tosses her spoon to the floor and waits in anticipation for her parent to retrieve it and continue the game is expressing something different than an infant who tosses her spoon to the floor and squirms to get out of her high chair.

Praxis (PRAK-sis)
The ability to plan and perform movements.
  Refer to **Dyspraxia**.

pre-
A prefix meaning before or in front of.

Precipitous Delivery
The sudden, uncontrolled delivery of an infant.

Precise Finger Opposition
  Refer to **Opposition Movements** *and* **Neat Pincer Grasp**.

Prednisone (PRED-ni-sone)
A *corticosteroid drug* used to treat inflammation associated with different disorders including severe *asthma*.

Pre-eclampsia (pree-ee-KLAMP-see-uh)
A serious complication of the second half of pregnancy in which the woman develops high blood pressure and *edema*, and has protein in the

urine. Pre-eclampsia must be treated to prevent *eclampsia*, which can be fatal.

Also known as **Toxemia of Pregnancy**.

Compare **Eclampsia**.

Pregestamil™
A predigested protein formula (the protein is broken down), fed to infants with malabsorption problems, such as *celiac disease* or *cystic fibrosis*.

Prehension
The act of grasping or holding.

Refer to **Grasp**.

Prelingual Deafness
Loss of hearing occurring before the development of speech and language skills. Prelingual deafness may be *congenital* or *adventitious*.

Premature Infant
A baby born before 37 weeks gestation. The cause of premature delivery cannot always be determined, but often it is caused by maternal conditions such as bleeding, high blood pressure, or infection, or by fetal conditions such as a multiple pregnancy or *hydramnios* (excessive amniotic fluid). Babies have different problems depending on the reasons for and the amount of prematurity. These complications may include a *low birth weight*, *respiratory distress syndrome, apnea, bradycardia, patent ductus arteriosus*, feeding difficulties, *necrotizing enterocolitis, jaundice*, infection, *seizures*, and *brain damage*.

Also known as a **Premie/Preemie**.

Premie/Preemie (PREE-mee)
A premature infant.

Prenatal
Before birth.

Prenatally Exposed to Drugs (PED)
Referring to an infant who was exposed to drugs as a fetus due to maternal substance abuse. The effects of drug exposure can range from slight to severe, in part due to the many variables associated with substance abuse. They include the type and/or combination of drugs taken; the amount, frequency, and route of use; the gestational period in which the fetus was exposed to drugs; the *genetic* make-up of the fetus and prenatal care received; and the environment in which the newborn lives. Infants prenatally exposed to drugs often have a withdrawal period. They suffer damage to the central nervous system and display behaviors that reflect this physiological assault. These behaviors might include poor impulse control, being easily distracted or stimulated, delayed language skills, difficulty with following

directions, and difficulty with developing appropriate attachments to others. Some refer to the infant prenatally exposed to drugs as a ***Drug Baby***.
*Also known as **Infant of a Substance Abusing Mother**.*
*Refer to **Neonatal Abstinence Syndrome, Fetal Alcohol Effects,** and **Fetal Alcohol Syndrome**.*

Preoperational Stage
The second stage of Jean Piaget's theory of cognitive development in which the two- to seven-year-old child acquires a symbolic system to represent her world, based on her own perceptions. Much of her play involves imitation, symbolic play, drawing, and use of language.
*Compare **Sensory-Motor Stage**.*

Pressure Equalization Tube
*Refer to **Ear Tube**.*

Primary Caregiver/Caretaker
The adult who provides care for, and is best known and depended upon by the young child. The primary caregiver is usually the mother but may be another adult who provides quality love and attention to the child.

Primary Circular Reactions
According to Jean Piaget's theory of cognitive development, primary circular reactions describes the infant's repetition of an action involving her body that initially occurred as an accident. After the first accidental occurrence, the one- to four-month-old attempts and eventually succeeds at repeating the action (such as getting her fist to her mouth). Primary circular reactions is a substage of the *sensory-motor stage*.
*Compare **Secondary Circular Reactions**.*
*Refer to **Sensory-Motor Stage**.*

Primary Epilepsy
*Refer to **Idiopathic Epilepsy**.*

Primary Teeth
The first teeth, which are shed and replaced by permanent (*secondary*) *teeth*. There are 20 primary teeth, 10 in each jaw. The primary teeth usually begin to appear around six months of age.
*Also known as **Deciduous Teeth** and **Baby Teeth**.*
*Compare **Secondary Teeth**.*

Primidone (PRIM-i-doen)
An *antiepileptic drug*.

Primigravida (prie-mi-GRAV-i-duh or pri-mi-GRAV-i-duh)
A woman pregnant for the first time.
*Refer to **Gravida**.*

Primitive Reflex

A reflex response to a stimulus such as touch or movement that is normal in infants. The word "primitive" refers to the fact that these are involuntary survival responses with which infants are born. As the newborn moves through her first year of life, reflexive movement is replaced by (integrated into) voluntary movement. The absence of a primitive reflex at the age at which it should be present, or presence beyond the age at which it should disappear, can interfere with normal motor function and may be an indication of neurological damage. The *asymmetrical tonic neck reflex* (ATNR), the *grasp reflex*, and the *suck reflex* are examples of primitive reflexes.

Compare **Automatic Reflex**.

pro-

A prefix meaning before or prior to.

Problem Solving

Experimenting with different methods and/or materials to reach a goal. Standing on a stack of books to obtain a toy that is out of reach is an example of problem solving.

Process-Oriented Measure

A type of assessment tool used to evaluate the child's problem-solving techniques. The process involved in task completion is the focus.

procto-

A prefix meaning anus or rectum.

Proctoscopy (prok-TOS-koe-pee)

Refer to **Rectoscopy**.

Progeria (proe-JEE-ree-uh)

Premature old age, characterized by graying hair, baldness, loss of fat, a wizened face, and sagging skin. The cause of this extremely rare condition is unknown.

Progesterone (proe-JES-tuhr-oen)

A female sex hormone essential to pregnancy and the menstrual cycle.

Prognosis (Px)

An estimate of the course and outcome of a disease, including the chance of recovery.

Prolapse (PROE-laps or proe-LAPS)

A condition in which an organ has fallen or slid from its normal position in the body. An example of a prolapsed organ is rectal prolapse, in which bowel tissue has pushed down through the anus.

Prolonged Regard
The newborn's ability to look at someone or something for four to five seconds.

Prompt
Input that encourages the child to perform a movement or activity. A prompt may be verbal, gestural, or physical. An example of a prompt is tapping beneath one's chin as a visual reminder to the child to close her mouth to prevent drooling.
*Also known as a **Cue**.*

Pronation
Turning of the hand or foot so the palm faces downward or the sole faces outward.
*Compare **Supination**.*

Prone
Lying with the face down, on the abdomen.
*Compare **Supine**.*

Prone Board
A padded board to which the front side of the child's body is strapped so she is positioned in properly aligned standing. This piece of equipment allows the child to bear some of her own weight (leaning at an angle, such as against a table), and to engage in table activities while developing head control.
*Also known as a **Prone Stander**.*

Prone On Elbows (POE Position)
Lying on the abdomen with weight on the elbows.

Prone Pivoting
Moving in a circular pattern (as opposed to forward and backward movement) while lying on the abdomen. The infant's arm and leg movements pivot her before she is able to crawl.

Prone Stander
*Refer to **Prone Board**.*

Prophylactic Therapy (proe-fi-LAK-tik)
Treatment to prevent disease, including use of drugs, equipment, or procedures. Using drugs to prevent *seizures* is an example of prophylactic therapy.

Proprioception (proe-pree-oe-SEP-shuhn)
The body's conscious or unconscious awareness of its position, movement, posture, and balance in relation to the surrounding environment. Nerve

sensors (proprioceptors) within the inner ear, muscles, tendons, and joints provide information about the body's position in space.

Proptosis (prop-TOE-sis)
An abnormal protrusion of a body organ, usually referring to the eye.

Prosobee™
A milk-free protein formula for infants sensitive to milk.

Prosodic Pattern
The stress and intonation aspects of speech production. For example, the same sentence can convey more than one meaning depending on how and which words are stressed "We're having a baby!" (excitement) versus "We're having a baby?" (surprise).

Prostaglandin (PROS-tuh-gland-in)
A fatty acid substance found in body tissues that functions in many ways within the body, including to stimulate labor contractions and to widen or constrict certain blood vessels.

Prosthesis (PROS-thee-sis or pros-THEE-sis)
An artificial replacement for a missing body part, such as a leg, arm, or eye. Prostheses may be designed to restore normal function of the missing body part, or for cosmetic enhancement.

Protective Extension
A response to a sudden body movement that upsets balance, in which the arm(s) and/or leg(s) extend to try to protect oneself from a fall. An example of protective extension is the *parachute reflex*. Another example is extending one arm to the side while sitting on the floor to avoid falling all the way over when one's balance is lost.
   *Refer to **Automatic Reflex**.*

Protein (PROE-teen or PROE-tee-in)
An organic compound that is made up of linked *amino acids* and is necessary for life. Protein is a part of many body tissues and is an essential component of a balanced diet.

Protein Binding
The process by which proteins in the blood attach to and carry medications and other chemicals through the bloodstream. This is a major factor determining distribution of various molecules (the smallest portion into which a substance can be divided and still retain its properties) to different organs of the body.

Protraction

To move the shoulder or hip forward from its natural resting position, such as reaching forward toward something just out of reach with the arm extended at shoulder level.

Proventil™ (proe-VEN-til)

Refer to **Albuterol**.

Proximal (PROK-suh-muhl)

Referring to the body parts that are closest to the point of attachment to, or to the center part of, the body. For example, the elbow is proximal to the shoulder while the fingers are *distal* to the shoulder. The development of movement skills follows a pattern of proximal to distal development, meaning that skills involving proximal body parts (such as the elbow) are acquired before skills involving distal body parts (such as the fingers).

Compare **Distal**.

pseudo-

A prefix meaning false.

Pseudohypertrophic Muscular Dystrophy (soo-doe-hie-puhr-TROE-fik)

Refer to **Duchenne Muscular Dystrophy**.

Pseudomonas (soo-doe-MOE-nas or soo-DOM-uh-nas)

A type of bacteria often found in urinary tract infections and in wounds.

Psychiatrist (sie-KIE-uh-trist)

A physician who specializes in diagnosing and treating mental illness. The psychiatrist can prescribe medications (unlike the psychologist, who is not a medical doctor).

psycho-

A prefix meaning mind.

Psychologist (sie-KOL-uh-jist)

A professional who specializes in the study of human behavior and the function of the brain, including intelligence. There are several types of psychologists, including clinical psychologists, who test and counsel children with emotional or behavioral disorders; school psychologists, who give standardized tests and make recommendations regarding school placement for the child with special needs; and developmental psychologists, who assess the child's intellectual development.

Psychomotor (sie-kuh-MOE-tuhr)

An educational term meaning voluntary motor activity. Sitting up and bladder control are examples of psychomotor skills.

Psychomotor Development Index (PDI)
The score given to the Motor Scale section of The Bayley Scales of Infant Development-II.

Psychomotor Seizure
Refer to **Complex Partial Seizure, Partial Seizure,** *and* **Epilepsy.**

Psychosis (sie-KOE-sis)
A severe mental disorder that alters the child's understanding of reality and ability to participate normally with others. The child may exhibit personality changes, loss of *affect*, disturbed thought processes, depression, confusion, a decrease in language skills, aggression, agitation, delusions, or hallucinations. (Individual symptoms can occur with disorders other than psychoses, as well.) *Schizophrenia* is an example of a psychosis.

pt
The abbreviation for patient.

PT
The abbreviation for physical therapy or physical therapist.

pto-
A prefix meaning fall.

-ptosis
A suffix meaning *prolapse* or drooping of an organ or body part.

Ptosis (TOE-sis)
A drooping down of an organ or body part, usually referring to the drooping of the upper eyelid. Ptosis of the eye can occur *congenitally* or be caused by injury or disease to the muscle or nerve supply to the eye.

Pubis (PYOO-bis)
The most anterior bone in the pelvis.

Public Law 94–142
Refer to **Education for All Handicapped Children Act.**

Public Law 99–457
Refer to **Education of the Handicapped Amendments of 1986.**

Public Law 101–336
Refer to **Americans with Disabilities Act.**

Public Law 101–476
Refer to **Individuals with Disabilities Education Act.**

pulmo-
A prefix meaning lung.

Pulmonary (PUL-muh-ner-ee)
Referring to the lungs.

Pulmonary Artery
The main vessel that delivers blood from the right side of the heart to the lungs to be oxygenated.

Pulmonary Function Test
A set of several tests to assess lung function, including determination of the volume of air that moves in and out of the lungs, the ability of the lungs to exchange oxygen and carbon dioxide, and the degree of airway obstruction.

Pulmonary Hypertension
High blood pressure in the vessels supplying blood to the lungs caused by inadequate blood flow through the lungs. High blood pressure occurs when the heart must pump harder to maintain proper blood flow and results in enlargement of the heart muscle. The underlying problem of inadequate blood flow can be caused by a decreased supply of oxygen to the lungs or other lung disease.

Pulmonary Interstitial Emphysema (PIE) (PUL-muh-ner-ee in-tuhr-STISH-uhl em-fuh-SEE-muh)
A condition in which air bubbles leak from the lungs into the tissue of the lungs. It can be caused by high pressure to the lungs associated with use of a *ventilator*. Pulmonary interstitial emphysema usually improves after respirator pressure is decreased.

Pulmonary Stenosis (PUL-muh-ner-ee sti-NOE-sis)
An obstruction of the outflow from the right ventricle of the heart, which causes the heart to pump harder to move blood to the lungs. Pulmonary stenosis is usually a *congenital* condition, and may be caused by narrowing of the pulmonary valve, the pulmonary artery, or part of the right ventricle, but obstruction can develop after birth. In severe cases, the obstruction (narrowing) can be improved through surgery.

Pulmonary Valve
One of the four valves in the heart that open and close with each heart beat to control the flow of blood. Blood exits each chamber of the heart through one of the valves. The pulmonary valve is located between the pulmonary artery and the right ventricle. The three cusps (small flaps) of the pulmonary valve close during each heart beat to prevent blood from flowing back into the right ventricle.
   Compare **Aortic Valve**, **Mitral Valve**, *and* **Tricuspid Valve**.

Pulmonary Vein
One of four blood vessels that return oxygenated blood from the lungs to the left *atrium* of the heart.

Pulse
The expansion and contraction of an artery caused by the pumping of blood through it, by the heart. Each pulse beat reflects a beat of the heart.

Pupil
The opening in the center of the iris of the eye through which light enters. The iris constricts to change the size of the pupil. The pupil becomes smaller, or constricted, in bright lighting to decrease the amount of light entering the eye, and becomes larger, or dilated, in dim lighting to admit more light.
Refer to Eye.

Puppy Position
The *prone* position with weight on the forearms and the head up.

Purulent (PUR-yoo-lent)
Containing or producing pus.

Pus
A creamy substance indicating the site of inflammation. Pus contains dead white blood cells and cellular debris.

Px
The medical abbreviation for prognosis.

pyelo-
A prefix meaning kidney or pelvis.

Pyelogram (PIE-uh-loe-gram)
An X-ray picture of the organs within the urinary system, including the kidneys, ureters (tubes that carry urine from the kidneys to the bladder), and bladder. The X-rays are taken after a contrast material has been injected into the bloodstream.

Pyknodysostosis (pik-noe-dis-os-TOE-sis)
Refer to Maroteaux-Lamy Syndrome II.

Pyloric Stenosis (pie-LOR-ik sti-NOE-sis)
A relative narrowing of the pyloric orifice (the opening between the stomach and the *duodenum*), where food passes from the stomach into the small intestine. The narrowing is caused by a thickening of the pyloric muscle, which obstructs the passage of food from the stomach. This results in persistent vomiting, constipation, and failure to gain (or loss of) weight. Pyloric stenosis is sometimes improved with medication, but often surgery is required to correct the narrowing.

pyo-
A prefix meaning pus.

Pyramidal Cerebral Palsy (pi-RAM-i-duhl)

Cerebral palsy that results from damage to the part of the brain that controls the initiation of voluntary movement or to the nerve pathways that transmit these motor impulses from the brain to the spinal cord. Pyramidal cerebral palsy is characterized by *spasticity* (stiffness) in certain muscle groups. It is the most common type of cerebral palsy and can take the form of *monoplegia, diplegia, hemiplegia, paraplegia, quadriplegia,* or *double hemiplegia* depending on the location of *brain damage.*

Also known as **Spastic Cerebral Palsy.**

Compare **Extrapyramidal Cerebral Palsy.**

Refer to **Cerebral Palsy.**

Pyramidal Tract

The nerve pathways that transmit impulses for initiating voluntary movement from the brain to the spinal cord.

Compare **Extrapyramidal Tract.**

q
1. The abbreviation for every.
2. Referring to the long arm of a *chromosome*.

q-
Referring to the partial deletion of the long arm of a *chromosome*. For example, *13q- syndrome* occurs when part of the long arm of a number 13 chromosome is deleted.

qd
The abbreviation for every day.

qh
The abbreviation for every hour.

qid
The abbreviation for four times a day.

qns
The abbreviation for quantity not sufficient.

qod
The abbreviation for every other day.

qq
The abbreviation for each or every.

qs
The abbreviation for quantity sufficient.

Quadriceps (KWOD-ri-seps)
The large muscle on the front of the thigh. The quadriceps is made up of four sections which function to extend the leg at the knee.

Quadriplegia (kwod-ruh-PLEE-jee-uh)
Weakness or *paralysis* in both arms and both legs, and often the head or face and the trunk, caused by disease or injury to the nerves of the brain or spinal cord that stimulate the muscles or by disease of the muscles themselves. Sometimes the word quadriplegia is used to describe *cerebral palsy* in which the legs, arms, face, and trunk are affected, with the legs and feet (and often the face) most affected.
   Refer to **Paralysis** *and* **Pyramidal Cerebral Palsy**.

Quadruped (KWOD-roo-ped)
Referring to an "all fours" (hands and knees) position.

Qualitative Developmental Assessment

An evaluation of the quality, rather than the quantity, of a child's cognitive skills.

qwk

The abbreviation for every week.

R
The abbreviation for respiration or response.

Radial (RAY-dee-uhl)
Referring to the thumb side of the forearm and the hand.

Radial Digital Grasp
Grasp of an object using the middle and index fingers and the thumb (without the use of the palm of the hand). The radial digital grasp usually develops between seven and nine months of age.
  Refer to **Grasp**.

Radial Palmar Grasp
Grasp of an object using the thumb, index, and middle fingers, and the palm of the hand. The radial palmar grasp usually develops between four and one-half and six months of age.
  Refer to **Grasp**.

Radius
The long bone on the thumb side of the forearm, extending from the elbow to the wrist. The radius is the smaller of the two forearm bones. (The other bone is the ulna.)

Rale
An abnormal breathing sound heard through a stethoscope placed at the chest. Breathing is heard as a crackling sound when air passes through bronchial tubes congested with fluid.

Range of Motion
The total distance through which a joint can be moved in natural directions. An example of the effects of a limited range of motion is seen in the child who has *spastic cerebral palsy*.

Rash
A skin eruption. A rash can be a sign of a childhood disease, a skin disorder, an infection, or an allergic reaction.

Raw Score
The number of test items "passed."

RBC
The abbreviation for red blood cell.

RDS
The abbreviation for respiratory distress syndrome.

RE
The abbreviation for right extremity.

Receptive Aphasia
Refer to Aphasia.

Receptive-Expressive Emergent Language Scale (REEL)
A screening tool used to assess the verbal abilities of young children. A parent interview format is used.

Receptive Language
The ability to understand what is being expressed, including verbal and nonverbal communication, such as *sign language.*
Compare Expressive Language.

Recessive Gene
A *gene* (unit of heredity) capable of producing an effect in the organism (such as the human body), only when it is transmitted to the offspring by both parents.
Refer to Autosomal Recessive Disorder.

Reciprocal Movement
Alternating movements of the arms and legs, such as the movement involved in walking or in creeping on the hands and knees. With creeping, the right arm and left leg move forward more or less simultaneously, then the left arm and right leg move forward at the same time. Both sides of the body are involved in reciprocal movement.

Reciprocating Gait Orthosis (RGO)
An *orthotic* device that assists with reciprocal walking. This brace provides support at the chest, hips, knees, ankles, and feet, and through the use of attached cables, allows the child to swing one leg forward at a time in a reciprocal motion.
Refer to Reciprocal Movement.

Recklinghausen Disease (REK-ling-hou-zen)
Refer to Neurofibromatosis.

Rectal Administration
Administration of a drug via the rectum. Absorption is much faster than by intramuscular injection or by mouth and is very useful when IV access cannot be obtained.

Rectal Fissure
Refer to Fissure.

Rectal Prolapse
Refer to Prolapse.

Rectal Temperature
The temperature reading when the thermometer is placed in the rectum. It runs approximately one-half to one degree higher than the oral temperature.

recto-
A prefix meaning rectum.

Rectoscopy (rek-TOS-kuh-pee)
A diagnostic technique for examining the rectum and anus in which a long, narrow, flexible tube is inserted into the rectum so the inside tissues can be seen. Tissue samples can also be obtained during this procedure.
*Also known as **Proctoscopy**.*

Rectum
The lowest part of the large intestine just before the anal canal and anus. The rectum moves fecal matter toward the anus for elimination from the body.

Rectus Femoris
One of four muscle sections that make up the *quadriceps*.

Red Blood Cells (RBC)
One of three types of blood cells. RBCs have hemoglobin, which picks up oxygen from the lungs and carries it to body tissues.
*Also known as an **Erythrocyte**.*

REEL
The abbreviation for Receptive-Expressive Emergent Language Scale.

Reflex
An automatic response to a stimulus that occurs without thinking. Removing the hand when something hot is touched and the knee-jerk reflex are examples of reflexes. Some reflexes (*primitive reflexes*) are normally only present in infants.
*Refer to **Primitive Reflex** and **Automatic Reflex**.*

Reflux
A backward flow. An example is *gastroesophageal reflux*.

Refraction
1. The bending of light rays as they pass into a medium of different density. Refraction is part of the process of vision which allows images to be focused on the retina.
2. The examination of the eye to determine if there is a refractive eye defect, such as *myopia*, and if there is a need for prescription glasses.

Refractive Error

An eye defect that causes decreased *visual acuity*. Examples of refractive errors include *myopia* (nearsightedness, or blurred vision of distant objects), in which the lens focuses distant objects in front of the retina because the eyeball is too long, and *hyperopia* (blurred vision of close objects), in which the lens focuses close objects behind the retina because the eyeball is too short.

Refer to **Refraction.**

Regard

To look or gaze.

Registered Nurse (RN)

A professional *nurse* who has completed the educational requirements (usually a bachelor's degree) and passed the necessary examination. RNs are licensed and registered by the state.

Compare **Licensed Practical Nurse** *and* **Licensed Vocational Nurse.**

Reglan™ (REG-lan)

Refer to **Metoclopramide.**

Regression

Reverting to a more immature form of behavior or decreased skill level. For example, the young child who resumes sucking her thumb after a substantial period (months or years) of no thumb-sucking. Regression is usually felt to be an unconscious protective mechanism.

Regurgitate

To flow backwards, as when swallowed food or liquid flows back into the mouth from the stomach. Regurgitation also refers to blood flow back through a defective heart valve.

Rehabilitate

To provide an individual with treatment, education, and/or training designed to help her attain or restore her potential for normal living, including learning the skills necessary for *activities of daily living*, working, and engaging in social or leisure activities.

Reinforcement

A behavior modification technique used to increase the likelihood of a desired response or behavior. Positive reinforcement is accomplished by immediately strengthening or rewarding a desirable behavior. The reward can be a social reinforcer, such as praise or a hug, or it can be material, such as a sticker or cookie. Negative reinforcement is accomplished by removing the usual unpleasant consequence of the child's behavior (such as yelling "NO") and, instead, ignoring the behavior. (It could be that the child is seeking the attention she gets for her undesirable behavior and so the adult's response actually reinforces, or encourages, the behavior.) For example, if the child typically hears "No!" every time she throws her cup on the floor, negative reinforcement would be to ignore her behavior, thereby depriving her of the satisfaction of the adult's attention. As might be expected, positive reinforcement is generally more effective than negative reinforcement.

Related Services
Services that enable a child to take advantage of special education. Related services include speech, occupational, and physical therapies, as well as transportation, and are required under the *IDEA*.
Also known as **Support Services**.

Reliability
The consistency of the results of a particular test instrument.

Remission
1. A decrease in the severity of the symptoms of a disease, such as cancer.
2. The period in which symptoms of a disease improve.

ren-, reno-
Prefixes meaning kidney.

Renal (REE-nuhl)
Pertaining to the kidney.

Renal Failure
Reduced function of the kidney. The kidney's ability to filter waste products from the blood and excrete them in the urine, to control the body's water and salt balance, and to regulate the blood pressure is diminished. Renal failure can be an *acute* or *chronic* condition. Acute renal failure is usually a temporary condition, and, once the underlying cause is treated, full kidney function returns. There are several causes of acute renal failure, including fluid and *electrolyte* depletion, hemorrhage, a tumor of the bladder, nephritis (inflammation of the kidney), *arterial* or *venous* obstruction, and severe injury, such as a burn. Chronic renal failure may result from any cause of significant renal dysfunction, such as *congestive heart failure*, infection, *hypercalcemia*, or obstruction, and it leads to *uremia*. If chronic renal failure is caused by a progressive and untreatable disorder, it usually progresses to complete loss of kidney function.
Also known as **Kidney Failure**.

Representation
The use of a symbol to stand for an actual object or activity. An example of representation is understanding that a picture of a dog is a symbol for an actual dog.
Also known as **Symbolic Representation**.

Resident
A physician in his or her second or third year of postgraduate training at a hospital.

Residential Program
An educational or other treatment program that provides room and board for its clients.

Residual Hearing
The level at which the child can hear after impairment or injury, without amplification.
*Refer to **Auditory Impairment**.*

Resource Specialist
A teacher who provides special education instruction to children who are taught by regular classroom teachers for the majority of the school day.

Respiration (res-puh-RAY-shuhn)
Breathing. The process of inhaling and exhaling by which oxygen is delivered to the lungs and carbon dioxide is eliminated.

Respirator
*Refer to **Ventilator**.*

Respiratory Distress Syndrome (RDS)
A lung disorder that results in breathing difficulties and an insufficient level of oxygen in the blood. RDS is common in *premature infants* because the infant is born too early to have produced enough *surfactant*, which is the agent needed to keep the lungs' air sacs open for breathing.
*Also known as **Hyaline Membrane Disease**.*

Respiratory Suctioning
*Refer to **Suctioning**.*

Respiratory Syncytial Virus (RSV) (sin-SI-shuhl)
A type of virus that causes acute respiratory disease (such as *pneumonia*) in children.

Respiratory Therapist
A specialist who uses various techniques to preserve or improve the breathing abilities of children with breathing problems, such as infants who are *ventilator*-dependent or children with other types of lung disease.

Respite Care (RES-pit)
Skilled caregiving service that can be provided to the parent of a disabled or seriously ill child. Respite care allows the parent time away from home for several hours or overnight to rest or attend to other needs. Respite care is provided in the family's home or in the home of a care-provider. The

duties of the respite worker usually include feeding and hygiene care and companionship for the child.

Restraint
A device used to prevent a child from moving in such a way that she could injure herself. A restraint might be used when the child who has *seizures*, or is unable to sit without support, is placed in a chair.

Resuscitation (ri-sus-i-TAY-shuhn)
Refer to **Cardiopulmonary Resuscitation**.

Retardation
Refer to **Mental Retardation**.

reti-, reticulo-
Prefixes meaning network.

Retina (RET-i-nuh)
The membrane lining the back of the inside of the eyeball on which images from the cornea and lens of the eye are focused and transmitted to the brain for vision.
Refer to **Eye**.

Retinitis Pigmentosa (ret-in-IE-tis pig-men-TOE-suh)
A disorder in which there is degeneration in the retinas of both eyes (with corresponding areas of abnormal pigment accumulation) that leads to varying degrees of visual impairment. Retinitis pigmentosa usually occurs due to *genetic* factors.

Retinoblastoma (ret-i-noe-blas-TOE-muh)
A *malignant congenital* tumor of the retina of the eye that affects the infant's vision. Retinoblastoma sometimes occurs due to *genetic* factors. Treatment involves radiation therapy or removal of the diseased eye.

Retinoic Acid
A drug used for treating severe acne that has been associated with brain malformation of children whose mothers used it during pregnancy.

Retinopathy of Prematurity (ROP) (ret-in-OP-uh-thee)
An eye disorder that can develop in *premature infants*. The *etiology* is not quite clear, but there is an increased incidence in infants who are given high levels of oxygen for long periods of time to treat *respiratory distress*. Most ROP gradually resolves. Some patients may develop other visual problems later in life. A small percentage of patients have progressive disease and in the most severe cases eventually have retinal detachment and/or blindness.
Also known as **Retrolental Fibroplasia**.

Retraction
1. An abnormal sinking in of the chest that occurs when the infant is making great efforts to breathe.
2. A drawing back of a body part (usually referring to the hips or shoulders), to a point behind its normal resting position.

retro-
A prefix meaning backward.

Retrolental Fibroplasia (RLF) (ret-roe-LEN-tuhl fie-broe-PLAY-zee-uh)
Refer to **Retinopathy of Prematurity**.

RGO
The abbreviation for reciprocating gait orthosis.

Rheumatic Fever (roo-MAT-ik)
A disease in which there is tissue inflammation, especially of the larger joints of the body. It may develop after infection with certain strains of streptococcal bacteria. Rheumatic fever is characterized by the sudden occurrence of fever and pain and stiffness of the joints; small, solid nodules (masses) under the skin; involuntary movements that affect the gait, arm movements, and speech; *erythema* (an inflammation of the skin resulting in redness); and occasionally heart damage of varying degrees.

Rheumatic Heart Disease
Heart disease caused by *rheumatic fever*. Damage to the heart usually is related to the valves and causes heart murmurs.

Rh Factor
A type of protein that is present on the red blood cells of people who have Rh positive blood. The Rh factor is an *inherited* trait. The Rh factor is important in blood transfusion (Rh negative recipients cannot receive Rh positive blood) and in pregnant women who are Rh negative with an Rh positive fetus.
Refer to **Rh Incompatibility**.

rhin-
A prefix meaning nose.

Rh Incompatibility
A condition that occurs when a woman with Rh negative blood is pregnant with an infant with Rh positive blood (an *inherited* trait from the baby's father). Some of the baby's Rh positive blood may enter the mother's circulation at the time of birth or miscarriage, causing the mother to develop *antibodies* against Rh positive blood. In subsequent pregnancies with an Rh positive fetus, the antibodies are passed through the placenta to the fetus, destroying the fetus's red blood cells. Injections can and should be given to

prevent Rh disease in future pregnancies. Rh incompatibility can also occur if a woman with Rh negative blood mistakenly receives a transfusion of Rh positive blood.

Refer to **Rh Factor.**

rhino-
A prefix meaning nose.

Rhinorrhea (rie-noe-REE-uh)
The discharge of mucus from the nose.

Rhizotomy (rie-ZOT-uh-mee)
Refer to **Dorsal Rhizotomy.**

Riboflavin (rie-boe-FLAY-vin)
Vitamin B_2, a component of the B vitamin complex. Riboflavin deficiency causes problems with vision, skin changes, and even problems with growth.

Rickets
A condition caused by vitamin D deficiency. It is characterized by abnormalities in the shape and structure of bones, delayed closure of the *fontanelles* (the two soft spots on the top of the infant's head), body pain or tenderness, sweating of the head, and an enlarged liver and spleen. Rickets is treated with vitamin D, sunlight, and adequate diet.

Ride-On Toy
A wheel toy on which the child can sit and move about, using his feet on the floor to propel himself forward.

Righting Reaction
An automatic movement response to bring or restore the head and body to an upright position. Righting reactions are normal responses. An example of a righting reaction is the automatic response of holding the head upright even if the body is tilted.

Refer to **Automatic Reflex.**

Rigid Cerebral Palsy
A form of *extrapyramidal cerebral palsy* characterized by extremely high *muscle tone*. Rigid cerebral palsy is caused by damage to the nerve pathways that transmit impulses for controlling movement and maintaining posture from the brain to the spinal cord.

Refer to **Extrapyramidal Cerebral Palsy.**

Rigidity
Extremely high *muscle tone* in any position, combined with very limited movement.

Riley-Day Syndrome

An *autosomal recessive disorder*, most commonly seen in Ashkenazi Jews, characterized by difficulty with swallowing, *aspiration pneumonia*, excessive salivation and sweating, unstable temperature, taste deficiency, insensitivity to pain, *dysarthria*, emotional instability, *mental retardation*, and ulceration of the cornea (in fifty percent of cases).

Also known as Familial Dysautonomia.

Ring Sit

Sitting on the buttocks with the knees bent and the bottoms of the feet together.

Ritalin™ (RIT-uh-lin)

Refer to Methylphenidate.

RLE

The abbreviation for right lower extremity.

RLF

The abbreviation for retrolental fibroplasia.

RN

The abbreviation for Registered Nurse.

Rocker-Bottom Foot

Refer to Vertical Talus.

Rolandic Epilepsy

An epileptic syndrome affecting children up to ten years of age, characterized by *partial seizures* that usually occur at night.

Roll

A cylindrical piece of equipment (often made of foam) on which the infant with special needs is placed to help develop muscle strength and control, balance and protective reactions, the ability to assume and maintain new positions, and/or weight-bearing and weight-shifting skills. The infant may be placed over the roll on his abdomen, he may be placed on the roll in a straddle position, or he may be placed on the roll in a sitting position with the legs together.

Also known as a Bolster and Therapy Roll.

Rollator™

An adjustable walker that only has wheels on the front two legs.

Room Air

The regular air we breathe. Room air is 21% oxygen by volume.

Rooting Reflex
A normal response in infants up to four months of age in which, when the baby's cheek is stroked, the head turns to the same side as the stroked cheek and the baby begins to suck. The rooting reflex is present until approximately 12 months of age in the sleeping baby.
Refer to **Primitive Reflex.**

ROP
The abbreviation for retinopathy of prematurity.

Roseola (roe-zee-OE-luh or roe-ZEE-oe-luh)
1. A viral infection that mainly affects children between six months and two years of age. Roseola causes a high spiking fever that lasts for usually three but up to five days, and is followed by a rash over most of the body. The rash usually appears after the fever disappears.
2. Any rose-colored rash.

Rotary Chewing
Normal chewing in which there is rotary jaw movement, rather than an up-and-down biting motion. The tongue moves food within the mouth from side to side and front to back. Rotary chewing typically develops between 18 and 24 months of age.
Refer to **Chewing.**

Rotation Movement
A turning or twisting movement between two body parts. Examples of rotation include the head turning from side to side, or the trunk twisting. Rotation is one of the four basic kinds of movement by the joints of the body.
Compare **Angular,** **Circumduction,** *and* **Gliding.**

Roussy-Levy Syndrome (roo-SEE LAY-vee)
A slowly progressive *familial* disorder characterized by muscle wasting, especially of the calves and the hands; *scoliosis*; *mental retardation*; and *ataxia* (an inability to coordinate muscles in voluntary movement).

RR
The abbreviation for respiration rate.

-rrhagia
A suffix meaning excessive discharge.

-rrhaphy
A suffix meaning suture or sew.

-rrhea
A suffix meaning flowing.

-rrhexia
A suffix meaning break or rupture.

RSV
The abbreviation for respiratory syncytial virus.

Rubella (roo-BEL-luh)
A mild, contagious viral infection symptomized by rash, fever, enlarged lymph nodes, and respiratory symptoms. Rubella is only serious in the pregnant woman who is infected during the first four months of pregnancy, when the virus can cause fetal abnormalities including *mental retardation*, heart disease, deafness, and eye disorders. The rubella vaccination provides *immunity* to the virus.

> *Also known as* **Three-Day Measles** *and* **German Measles**.
> *Compare* **Measles (Rubeola)**.

Rubenstein-Taybi Syndrome
A *congenital* disorder characterized by *short stature*; *anomalies* of the vertebrae and sternum; small head; facial anomalies including *ptosis* (drooping of the upper eyelid), slanting eyes, *exophthalmos* (abnormal protrusion of the eyeball), *epicanthal folds* (a vertical skin fold at the inner corner of the eyes), *strabismus* (a condition in which the eyes do not work together), a thin beaked nose, high arched palate, and underdeveloped upper jaw; low-set and/or deformed ears; occasional cardiac anomaly; broad thumbs and great toes; undescended testes; and *mental retardation*.

Rubeola
> *Refer to* **Measles**.

RUE
The abbreviation for right upper extremity.

Rx
The abbreviation for prescription.

S

---

s
The abbreviation for without.

Sabin Vaccine (SAY-bin)
Refer to **Oral Polio Vaccine**.

Sacrum (SA-kruhm)
The five fused vertebrae of the lower back which form the back part of the pelvis. The sacrum is triangular in shape and is located between the two hip bones.

Saline Solution
A solution containing salt (sodium chloride).

salpingo-
A prefix meaning fallopian tube.

Sanfilippo Syndrome
An *autosomal recessive mucopolysaccharidosis* disorder characterized by *short stature*, coarse facial features, *hirsutism* (excessive body hair), mildly stiff joints, normal growth for one to three years followed by slowed growth, and *mental retardation* by one and one-half to three years of age. The child with this disorder tends to have severe mental retardation, and to deteriorate in motor, speech, and social skills.
Also known as **Mucopolysaccharidosis III**.

sarc-
A prefix meaning similar to or resembling flesh.

Scalp IV
The placement of an intravenous needle in a vein in the scalp. The scalp is often chosen as the location for IV placement in an infant because the scalp has an abundance of surface veins and because an IV placed there does not restrict the baby's arm and leg movements.

Scaphoid Pad (SKAF-oid)
Refer to **Cookie Insert**.

Scapula (SKAP-yuh-luh)
The shoulder blade.

Scarlet Fever
A contagious childhood disease characterized by a widespread red rash, sore throat, and fever. It is caused by a type of streptococcal (strep throat) bacteria which can be treated with *antibiotics*.

Scattered Scores

Scores on an assessment that range between high scores and low scores. Achieving high scores in some developmental areas and low scores in other areas shows an uneven quality to the child's development and may indicate that the child is at-risk or developmentally delayed.

Scheie Syndrome (shie or shay)

An *autosomal recessive mucopolysaccharidosis* disorder characterized by a broad mouth with full lips that develops between five and eight years of age, opacity of the corneas of the eyes, *retinitis pigmentosa*, joint limitation, mild deformities of the bones, including broad and short hands and feet, cardiac defect, *hirsutism* (excessive body hair), a short neck, and normal intelligence.

Also known as **Mucopolysaccharidosis V**.

Schizophrenia (skit-suh-FREE-nee-uh or skit-suh-FREN-ee-uh)

Any of a group of mental illnesses in which the individual displays characteristic psychotic symptoms (such as delusions, hallucinations, and *flat affect*) and functions at a lower level than before the onset of the disturbance (or, in the case of children and adolescents, fails to achieve the social skills expected of their age group). The individual with schizophrenia usually withdraws and displays thoughts and feelings that do not relate to each other in a normal way. Schizophrenia usually appears during adolescence or early adulthood. Investigators have found both *genetic* and non-genetic causes associated with schizophrenia.

Schwa (shwah)

The vowel sound produced when the lips and tongue are relaxed (the /uh/ sound).

Scissoring

Bringing the extended legs together so they are tightly crossed at the knees. Scissoring can occur if there is extreme tightness of the *adductor* muscles in the inner thighs. The child with spastic *cerebral palsy* may scissor his legs.

Sclera (SKLER-uh)

The tough, dense white membrane starting at the edges of the cornea and covering most of the back of the eyeball.

sclero-

A prefix meaning hardening.

Sclerosis (skluh-ROE-sis)

A condition in which there is hardening of body tissue. The cause is not always understood but it can be caused by chronic inflammation or by plaque formation (raised areas). *Atherosclerosis* (thickening of the inside walls of the arteries) and *multiple sclerosis* (a progressive central nervous system disease that affects adults and may result in *paralysis*) are examples.

Scoliosis (skoe-lee-OE-sis)
A C-shaped or S-shaped lateral (sideways) curve of the spine. Scoliosis can occur as a result of *poliomyelitis* or other *neuromuscular* disease, of *paralysis* of spinal muscles, of one leg being shorter than the other, or due to a *congenital* abnormality of the vertebrae. Often the cause of scoliosis is unknown.
    Compare **Kyphosis** *and* **Lordosis**.

Scooter Board
A mobility aid that holds the child in proper alignment to allow him to move about and explore his environment. The child lies on his abdomen on a board with casters and uses his hands to propel forward. Adaptations may be necessary depending on the child's muscle tone, head control, tendency to *scissor* his legs, etc.

Screening Test
1. Any test designed to minimize *false negatives* (to not miss any patient with a particular condition).
2. An evaluation tool designed to identify children who are at- risk for having or developing a *developmental disability*. The Denver Developmental Screening Test is an example of a screening test.
    Compare **Criterion-Referenced Test** *and* **Norm-Referenced Test**.

SE
The abbreviation for Signed English.

Seborrheic Dermatitis (seb-oe-REE-ik dur-muh-TIE-tis)
A common skin condition affecting the scalp and face. It consists of thick, yellow scales and *erythema* (inflammation of the skin resulting in redness) on the scalp, and occasionally the face, neck, chest, or the infant's diaper area. The cause is unknown.
    Also known as **Cradle Cap** *(in infants)*.

Seckel Syndrome
An *autosomal recessive disorder* characterized by *short stature* (prenatal onset of growth deficiency), *microcephaly* (an abnormally small head size), *strabismus* (a condition in which the eyes do not work together), prominent beaked nose, low-set and/or malformed ears, *simian crease* (a single crease across the palm of the hand), absent thumb, *clinodactyly* (an incurved fifth finger), *hip dislocation*, and moderate to severe *mental retardation*.

Secondary Circular Reactions
According to Jean Piaget's theory of cognitive development, the infant's repeating of an action involving an object that initially occurred as an accident. After the first accidental occurrence, the four- to eight-month-old at-

tempts and succeeds at repeating the action (such as batting a toy that makes noise). Secondary circular reactions is a substage of the *sensory-motor stage*.

Compare **Primary Circular Reactions.**
Refer to **Sensory-Motor Stage.**

Secondary Seizure
Refer to **Symptomatic Epilepsy.**

Secondary Teeth
The permanent teeth which begin to replace the primary teeth (baby teeth) starting around six years of age. There are 32 secondary teeth, 16 in each jaw.

Also known as **Permanent Teeth.**
Compare **Primary Teeth.**

Secrete
To release cell products for use in the body.

Compare **Excrete.**
Refer to **Gland.**

-sect
A suffix meaning cut or divide.

SEE
The abbreviation for Signed Exact English.

Segmental Rolling
Rolling in which the body moves sequentially; i.e., the head moves first, then the shoulders, then the hips.

Seizure (SEE-zhur)
Involuntary movement or changes in consciousness or behavior brought on by abnormal bursts of electrical activity in the brain.

Refer to **Convulsion** *and* **Epilepsy.**

Seizure Disorder
Refer to **Epilepsy.**

Selective Dorsal Rhizotomy
Refer to **Dorsal Rhizotomy.**

Selective Posterior Rhizotomy
Refer to **Dorsal Rhizotomy.**

Self-Comforting Behavior
Activity in which the baby engages to comfort himself, such as sucking on his fist or fingers.

Self-Help
The developmental area that involves skills which enable the child to care for his own needs, such as feeding, bathing, and dressing himself.

Self-Injurious Behavior (SIB)
Abnormal behaviors that are harmful to oneself, such as head- banging or scratching or biting oneself.
Refer to Self-Stimulation.

Self-Stimulation
Abnormal behaviors such as head banging (which is also *self- injurious*), watching the fingers wiggle, or rocking side to side that interfere with the child's ability to "sit still" and pay attention or to participate in meaningful activity. It may also be considered self-stimulation if the child plays with a toy, but without purpose, such as only spinning the wheels on a toy truck rather than exploring it in other ways as well. The child may engage in self-stimulatory behavior (often referred to as "stimming") if he cannot readily participate with people and objects in his environment. Self-stimulation is most common in children who have *mental retardation*, *autism*, or a *psychosis*.

Semantics
The study of the meaning of language, specifically the understanding of the relationship between words (not just of the meaning of individual words). An example of semantics is the understanding that "kick the ball" is different than "throw the ball." The child must not only be able to identify the ball, but also understand how to act upon it.

semi-
A prefix meaning half.

Sensorimotor (sen-suh-ree-MOE-tuhr)
Referring to input from the senses, in conjunction with purposeful motor responses. For example, catching a ball is a sensorimotor activity because both vision and raising the arms to the right place and at the right time are required.

Sensorimotor Integration
The ability to receive input from the various individual senses, organize them into a meaningful whole, and produce a purposeful motor response. For example, when running, leaning forward as the ground slopes upward. (This response may not be on a conscious level.)

Sensorineural Hearing Loss (sen-suh-ree-NOOR-uhl)
Auditory impairment that results from permanent damage to the inner ear or to the auditory nerve which transmits sound stimuli (in the form of electrical impulses) to the brain. Sensorineural hearing loss can occur *congenitally* or be *acquired*. If sensorineural hearing loss is acquired (such as from a

tumor of the auditory nerve) and if the child receives treatment before sustaining permanent damage, his hearing may improve.

Compare **Conductive Hearing Loss** and **Mixed Hearing Loss**.

Sensory Impairment

A problem with receiving information through one or more of the senses (sight, hearing, touch, etc.). For example, *deafness* is a sensory impairment.

Sensory Integration

The ability of the central nervous system to receive, process, and learn from sensations (such as touch, movement, sight, sound, smell, and the pull of gravity) in order to develop skills.

Sensory-Motor Stage

The first stage of Jean Piaget's theory of cognitive development in which the birth to two-year-old child learns about objects and events in the environment and how to respond to and manipulate them. As the child progresses through the sensory-motor stage, he refines his reflexive movements and his actions become more purposeful. It is during this stage that the infant understands *object permanence*.

Compare **Preoperational Stage**.

Sensory Nerve

Refer to **Peripheral Nervous System**.

Sensory Overload

The condition that occurs when one or more of the senses have been overstimulated beyond the child's level of tolerance. The sensory input is overwhelming, and the infant or child may respond by becoming over-active or unable to attend to an activity or to speech, or by withdrawing. The infant or child who is overstimulated also has a difficult time being comforted and utilizing sensory information. Sensory overload may occur as the result of too much noise, light, or movement.

Also known as **Overstimulated**.

Sensory Seizure

A type of *partial seizure* which produces dizziness or disturbances in vision, hearing, taste, smell, or other senses. For example, the child may hear sounds or see images which are not actually occurring.

Refer to **Partial Seizure** and **Epilepsy**.

Sensory Stimulation

Any arousal of one or more of the senses. For example, a play activity that includes touching strips of shiny cellophane, listening to them crinkle, and watching while a bright light is shining on them against a contrasting background might be a fun and stimulating activity for the child with low vision.

sep-
A prefix meaning decay.

Sepsis (SEP-sis)
A bacterial infection.

Septal Defect
A hole in the septum (wall) that divides the right and left *atria* or the right and left *ventricles* of the heart.
Also known as a Hole in the Heart.
Refer to Atrial Septal Defect and Ventricular Septal Defect.

-septic
A suffix meaning infection.

Septic
Related to sepsis (a bacterial infection).

septo-
A prefix meaning fence.

Septra™
A trademark for a drug made of two *antibacterial* drugs (Sulfamethoxazole and Trimethoprim) to treat certain bacterial infections such as urinary tract, respiratory, or middle ear infections.

Septum
A dividing wall in the body, such as in the chambers of the heart or in the nose dividing the nostrils.

Sequela (see-KWEE-luh)
A condition that follows as a consequence of disease, injury, or disorder. An example of a sequela is *bronchitis*, which can be a complication of the *common cold*.

Serology (see-ROL-uh-jee)
The medical science involved with studying blood *serum*.

Serous (SIR-uhs)
Pertaining to, producing, or containing serum (a thin, watery fluid).
Refer to Serum.

Serous Otitis Media (SIR-uhs oe-TIE-tis MEE-dee-uh)
An acute or chronic ear condition in which fluid collects in the middle ear causing inflammation, but not an infection. The condition usually is pain-less. It can cause some degree of temporary *conductive hearing loss*, or cause permanent hearing loss if, over time, untreated serous otitis damages the bones of the middle ear.

Serum (SIR-uhm)
1. The clear, sticky, fluid part of blood that remains after clotting and removal of the blood cells.
2. Any thin, watery fluid that has been separated from its more solid elements.
3. A *vaccine* made from the serum of a patient with a particular disease and used to protect someone else from the same disease.
   Compare **Plasma**.

Serum Hepatitis
Refer to **Hepatitis B Virus**.

Sex Chromosome
One of a pair of chromosomes that determines gender. It may carry *genes* that transmit *sex-linked* traits and disorders. In humans, the normal *chromosome* combination for females is XX and the normal chromosome combination for males is XY.

Sex-Linked Disorder
Any disease or abnormal condition that is caused by a defect in the *sex chromosomes* or in the *genes* of the sex chromosomes. Sex-linked disorder is often used interchangeably with X-linked disorder since no known disorders are associated with genes of the Y chromosome (the other sex chromosome). *Turner syndrome* is an example of a sex-linked disorder.

Sexual Abuse
Acts of sexual molestation or exploitation of a minor. Signs of suspected sexual abuse in children include sexually transmitted diseases; evidence of injury to the genital or anal areas; vaginal discharge or blood in the diaper or underwear; frequent urinary or yeast infections; unusual sexual behavior, acting out, or knowledge; and sudden change in behavior or emotions such as moodiness, fear, regression, or withdrawal. (Signs of force or penetration are not the only indicators of sexual abuse.)
   Refer to **Child Abuse and Neglect** *and* **Mandated Reporter**.

Sexually Transmitted Disease (STD)
A contagious disease transmitted through sexual contact. STDs can also be transmitted other ways, such as through blood contact (as with drug users who share needles). An infant can be infected with an STD prenatally or during delivery as he passes through the birth canal and comes in contact with his infected mother's tissues or bodily fluids.
   Also known as **Venereal Disease**.

SGA
The abbreviation for small for gestational age.

Shaken Baby Syndrome
A group of symptoms that, occurring together, characterizes injury sustained by the infant who has been shaken (not necessarily with much force). The infant will have bleeding in his brain and also in the retinas of his eyes. Abusing an infant this way is likely to result in both mental and motor damage, and often death.
   Refer to **Child Abuse and Neglect** *and* **Mandated Reporter**.

Shaping
A method of teaching a new skill or behavior by reinforcing responses which most closely approximate the desired goal. The goal is broken down into small steps, and as each step is mastered, it is rewarded. For example, if the goal is for the child to make eye contact with the person speaking to him, he would be rewarded (reinforced) initially for directing his face toward the speaker, then after this skill is demonstrated consistently, it can be shaped into the even more appropriate response of making eye contact briefly, then shaped into the skill of holding eye contact for a designated period of time, etc., until the desired goal is attained.

Sheridan Tests for Young Children and Retardates
   Refer to **STYCAR**.

Shock
Reduced blood flow to vital organs that leads to low blood pressure, collapse, pale skin, sweating, and a fast pulse and rate of breathing. Untreated shock may result in unconsciousness or death. Shock may occur for many reasons, including failure of the heart to pump normally, severe *hypoxia* (a lack of sufficient oxygen in the body cells or blood), decreased blood volume, infection, severe injury, severe bleeding or burns, persistent vomiting or diarrhea, or poisoning.

Short Stature
Abnormal underdevelopment of the body. Body height is below the level obtained at that age by seventy percent of the population. Short stature can result from hormonal or nutritional deficiencies or from intrauterine growth retardation.
   Also known as **Dwarfism**.

Shoulder Presentation
The birth (delivery) of a baby in which the shoulder is the part of the body that first appears in the pelvis.
   Refer to **Fetal Presentation**.

Shunt
A surgical procedure in which a *catheter* (tube) is placed to divert an accumulation of fluid. For example, with increased fluid pressure in the brain, a catheter is placed through the skull to drain excess *cerebrospinal*

fluid from the ventricles of the brain. The fluid may be drained into the abdominal cavity (through a *ventriculoperitoneal shunt*) or into the right atrium of the heart (through a *ventriculoatrial shunt*), where it is absorbed. Draining the excess fluid relieves the pressure on the brain caused by the fluid. If the pressure is not relieved, hydrocephalus or brain damage may occur.

Refer to **Hydrocephalus**.

Shunt Revision
A surgical procedure to replace a *shunt* that is malfunctioning.

sial-
A prefix meaning saliva.

SIB
The abbreviation for self-injurious behavior.

Sickle Cell Anemia
An *autosomal recessive* hemoglobin abnormality characterized by the presence of crescent- or sickle-shaped red blood cells. It is a serious disease which can render the child vulnerable to bacterial infections (because the spleen functions poorly), painful crises (periods of obstructed capillary blood flow and inadequate oxygen supply that are symptomized by fever and pain in the joints and abdomen), and *aplastic anemia*. Sickle cell anemia occurs primarily in African-Americans and is an incurable disease.

Side Effect
A reaction to medication or therapy that occurs in addition to the desired effect. A side effect is usually, but not necessarily, an adverse effect. For example, drowsiness may be a side effect of *phenobarbital*, which is prescribed to control *seizures*.

Side Lyer
A piece of adaptive equipment that supports the child's body so he can bear weight on his side and bring his hands together at midline to play.

Side Sitting
Sitting with both knees bent and to one side of the body.

Sideways Walking
Refer to **Cruising**.

SIDS
The abbreviation for sudden infant death syndrome.

Sigmoidoscopy (sig-moi-DOS-koe-pee)
A procedure for examining the rectum and the sigmoid colon in which a lighted viewing tube is inserted through the rectum.

Sign (Sx)
An indication of a disease or a disorder that is noticed by a physician.
Compare Symptom.

Signed English (SE)
Refer to Manual English.

Signed Exact English (SEE)
Refer to Manual English.

Sign Language
One of several methods for communicating in which hand signs are used to express thoughts and feelings. American Sign Language and Manual English are examples of forms of sign language.

Simian Crease (SIM-ee-uhn)
A single crease across the palm of the hand. This is a common feature of Down syndrome and other syndromes.

Simple Partial Seizure
A type of *partial seizure* confined to one area of the brain which causes involuntary jerking of the muscle groups controlled by that brain region. During this type of seizure, the child remains conscious (unless the seizure spreads to involve the whole brain, in which case the seizure is described as secondarily generalized).
Compare Complex Partial Seizure.
Refer to Partial Seizure and Epilepsy.

Sinus
A cavity or hollow space.

Sjogren-Larsson Syndrome (SHOE-gren)
An *autosomal recessive disorder* characterized by *spasticity* (especially in the lower extremities), dry and scaly skin, brittle and sparse hair, *short stature*, and *mental retardation*.

Skin Graft
A procedure in which a piece of skin is transferred to an area where skin has been lost through burns, injury, or surgical removal of diseased tissue.

Skin Tag
A small flap of skin that may occur spontaneously or as the result of a wound that is not healing properly.

Sleep Study
Refer to Pneumogram.

Small For Dates
Refer to Small For Gestational Age.

Small For Gestational Age (SGA)

A newborn whose weight is low (below the tenth percentile) for his *gestational age*. This indicates that the baby has a low birth weight due to growth retardation while *in utero* (compared to the simple premature infant who has a low birth weight due to a shortened length of time in utero).

Also known as **Small For Dates.**
Compare **Appropriate for Gestational Age** *and* **Large for Gestational Age.**
Refer to **Intrauterine Growth Retardation.**

Small Intestine

The longest part of the digestive tract, extending from the stomach to the large intestine. The small intestine is approximately 21 feet long and is made up of three sections, the *duodenum*, the *jejunum*, and the *ileum*. Most absorption of nutrients takes place here.

Smith-Lemli-Opitz Syndrome

An *autosomal recessive disorder* characterized by *short stature, microcephaly* (an abnormally small head size), low-set or slanted ears, short nose with upturned nostrils, small jaw, arched palate, *ptosis* (drooping) of the eyelids, *epicanthal folds* (a vertical skin fold at the inner corner of the eyes), *strabismus* (a condition in which the eyes do not work together), *simian crease* (a single crease across the palm of the hand), fusion of second and third toes, *metatarsus adductus* (inward turning of the forefoot), short thumbs and toes, genital abnormalities, feeding problems, *failure to thrive*, irritability, and *mental retardation*.

SMO

The abbreviation for supra malleolar orthosis.

Social/Emotional

The developmental area that involves skills which enable the child to function in a group and to interact appropriately with others, such as playing a circle game with other children or comforting someone who is crying by offering a hug.

Social Maturity

The ability to function in a socially responsible manner appropriate to the child's age. An example is the ability of the three-year-old to cooperatively join other children in forming a circle so that the group can play a circle game.

Social Security Disability Insurance (SSDI)

A federally-funded disability insurance program. This money has been paid into the Social Security System through payroll deductions on earnings. Disabled workers are entitled to these benefits. People who become disabled before the age of 22 years may collect SSDI under a parent's account, if the parent is retired, disabled, or deceased. The applicant's financial need is not an eligibility consideration.

Social Worker

A professional who helps individuals manage within society. The social worker may function as a counselor or case manager, as well as help to secure services, such as counseling, financial assistance, respite care, or crisis intervention.

Sodium

A mineral needed in small amounts for the body's health.

Sodium Bicarbonate

A substance that helps neutralize excess acid in the blood.
   Also known as **Bicarbonate**.

Soft Palate

The movable structure made of muscular fibers and mucous membrane that is attached to the back edge of the hard palate (the bony front part of the roof of the mouth). The soft palate rises during sucking and swallowing to close off the nose and sinuses from the mouth and throat. The soft palate is also involved in the production of speech sounds such as the /g/ and /k/ sounds.
   Compare **Hard Palate**.
   Refer to **Palate**.

Soft Sign

Any of several neurological signs (indicators of disease or disorder that are noticeable by a physician) that, collectively, suggest the presence of damage to the central nervous system. Soft signs include a disturbance of balance or *proprioception*, visual motor difficulties, a lack of motor control or coordination, *associated reactions*, or *nystagmus*.

Soft Tissue

Tissue that surrounds bones and joints, including ligaments, tendons, and muscles.

Soft Tissue Release

A surgical procedure on the muscles, tendons, or ligaments (or a manual therapy technique called *myofascial release*) to correct deformities or improve positioning and movement.

soma-, somat-

Prefixes meaning body.

Somatic (soe-MAT-ik)

A word that means related to the body.

Somatic Growth Measurements
Refer to **Body Measurements**.

-some
A suffix meaning body.

Somophyllin-CRT™ (som-AH-fi-lin)
Refer to **Theophylline**.

Sonogram (SOE-noe-gram)
A two-dimensional image produced by *ultrasound*.

Sonography (soe-NOG-ruh-fee)
Refer to **Ultrasound Scanning**.

Spasm
A sudden, involuntary muscle contraction.

Spastic
Having increased *muscle tone,* or stiffness (resulting in difficult movements), and, usually, increased *deep tendon reflexes.*
Also known as **Hypertonic**.

Spastic Cerebral Palsy
Refer to **Pyramidal Cerebral Palsy**.

Spastic Diplegia
Refer to **Diplegia**.

Spasticity (spa-STIS-i-tee)
Increased *muscle tone* (stiffness) resulting in difficult movements.
Also known as **Hypertonicity** or **Hypertonia**.

Spastic Quadriplegia
Refer to **Quadriplegia**.

Spatial Relationships (SPAY-shuhl)
The understanding of the relationship between the position of an object and the infant's own body or another object. For example, when the infant plays at placing objects in and removing them from a container, he is experimenting with the spatial relationship between objects and his own hand.

Special Education
Specialized instruction tailor-made to fit the unique learning strengths and needs of the individual student with disabilities, from age three through high school. A major goal of special education is to teach the skills and knowledge the child needs to be as independent as possible. Consequently, special education programs do not just focus on academics, but also include special therapeutic and other *related services* to help the child overcome dif-

ficulties in all areas of development. Special education and related services may be provided in a variety of educational settings, but are required by the *IDEA* to be delivered in the *least restrictive environment*.

Refer to **IEP.**

Special Needs

Referring to the needs of the child who requires special services to assist with his acquisition of skills in one or more developmental areas: cognition, communication (language), gross motor, fine motor (perceptual), social, and self-help (adaptive). The needs are generated by the child's disability.

Refer to **Early Intervention.**

Speech and Language Pathologist

A therapist who works to improve the child's speech and language skills, as well as to improve oral motor abilities, such as feeding. Speech and language pathologists are required to have a master's degree in speech pathology and either a teaching credential to work in a school district setting or a state license to work in private practice or other agencies. (A therapist without this level of training is not a speech pathologist.)

Speech Disorder

A condition that affects the ability to speak. Speech disorders include *articulation* problems, such as sound substitutions (saying "wan" instead of "ran"); rate and rhythm problems, such as *stuttering*; and voice production (or resonance) disorders, such as a voice that is too soft or *hypernasal*. Speech disorders are often associated with another disorder, such as *cerebral palsy*, but can occur on their own.

Compare **Language Disorder.**

Speechreading

A form of communication for the child with *auditory impairment* in which the child uses visual input (watching the speaker's mouth) to help him understand what he cannot hear.

Speech Therapist

Refer to **Speech and Language Pathologist.**

Sperm

The male sex cell. An embryo can only develop if a sperm fertilizes an ovum (egg).

sperma-

A prefix meaning seed, or relating to sperm.

Sphenoid Bone (SFEE-noid)

The bone that makes up the front portion of the base of the skull and parts of the orbits (the bony sockets that contain the eyes) and nose.

Sphincter (SFINGK-tuhr)
A ring-like muscle around a natural body opening, such as the anal sphincter.

Sphingolipid (sfing-goe-LIP-id)
A lipid (fat) substance found in nervous system tissue, including the brain.

Sphingolipidosis (sfing-goe-lip-id-OE-sis)
One of a group of *hereditary* disorders of *lipid* (fat) metabolism in which a specific enzyme used in the breakdown of a specific lipid is missing, resulting in fat accumulation in body tissue. *Tay Sachs* disease is an example of a sphingolipidosis.

Sphingomyelin (sfing-goe-MIE-uh-lin)
A *sphingolipid* (a lipid, or fat, substance) that contains phosphorus and is found in nervous system tissue and in the *lipids* in the blood. It is also a component in *surfactant* (a substance formed in the lungs that is needed to keep the air sacs in the lungs open).

Spina Bifida (SPIE-nuh BIF-uh-duh)
A birth defect in which part of the spinal column (one or more vertebrae) fails to close completely, exposing the meninges (the membranes covering the spinal cord) or the meninges and the spinal cord. Sometimes the membranes and cord protrude out through the back of the spine. The severity of damage depends on the degree and the placement of the exposure, and can range from no apparent damage to *paralysis* below the level of the protrusion and severe *brain damage*. Spina bifida is often associated with *hydrocephalus*. The exact cause is not known, although it is believed that there are many contributing factors. There are four forms of spina bifida: *spina bifida occulta, meningocele, myelocele,* and *encephalocele*. (Encephalocele is actually a cranial defect in which the brain, the membranes covering the brain, or both protrude through an opening in the skull.)

Spina Bifida Occulta
A birth defect in which a minimal amount of spinal cord tissue is exposed due to the spinal column failing to form completely. This form of spina bifida may not be detected without an X-ray, but is often suspected because of a dimple or tuft of hair on the skin that lies over the defective vertebrae.
Refer to **Spina Bifida**.

Spinal Cerebellar Degeneration
Refer to **Friedreich Ataxia**.

Spinal Column
The 33 vertebrae that form the spine and the spongy disks that separate the vertebrae. The spinal column extends from the base of the skull to the pel-

vis and supports the trunk and head. It is within the spinal column that the spinal cord is located.

Also known as **Vertebral Column**.

Refer to **Vertebra**.

Spinal Cord

The nerve tissue located within the canal of the spinal column that runs from the base of the brain to the lower back area. The spinal cord passes sensory information to the brain and passes on motor signals from the brain. The spinal cord is also responsible for certain reflex actions that do not require brain involvement.

Spinal Fusion

A surgical procedure (*arthrodesis*) to join an unstable part of the spine (to reduce movement between two vertebrae). This may result in some loss of mobility.

Spinal Muscular Atrophy

A *genetic* disorder in which the muscles do not receive impulses from the spinal cord due to a wasting of motor *neurons* (nerve cells that convey impulses which initiate muscle contraction) of the spinal cord. This results in severe wasting of muscle, which can render the child unable to walk. There are several forms of this disease, including *Werdnig-Hoffmann Disease* and *Kugelberg-Welander Disease*. Some forms of spinal muscular atrophy are fatal.

Spinal Tap

Refer to **Lumbar Puncture**.

Spine

Refer to **Spinal Column**.

Spironolactone (spie-roe-noe-LAK-tone)

A *diuretic* (a drug that helps remove excess water from the body).

Spleen

The organ located in the upper left part of the abdomen beneath the diaphragm. The spleen produces blood cells in the fetus and, after birth, functions to destroy old blood cells and to help fight infection.

Splenomegaly (splee-noe-MEG-uh-lee)

An enlarged spleen that can result from many diseases, including certain types of *anemia, mononucleosis, thalassemia, leukemia,* and tumors in the spleen.

Splint

A device used to stretch soft tissues, prevent movement, or hold a limb in a position that makes movement easier. An example of a splint is an *opponens splint,* which may be prescribed for the child with *cerebral palsy* to hold the thumb in correct alignment.

spondyl-
A prefix meaning vertebra.

Spontaneous Abortion
*Refer to **Miscarriage**.*

Sporadic
Occurring only occasionally.

Squamous (SKWAY-muhs)
Scaly.

Squint
*Refer to **Strabismus**.*

S-R
The abbreviation for stimulus-response.

SSDI
The abbreviation for Social Security Disability Insurance.

SSI
The abbreviation for Supplemental Security Income.

Stammering
*Refer to **Stuttering**.*

Standard Deviation
A measurement of the degree to which a given test score differs from the mean (average) score. On an IQ test, for example, the majority of children score within 15 points above to 15 points below the mean score of 100, so one standard deviation is considered to be 15 points. That is, an IQ score of 85 is considered to be one standard deviation below the mean.

Standardization
The process of testing a sample population to establish general evaluative criteria (the average scores or standards against which the child is evaluated). For example, a test may be standardized to children of a specific age who have hearing impairments.

Standardized Test
A test that has set standards on which the child is evaluated, in addition to set administration and scoring procedures. The standardized test yields a score that may be used to compare the child's performance with those of others in his age group. *Norm-referenced* tests are standardized tests, as are some *criterion-referenced* tests.

Stanford-Binet Intelligence Scale
A standardized test used to evaluate the intelligence (verbal reasoning, abstract/visual reasoning, quantitative reasoning, and short-term memory) of children two years of age to adulthood.

Stapes (STAY-peez)
One of the three small bones of the inner ear. (The other two bones are the malleus and the incus.)
Also known as the Stirrup.
Refer to Ear.

Staph
The abbreviation for *staphylococcus.*

Staphylococcus (staf-il-oe-KOK-uhs)
An infection-causing bacterium.

Startle Reflex
A startle reaction normal in infants up to four months of age. The startle reflex is observed when the infant reacts to a sudden loud noise by bringing his arms and legs in close to his body.
Compare Moro Reflex.
Refer to Primitive Reflex.

Static Splint
A device that supports body parts, such as the wrist and hand, in correct alignment.
Compare Dynamic Splint.

Status Epilepticus (STAY-tuhs ep-i-LEP-ti-kuhs)
A single or series of *convulsive seizures* throughout which the child remains unconscious. If the seizures are not stopped, *brain damage* will result. (Untreated, they will last more than 30 minutes, even up to one hour.) Status epilepticus may be caused by the sudden withdrawal of seizure medication, erratic administering of medication, low blood sugar, a brain tumor, infection, head injury, or poisoning. Status epilepticus is a life-threatening condition and patients may have permanent neurologic *sequelae* (resulting damage).

STD
The abbreviation for sexually transmitted disease.

Steady State
A term that describes the drug level in the blood once it has reached a level around which it is fairly stable. Daily doses of medication maintain this level.

Stelazine™ (STEL-uh-zeen)
Refer to **Trifluoperazine**.

sten-
A prefix meaning narrow.

Stenosis (sti-NOE-sis)
Constriction or narrowing of an opening or passageway in the body, such as a blood vessel. An example is *aortic stenosis*.

Stepping Reflex
A normal response that occurs in newborns up to two months of age, and then again at six months of age, when the baby is held upright with the soles of the feet touching a firm surface. It causes the baby to simulate walking movements with each leg moving forward as weight is placed on the other leg.
Also known as the **Walking Reflex**.
Refer to **Primitive Reflex**.

Stereotypic Behavior
Persistent repetitive actions or vocalizations that appear to have no meaning or logical motivation. Hand flapping and rocking back and forth are examples.

Sternum (STUR-nuhm)
The breastbone.

Steroids
A group of chemical substances including natural and synthetic compounds. They may be prescribed to replace natural corticosteroid hormone (one of the hormones produced by the adrenal glands) or to treat inflammatory disorders. These are *corticosteroid drugs*. Another type of steroid works in a manner similar to male sex hormones. These are called *anabolic steroids*. Anabolic steroids are any of a group of synthetic derivatives of testosterone. They are used primarily to repair and build tissue and to promote body growth. They are also used to treat some types of *anemia* and *leukemia*.

Stiffness
Refer to **Hypertonia**.

Stigma (STIG-muh)
A physical mark or sign that serves to identify a disease or condition, such as a limp or unusual gait which may be a manifestation of an individual's disability.

Stillbirth

An infant who dies *in utero* and is born dead. In many cases, the cause of stillbirth is unknown, but seriously malformed infants (such as infants with *anencephaly*) account for a significant number of stillbirths. Other causes include maternal disease (such as *cytomegalovirus* or high blood pressure), fetal oxygen deprivation, and *Rh incompatibility*.

Stimming

*Refer to **Self-Stimulation**.*

Stimulant Drug

A drug that increases nerve activity in the brain. An example of a stimulant drug is caffeine.

Stimulus

A physical object or an environmental event that may affect an individual's behavior. Some stimuli are internal (such as earache pain), while others are external (such as a smile from a loved one).

Stirrup

*Refer to the **Stapes**.*

Stoma (STOE-muh)

A surgically created opening from an internal organ (such as the colon) to the surface of the body. For example, a stoma is created at the site of a *colostomy* to allow feces to be passed from the body when it cannot be passed through all of the colon or through the colon and rectum.

Stomach

The organ located in the left upper part of the abdomen that is connected to the esophagus and small intestine. The stomach is the main organ of enzymatic digestion and also functions to receive food.

stomato-

A prefix meaning mouth.

Stop

A consonant sound that is made when the flow of air is stopped as it passes through the mouth. Usually the tongue (and sometimes the lips) is what stops the air stream, such as when producing the /t/, /d/, /p/, and /b/ sounds.

STORCH Infections

A group of *congenital* infections, each responsible for causing illness, disabling conditions, or death: Syphilis, Toxoplasmosis, Other Infections (such as *HIV* and *hepatitis B*), Rubella, Cytomegalic Inclusion Disease, and Herpes.
    *Also known as **TORCH-S**.*

Strabismus (struh-BIZ-muhs)
A condition in which the eyes do not work together, in that one eye deviates (wanders) from its position, relative to the other eye. Strabismus may be convergent (deviate inward, also known as *esotropia*, or cross-eye), or divergent (deviate outward, also known as *exotropia*, or wall-eye). It may result from an inability of the muscles to align the eyes, from a defect such as *cataract*, or from a *visual acuity* problem.
Also known as **Squint***.*

Strawberry Mark
A raised red birthmark. Strawberry marks nearly always resolve spontaneously.
Also known as a **Capillary Hemangioma***.*
Refer to **Hemangioma***.*

Strep Throat
A throat infection caused by streptococcal bacteria. Strep throat is spread by airborne droplets and usually causes a sore throat, fever, enlarged lymph nodes in the neck, and general discomfort. Strep throat is treated with antibiotics.

Streptococcus (strep-toe-KOK-uhs)
An infection-causing bacterium.

Streptomycin (strep-toe-MIE-sin)
An *antibiotic drug* used to treat infections.

Stress Test
1. A test to record the fetus's heart rate patterns in response to the stress of uterine contractions. The drug oxytocin is usually given to induce the contractions, which are monitored by a device worn around the mother's abdomen. A stress test is done during certain types of high risk pregnancies, but should not be used with women who have a history of premature labor. 2. A test to measure a body system's response to carefully controlled stress, such as the heart's response to monitored exercise.

Stricture (STRIK-chur)
A narrowing of a tube, duct, hollow organ, or other passage within the body. A stricture may be a *congenital* condition, or it may be the result of another condition, such as the growth of a tumor, inflammation, damage to the passage that results in scar tissue, or spasm of the muscles in the passage wall. For example, a stricture may develop in the esophagus or in a ureter.

Stridor (STRIE-dor)
An abnormal, high-pitched breath sound, caused by a blockage in the throat or larynx. Stridor may occur due to *croup*, growth of a tumor in the

larynx, laryngomalacia (softening of the tissues of the larynx), or a foreign object that has been inhaled.

Stroke
Damage of sudden onset to part of the brain that can occur if the area does not receive its blood supply or if there is bleeding within or over the surface of the brain. Stroke does not always result in other problems, but problems that may occur range from language disability and/or motor impairment to death.

Structure
1. An organ, a body part, or a complete organism.
2. The parts and their arrangement in forming a whole.

Sturge-Weber Syndrome
A *congenital neurological disorder* characterized by a *port wine stain* (a flat, purple-red birthmark), commonly on one side of the face, and a *hemangioma* (a usually harmless tumor caused by an abnormal distribution of blood vessels) of the brain. The brain hemangioma may result in a lack of brain growth and development (progressive *mental retardation*), *seizures*, and motor impairment caused by weakness. Other features include *exophthalmos* (abnormal protrusion of the eyeballs), *optic atrophy* (wasting of the optic nerve fibers that leads to visual impairment), *glaucoma*, and malformation of blood vessels.

Stuttering
A speech disorder, usually beginning by eight years of age and sometimes continuing into adulthood, in which the person's speech has many hesitations, repetitions of syllables or words, and prolonged sounds. Stuttering may be associated with certain *learning disabilities* or with *mental retardation*, but it also occurs in children who have no other disability. Stuttering most commonly occurs in children between two and four years of age, as a temporary condition.

Also known as **Stammering**.

STYCAR
A test for assessing *visual acuity* in which the preschool-aged child is asked to name objects he is shown. Although the test is often referred to as the STYCAR, the actual test name is Sheridan Tests for Young Children and Retardates.

sub-
A prefix meaning under.

Subarachnoid Hemorrhage (sub-uh-RAK-noid HEM-uhr-ij)

Bleeding in the subarachnoid space (the space inside the arachnoid membranes that surround the brain).

Compare **Intracranial Hemorrhage**, **Intraventricular Hemorrhage**, *and* **Periventricular Hemorrhage**.

Refer to **Intracranial Hemorrhage**.

Subclinical

Denoting the presence of disease without *symptoms* or *signs* (disease that cannot be noted clinically), either because the disease is mild or because the disease is in an early stage.

Subcutaneous (sub-kyoo-TAY-nee-uhs)

Beneath the skin.

Subependymal Hemorrhage (sub-ep-EN-di-muhl HEM-uhr-ij)

Refer to **Intraventricular Hemorrhage**.

Subglottic (sub-GLOT-ik)

Referring to beneath the glottis (the vocal cords and the slit-like opening between them).

Subglottic Stenosis

A narrowing of the area beneath the glottis (the vocal cords and the slit-like opening between them).

Subluxation (sub-luks-AY-shuhn)

A partial *dislocation* of the two bones of a joint. The bone surfaces are displaced to the degree that they are only partly in contact.

Compare **Dislocation**.

Subluxed Hip

A partially dislocated hip.

Refer to **Subluxation**.

Suck Reflex

A normal response in infants up to 12 months in which the baby starts sucking when something is placed in the mouth. Sucking is sometimes noticed during sleep, also.

Refer to **Primitive Reflex**.

Sucrose (SOO-krose)

Sugar derived mainly from sugar cane and sugar beets.

Suctioning

A procedure to rid the body of unwanted or excess fluid, often referring to a procedure to remove excess mucus from the respiratory tract. Suctioning may be done with a syringe and hollow needle, a bulb syringe, or with one end of a narrow tube inserted into the respiratory tract and the other end attached to a machine that suctions out fluid.

Also known as **Respiratory Suctioning**.

Sudden Infant Death Syndrome (SIDS)

The unexpected and sudden death of an infant who had appeared to be healthy. SIDS occurs during sleep (this is why it is also known as crib death), and is the most common cause of death in children between one month and one year of age. Peak incidence occurs between two and four months. The cause of SIDS is still unknown. A number of hypotheses have been offered (such as a heart rate or breathing problem) but nothing has been proven and post-mortem examination fails to demonstrate the cause of death.

Suffocation

Refer to **Asphyxia**.

Sulfamethoxazole (sul-fuh-meth-OKS-uh-zole)

An *antibacterial drug*.

Sulfisoxazole (sul-fi-SOK-suh-zole)

An *antibacterial drug* used to treat *conjunctivitis* and urinary tract infections.

super-

A prefix meaning above or extreme.

Superior

Situated above.

Superior Vena Cava

Refer to **Vena Cava**.

Supination (soo-pin-AY-shuhn)

Turning the forearm so the palm faces upward.

Compare **Pronation**.

Supine (SOO-pine)

Lying on the back.

Compare **Prone**.

Supplemental Security Income (SSI)

A federally-funded public assistance program to people who are 65 or older or people of any age who are blind or disabled. The individual's income is an eligibility consideration.

Support Services

Refer to **Related Services**.

Support Trust
A trust that requires that funds be expended to pay for the beneficiary's expenses of living, such as housing, food, and transportation.

Suppository
A bullet-shaped mixture of an easily-melted material (such as cocoa butter) and a drug that is placed in the rectum or vagina when the drug cannot be administered orally, or if the drug is for treating rectal or vaginal disorders. A suppository is a useful means of administering medication to infants and young children.

supra-
A prefix meaning above or extreme.

Supra Malleolar Orthosis (SMO)
A *brace* that provides support to the ankle joint and the foot.

Surfactant (sur-FAK-tuhnt)
A substance formed in the lungs that is needed to keep the alveoli (air sacs) in the lungs open. Without surfactant, the alveoli would collapse at the end of each exhalation and stick together. A fetus born before 36 weeks gestation usually has not produced enough surfactant and often develops *respiratory distress syndrome*.

Surgeon
A medical doctor who performs operations that involve cutting body tissue for the treatment of disease, deformity, or injury.

Suture (SOO-chur)
1. The border (joint) of the bones of the skull.
2. A surgical stitch.

Sway-Back
Refer to **Lordosis**.

Sweat Test
A test to measure the concentration of sodium and chloride in the child's sweat to diagnose *cystic fibrosis*.

Swimming Position
A position that the four- to six-month-old may assume while lying on his stomach in which he extends and lifts his arms and legs, and supports most of his weight on his abdomen.

Swivel Walker
A type of walker consisting of a supportive body brace secured to a base that has two foot plates that rise and swivel forward.

Sx
The abbreviation for symptom or sign.

Symbolic Representation
*Refer to **Representation**.*

Symmetrical (si-MET-ri-kuhl)
Referring to parts of the body that are equal in size or shape, or are similar in arrangement or movement patterns.
*Compare **Asymmetrical**.*

Symmetrical Movements
Moving corresponding parts of the body, such as both arms, at the same time and in the same movement pattern.

Symmetrical Tonic Neck Reflex
A normal reflex in infants up to six months of age in which both arms extend when the head is extended backwards.
*Compare **Asymmetrical Tonic Neck Reflex**.*
*Refer to **Primitive Reflex**.*

Symptom (Sx)
An indication of a disease or disorder that is noticed by the patient. For example, a sore throat may be a symptom of an *upper respiratory infection*.
*Compare **Sign**.*

Symptomatic
Pertaining to a *symptom* or a condition that is indicative or characteristic of a particular disease or disorder. For example, emesis (vomiting) is symptomatic of abdominal disorders.

Symptomatic Epilepsy
Epilepsy that has an identifiable cause, such as an infection, a tumor, a reaction to a toxin, or a metabolic disturbance.
*Also known as **Secondary Epilepsy**.*
*Refer to **Epilepsy**.*

syn-
A prefix meaning with or together.

Synapse (SIN-aps)
A junctional region between two nerve cells (*neurons*), forming the place across which a nerve impulse is transmitted from one neuron to another by chemical neurotransmitting substances.
*Refer to **Neurotransmitter**.*

Syncopal (SIN-kuh-puhl or SING-kuh-puhl)
Referring to a short period of unconsciousness (fainting).

Syncope (SIN-kuh-pee or SING-kuh-pee)
Fainting or a short period of unconsciousness caused by poor blood supply to the brain.

Syndactyly (sin-DAK-tuh-lee)
A *congenital anomaly* in which there is partial or complete *webbing* or fusion of fingers or toes.

Syndrome
A group of *signs* and *symptoms*, or *genetic* traits, that, occurring together, are characteristic of (describe) a particular disease or disorder.

Synergy (SIN-uhr-jee)
The action of two drugs or body structures which, working together, can achieve an effect that is greater than the simple addition of the two actions. An example is two muscles which must work together to produce a certain movement.

Syntax
The rules that govern the way in which words are arranged to form meaningful sentences or phrases. For example, "He ran outside" compared to, "Outside ran he."

Synthroid™ (SIN-throid)
Refer to **Levothyroxine**.

Syphilis (SIF-uh-lis)
Refer to **Congenital Syphilis**.

Systemic (sis-TEM-ik)
Of, or relating to, the whole body rather than a specific area or part of it.

Systole (SIS-tuh-lee)
The muscular contraction phase of the heart. (The heart rests in between contractions.) During systole, blood is pumped out of the heart to the rest of the body. The systole is what is felt when the pulse is taken and is the first sound of the heartbeat.
Compare **Diastole**.
Refer to **Blood Pressure**.

Systolic Murmur (sis-TOL-ik)
A type of *heart murmur* that occurs during heart contraction. This type of murmur is commonly harmless and does not necessarily indicate heart disease.

T

t
The abbreviation for time.

T
The abbreviation for temperature.

T & A
The abbreviation for tonsillectomy and adenoidectomy.

tachy-
A prefix meaning fast.

Tachycardia (tak-ee-KAR-dee-uh)
A condition in which the heart rate is too fast (although the rhythm of the heart's contractions is normal). For an infant, tachycardia is a heart rate over 180 to 200 beats per minute. (A healthy newborn heart rate is over 100 beats per minute.) Tachycardia occurs when the infant is upset or excited, but can also be an indication of infection, heart disease, or breathing problems. An increased heart rate may also be a side effect of certain drugs or fever. (For an adult, tachycardia is a resting heart rate of more than 100 beats per minute.)

Tachypnea (tak-ip-NEE-uh)
An abnormally rapid rate of breathing. An infant whose breathing rate is over 60 breaths per minute is experiencing tachypnea. (A newborn baby breathes at an approximate rate of 40 breaths per minute.) Tachypnea occurs when the infant is upset or excited, but can also be an indication of respiratory distress, heart disease, or infection.

Tactile (TAK-til)
Pertaining to touch.

Tactile Defensiveness
An abnormal sensitivity to touch, indicated by an infant's avoidance or rejection of touching and handling. The infant who has tactile defensiveness may resist touching or being touched by something that is wet, that is an unusual texture, or that is of an unfamiliar temperature or pressure. Tactile defensiveness may be the result of having difficulty with processing and discriminating tactile stimulation.

Tactile Discrimination
The ability to perceive the differences between various stimuli to the skin, either when touching objects or when being touched by someone or something.

Tailor Sitting
Sitting with the buttocks on the floor with the legs bent and feet crossed.

Talipes (TAL-i-peez)
Any deformity of the foot involving the talus (the foot bone that connects with the *tibia* and *fibula* to form the ankle).
Refer to **Clubfoot**.

Talipes Equinovalgus (TAL-i-peez ee-kwie-noe-VAL-guhs)
A form of *clubfoot* in which the foot is bent downward and the heel is elevated and turned outward (away from the midline of the body).
Refer to **Clubfoot**.

Talipes Equinovarus (TAL-i-peez ee-kwie-noe-VER-uhs)
A foot deformity (the most common form of *clubfoot*) in which the foot is twisted in an abnormal position of *plantar flexion*, *adduction*, and *inversion* (the foot is bent downward and inward, with the heel turned inward as well). Talipes equinovarus should be treated as soon as possible after birth in order to restore the foot to the normal position.
Refer to **Clubfoot**.

Talus (TAY-luhs)
The foot bone that connects with the tibia and fibula (the bones of the lower leg) to form the ankle.

Tandem Walking
Walking forward in a straight line with the heel of one foot touching the toe of the opposite foot. (Heel-to-toe walking.)

Tantrum
A normal behavior exhibited especially by children under three years of age that is typically caused by the child's inability to tolerate frustration. To some adults, yelling or crying angrily constitutes a tantrum. To others, lying on the floor kicking and screaming for a long period of time is a tantrum. Most adults find it difficult to deal with a child who is having a tantrum. An important first step is to try to determine if the behavior is internally motivated (the child may be venting her frustration over trying to cope with some aspect of her environment), or if the tantrum is externally motivated (the child has learned that she will get something she wants, or avoid something she does not want to do, if she throws a tantrum).

Tarsal (TAR-suhl)
Pertaining to the tarsus, or ankle.

Tarsus (TAR-suhs)
The seven bones that form the instep part of the foot and ankle.

Task Analysis
Dividing a task into steps. In this way it can be determined which steps toward task completion a child has mastered. For example, task analysis can be used to determine whether the infant can feed herself a cracker. The child will be observed as to which, if any, of the following steps she can perform: extend her arm, voluntarily grasp a cracker, bring the cracker to her mouth, gum or bite the cracker, swallow the cracker. Task analysis enables the caregiver or teacher to know which skills need to be taught.

Taste
The sense of perceiving and distinguishing between different flavors (sweet, salty, sour, and bitter) that come in contact with the tongue. (The sense of smell is needed to discriminate between subtle variations of the four flavors.) When the taste receptor cells (taste buds, which are found mainly on the tongue) receive taste sensations, they send nerve impulses to special taste centers in the brain.

Taste Buds
The small cells found primarily on the tongue that detect different flavors (sweet, sour, bitter, and salty). The taste buds that are sensitive to sweet tastes are located at the center of the tip of the tongue; the taste buds that are sensitive to sour tastes are located on the sides of the tongue, at the front; the taste buds that are sensitive to salty tastes are located on the sides of the tongue, in the middle and toward the back; and the taste buds that are sensitive to bitter tastes are located across the back of most of the tongue.

tax-
A prefix meaning arrange or order.

Tay Sachs Disease (tay-SAKS)
An *autosomal recessive* brain disorder characterized by *failure to thrive*, blindness, *seizures*, and progressive *paralysis*. These symptoms begin by the time the infant is six months old, and are caused by a deficiency of the *enzyme* hexosaminidase, which results in an accumulation of a material that damages the brain. Tay Sachs is a fatal disease that usually results in death by four years of age.
   *Also known as **Infantile Cerebral Sphingolipidosis**.*

TB, tb
The abbreviation for tuberculosis.

Tegretol™ (TEG-ri-tahl)
   *Refer to **Carbamazepine**.*

Temporal Lobe Seizure (TEM-por-uhl)
   *Refer to **Complex Partial Seizure**, **Partial Seizure**, and **Epilepsy**.*

Tendon
The fibrous cord of connective tissue in which the fibers of a muscle end and by which a muscle is attached to a bone or other structure.

Tendon Lengthening
A surgical procedure to release muscle *contractures*. An example of a tendon lengthening procedure is heelcord (achilles tendon) lengthening.

Tenotomy (tuh-NOT-uh-mee)
A surgical procedure that involves cutting the tendon to release muscle *contractures* or to lengthen shortened muscles. This allows for better movement of the joint.

Tension
The state of being stretched.

Tent
A tent erected over the patient's bed into which humidified air and/or oxygen, vaporized drugs, or a cool mist of water is passed to treat certain respiratory conditions. An *oxygen tent* is an example.

Teratogen (tuh-RAT-uh-juhn or TER-uh-tuh-juhn)
An agent that affects normal embryonic and fetal development, when the pregnant mother is exposed. This disruption may cause abnormalities in the fetus. Examples of teratogens include certain drugs, the *Rubella* virus, and X-rays. The various teratogens cause a wide range of birth defects, including *brain damage,* missing or defective limbs, heart defect, and blindness.

Terbutaline (ter-BYOO-tuh-leen)
A drug that relaxes the uterus in order to prevent premature labor. It is also a *bronchodilator drug* used to treat *asthma*.

Term Infant
Any newborn infant born between the beginning of the 38th week and the end of the 42nd week of gestation. Term infants usually measure from 48–53 centimeters (approximately 19–21 inches) in length, and weigh between 2700 and 4000 grams (approximately five pounds, 15 ounces to eight pounds, 13 ounces).

Testes (TES-teez)
Plural of testis.

Testis (TES-tis)
One of a pair of male gonads, or sex glands, which forms spermatozoa cells, necessary for reproduction. The testes are normally situated in the scrotum.
    Compare **Ovary.**

Tetanus (TET-uh-nuhs)

A potentially fatal *neurological disease* caused by infection of a wound with the bacterium Clostridium tetani. Tetanus is characterized by painful muscle spasms, stiffness of the jaw (which is why tetanus is sometimes referred to as "lockjaw"), and stiffness in other muscle groups. Tetanus can be prevented with a *vaccine* (it is the "T" part of the DPT vaccine) given during infancy and childhood. To maintain *immunity* in individuals who have not been wounded, a booster shot is necessary every ten years. Individuals with burns or cuts should have a booster if one has not been given in the last five years.

Tetracycline (tet-ruh-SIE-kleen)

An *antibiotic drug* used to treat many conditions. It should not be given to children under eight years of age or to pregnant women because tetracycline may discolor developing teeth and affect developing bone.

Tetralogy of Fallot (te-TRAL-uh-jee of fal-OE)

A *congenital* heart defect that is made up of four *anomalies*: a narrowed pulmonary valve, a hole in the ventricular septum (*ventricular septal defect*), malposition of the aorta, and enlargement (thickened wall) of the right ventricle. Tetralogy of Fallot results in insufficiently oxygenated blood being pumped from the heart to the rest of the body, which causes *cyanosis* (a blue color to the skin caused by a lack of oxygen in the bloodstream). Surgery is necessary to correct these heart defects.

Thalamus (THAL-uh-muhs)

A part of the *diencephalon* of the brain that functions as a relay station for most sensory impulses going to the brain.

Thalassemia (thal-uh-SEE-mee-uh)

A group of *autosomal recessive disorders* of abnormal hemoglobin production rate or synthesis which leads to *anemia*. If a child inherits the defective *gene* that causes thalassemia from one parent, the condition is called thalassemia minor, and the symptoms are few, if any. If a child inherits defective genes from both parents, the condition is called thalassemia major, and the symptoms include *anemia, jaundice, failure to thrive*, spleen enlargement, lack of normal growth, and, if left untreated, death. The symptoms of thalassemia major appear during the first three to six months of life. Treatment is with blood transfusions.

Thalassemia major is also known as **Cooley's Anemia**.

thel-

A prefix meaning nipple.

Theophylline (thee-OF-uh-lin or thee-oe-FIL-een)

A *bronchodilator drug*.

Therapeutic Blood Level (ther-uh-PYOO-tik)
The level at which a drug is most effective but not toxic. For example, the dose of an *antiepileptic drug* is adjusted so that a level which provides effective protection against *seizures,* but a minimum of adverse side effects, is maintained.

Therapy Roll
Refer to **Roll.**

therm-, thermo-
Prefixes meaning heat.

Thermogenesis (thur-moe-JEN-uh-sis)
The production of heat by the cells of the body.

Thermoregulation (thur-moe-reg-yuh-LAY-shuhn)
The body's control of heat production and heat loss (maintenance of normal body temperature).

Thioridazine (thie-oe-RID-uh-zeen)
An *antipsychotic drug.*

Thiothixene (thie-oe-THIKS-een)
An *antipsychotic drug.*

Thomas Heel™
A shoe modification (a piece added to the heel of the shoe) that helps keep the foot in correct alignment and body weight centered while walking.

Thoracic Cavity (thuh-RAS-ik)
The chest cavity.

thoraco-
A prefix meaning chest.

Thoraco-Lumbar-Sacral Orthosis (TLSO)
A *brace* that supports the spine and is worn to prevent spinal deformities, such as *scoliosis,* from worsening. The TLSO is often a molded plastic shell that keeps the spine in a straightened position.

Thorax (THOR-aks)
The chest.

Thorazine™ (THOR-uh-zeen)
Refer to **Chlorpromazine.**

Three-Day Measles
Refer to **Rubella.**

Three Point Position
Positioned on three limbs.

thromb-, thrombo-
Prefixes meaning clot or lump.

Thrombocyte (THROM-boe-site)
Refer to **Platelet**.

Thrombocytopenia (throm-boe-sie-tuh-PEE-nee-uh)
An abnormal blood condition characterized by a reduced number of platelets (due to a decreased production of the platelets or an increased rate of destruction of the platelets) that results in bleeding and easy bruising. While the underlying cause is often unknown, thrombocytopenia may be associated with another disease, result from a drug reaction, or occur as a response to a severe infection in which platelets are consumed as part of the process of coagulation.

Thrush
Infection of the oral cavity with the fungus Candida Albicans.
Refer to **Candida Albicans**.

Thyroid Gland (THIE-roid)
The gland located in the front of the neck, below the larynx. The thyroid gland, under control by the pituitary gland, secretes hormones that play an important part in controlling body metabolism.

Tibia (TIB-ee-uh)
The shin bone. (The other bone of the lower leg is the fibula.)

Tic
A repetitive, uncontrolled movement of a muscle or small muscle group caused by muscle contraction. Tics most often occur in the facial, shoulder, or arm muscles. Purposeless blinking is an example of a tic.

tid
The abbreviation for the Latin words meaning three times a day.

Time-Out
A method of disciplining the child who is behaving in an unacceptable manner. Time-out is an opportunity for the child to regain control over her actions, so she can resume playing or interacting with others in appropriate ways. Time-out is accomplished by removing the child to a quiet place (it should always be the same place, if possible) where she won't be distracted. It is important that the child does not become frightened by time-out. Time away from playing with peers, or from adult interaction, need not be long; under one minute is usually enough time for a toddler and up to five minutes for a five-year-old (or until the child is calm and appears ready to

rejoin the group). Some educators and caregivers feel that one minute per year of life is the appropriate length of a time-out.

TLSO
The abbreviation for thoraco-lumbar-sacral orthosis.

TM
The abbreviation for tympanic membrane.

TNR
The abbreviation for tonic neck reflex.

Tocolytic Drug (toe-koe-LIT-ik)
Any drug used to stop premature labor.

Toe Grasp
The grasping (curling under) movement of the toes in response to pressure to the sole, such as by touching the floor.

Toeing In
A turning inward of the foot caused by the foot, tibia (shin bone), and/or femur (thigh bone) turning inward.
   Also known as **Pigeon-Toed.**

Toeing Out
A turning outward of the foot caused by the foot, tibia (shin bone), or femur (thigh bone) turning outward or by flatfeet.
   Also known as **Duck-Feet.**

Toe-Off
The action of the foot when, during walking, it points downward, pushing off from the floor.

Toe Walking
Walking up on the toes rather than on the whole foot. Toe walking may be used by the child who develops *contractures* in the calf muscles and tendons and cannot place the whole foot on the floor. It can also be a sign of *muscular dystrophy.*

Tofranil™ (toe-FRAY-nil)
   Refer to **Imipramine.**

Tomography (tuh-MOG-ruh-fee)
   Refer to **CT Scanning.**

-tomy
A suffix meaning cutting.

Tone
Refer to **Tonus**, **Muscle Tone**, **Hypertonia**, *and* **Hypotonia**.

Tongue Protrusion Reflex
Refer to **Tongue Thrust**.

Tongue Thrust
The strong, involuntary (reflexive) protrusion of the tongue. Tongue thrust interferes with eating because food is pushed out of the mouth. It also creates dental problems because the tongue pushes against the back of the upper teeth. Children with some forms of *cerebral palsy* may exhibit this reflex. (The child with *Down syndrome* may have a protruding tongue, too, but this is not a tongue thrust. It is likely due to having a smaller mouth size with a more shallow roof, and/or due to having low muscle tone; it is not the result of the child having a too-large tongue. The child can learn to bring/keep her tongue in her mouth.)
Also known as **Tongue Protrusion Reflex**.

Tonic (TON-ik)
Having continuous muscular contraction.

Tonic-Clonic Seizure (TON-ik KLON-ik)
A form of *generalized seizure* that is named after the two phases involved in the seizure: the tonic phase and the clonic phase. Before a tonic-clonic seizure begins, the child may experience a warning called an *aura*. During the tonic phase there is usually loss of consciousness and the child falls to the floor. Her body stiffens, and she may experience irregular breathing and may drool and lose bladder control. The tonic phase usually lasts ten to thirty seconds and is followed immediately by the clonic phase. It is characterized by alternating rigidity and relaxation (jerking) of the muscles. After the clonic phase, the child is usually sleepy or disoriented, and may have a headache or other discomfort.
Also known as a **Grand Mal Seizure**.
Refer to **Epilepsy**.

Tonic Labyrinthine Reflex (TON-ik lab-uh-RIN-thin or lab-uh-RIN-theen or lab-uh-RIN-thine)
A normal reflex in the birth to four-month-old that is elicited by a change in position of the *labyrinth* inside the inner ear. (The labyrinth position is changed when the neck flexes or extends and the head moves.) Testing for the presence of this *primitive reflex* in an older child can be done while the child is lying on her back or on her stomach. While lying on her back with her neck in an extended position, the reflex is seen when the child's arms and legs extend and her shoulders pull back toward the surface on which she is lying (her shoulders retract). When the child is lying on her stomach with her neck in a flexed position, the reflex is seen when the child's arms, legs, and hips bend and the shoulders move forward (her shoulders

protract). In either position (lying on the back or on the stomach), an involuntary increase in *muscle tone*, even if there is no actual movement of the arms or legs to a new position, indicates that the reflex is present. A positive response beyond the age at which the reflex is normally present may be a sign of *brain damage*, such as occurs with *cerebral palsy*.

*Refer to **Primitive Reflex**.*

Tonic Neck Reflex (TNR)

*Refer to **Asymmetrical Tonic Neck Reflex** and **Symmetrical Tonic Neck Reflex**.*

Tonsil

One of two tissue masses located at each side of the back of the throat. The tonsils provide the first defense against *microorganisms* capable of producing respiratory disease.

Tonus (Tone) (TOE-nuhs)

The slight, continuous balanced contraction of muscles. For example, tonus is involved in the ability to maintain posture and to return blood to the heart.

TORCH-S

*Refer to **STORCH Infections**.*

tors-

A prefix meaning twist.

Torsion (TOR-shuhn)

The process of twisting or being turned.

Torticollis (tor-ti-KOL-is)

A condition in which the head tends to tilt to one side as a result of the muscles contracting on that side of the neck. It can be caused by injury to the nerves or muscles of the neck or be the result of a muscle spasm. It can also be caused by a high degree of *astigmatism* or by eye muscle *palsy* (partial *paralysis*).

*Also known as **Wryneck**.*

Total Anomalous Pulmonary Venous Return (uh-NOM-uh-luhs PUL-muh-ner-ee VEE-nuhs)

A *congenital* heart defect in which the pulmonary veins are unable to bring oxygenated blood back to the left side of the heart (and thus to the rest of the body) from the lungs.

*Also known as **Anomalous Pulmonary Venous Return**.*

Total Communication

A method of communicating by using a combination of any of the existing forms of communication, including facial expression, gesture, *sign language*, *fingerspelling*, lipreading, speech, writing, and augmentative communication devices.

Total Parenteral Nutrition (TPN) (puh-REN-tuhr-uhl)

The process of feeding a child fluids via an *intravenous catheter* (such as a central line which is threaded through a vein to the heart, or peripheral lines which are inserted into peripheral blood vessels such as those in the hands, feet, or scalp). The catheter is left in place (not removed and then replaced at each feeding), and an *infusion pump* regulates the flow of the fluids. Feeding (continuous infusion) may take place over 10 to 24 hours. The intravenous solution is called *hyperalimentation* and it can include sugar, amino acids, electrolytes, minerals, vitamins, and fats.

*Also known as **Central Venous Nutrition (CVN)**.*

Toxemia of Pregnancy (tok-SEE-mee-uh)

*Refer to **Pre-eclampsia**.*

Toxic

Poisonous.

Toxicology Screen (tok-si-KOL-uh-jee)

A test of urine or blood samples to determine the presence of drugs or alcohol.

*Refer to **Prenatally Exposed to Drugs**.*

Toxin

A poison produced by a plant, animal, or bacteria.

Toxoplasmosis (tok-soe-plaz-MOE-sis)

A common infection caused by the *microorganism* Toxoplasma gondii. The infection is harmless in an immunologically intact individual, except when transmitted by the pregnant woman to her fetus through the placenta (especially early in the pregnancy). This condition, known as *congenital* toxoplasmosis, may result in miscarriage or stillbirth. The infant who survives may have a premature birth, *low birth weight, jaundice,* an enlarged liver and spleen, *brain damage, hydrocephalus, seizures,* blindness, *microcephaly,* and *mental retardation.* Congenital toxoplasmosis can be fatal to the infant. Toxoplasmosis is also a serious infection in people who have an immune system disorder, such as *AIDS.* Toxoplasmosis may be contracted by eating undercooked meat or eggs of animals containing the microorganism, or by coming in contact with an infected cat or with animal feces.

TPN

The abbreviation for total parenteral nutrition.

TPR

The abbreviation for temperature, pulse, respiration.

Trach (trayk)
An informal word for *tracheostomy* or tracheal tube.

Trachea (TRAY-kee-uh)
The tube that extends from the larynx (voice box) downward toward the lungs, dividing into the two bronchi of the lungs. The trachea functions as the passageway for air in and out of the body for breathing.
Also known as the **Windpipe***.*

Tracheal Catheter (TRAY-kee-uhl)
A *catheter* used to remove mucus from the trachea by a machine that applies suction.

Tracheal Tube
A tube placed into the opening created by a *tracheostomy*.
Refer to **Tracheostomy***.*

tracheo-
A prefix meaning windpipe.

Tracheoesophageal Fistula (tray-kee-oe-ee-sof-uh-JEE-uhl FIS-chuh-luh)
A birth defect in which the baby is born with an abnormal passage that connects the trachea (the windpipe) and the esophagus (the tube that carries food from the throat to the stomach). The fistula causes the baby to cough and become cyanotic (develop a blue color to the skin due to a lack of oxygen in the bloodstream) when attempting to swallow saliva. It also causes the baby to regurgitate food. Food may also enter the infant's lungs, causing her to develop *aspiration pneumonia*. This type of birth defect can be corrected surgically.
Refer to **Fistula***.*

Tracheostomy (tray-kee-OS-tuh-mee)
A surgical procedure in which an opening is made through the base of the throat and into the trachea to create an airway. A *tracheal tube* (the tube through which the child breathes) is inserted into the opening and the child will then either breathe room air, or, if she cannot breathe without assistance, have her tube connected to a *ventilator*.
Compare **Tracheotomy***.*

Tracheotomy (tray-kee-OT-uh-mee)
Cutting into the trachea to create an airway, usually below a blockage in the trachea.
Compare **Tracheostomy***.*

Traction (TRAK-shuhn)
A pulling force to hold two body parts in the correct position relative to each other, or to correct their alignment. Traction involves the use of tension to immobilize the body parts being treated.

Tranquilizer Drug
A drug that has a sedative (calming) effect.

trans-
A prefix meaning across or through.

Transfer
1. To move an object held in one hand to the other hand. The ability to transfer an object from one hand to the other emerges around six to seven months of age.
2. To move from one position to another, such as from a wheelchair to bed.

Transition
The purposeful, organized process of helping children who are at-risk or have developmental disabilities move from one program to the next, such as from the hospital to home or from an infant development program to a preschool program for children with special needs. The child's parents and *multidisciplinary team* are involved in the process of selecting the program/class that would best meet the child's needs and in preparing for the change.

Translocation (tranz-loe-KAY-shuhn)
*Refer to **Chromosomal Translocation**.*

Translocation Trisomy 21
The attachment of an extra (a third) *chromosome* 21 to another chromosome.
*Refer to **Down Syndrome**.*

Transposition of the Great Vessels (tranz-poe-ZI-shuhn)
A *congenital* heart defect in which the aorta and pulmonary artery are attached to the wrong ventricles, resulting in an insufficient amount of oxygenated blood being delivered to the body and oxygenated blood returning to the lungs. This defect must be repaired surgically. Once corrected, the child should be able to live an active life.

Tranxene™ (TRAN-zeen)
*Refer to **Benzodiazepine**.*

Trauma
A physical injury caused by external force (such as a car accident or an act of violence) or a severe emotional shock.

Treacher Collins Syndrome

An *autosomal dominant disorder* characterized by a flattening of the cheek bones, an underdeveloped jaw, external ear malformation, *congenital* hearing loss, lower eyelid *coloboma* (a defect in which there is a space, or cleft, of part of the eyelid), *cleft palate*, scalp hair growth on the cheek, and respiratory problems. The child usually has normal intelligence.

Tremor

Involuntary, rhythmic, quivering movements caused by the contraction and relaxation of a group of muscles.

tri-

A prefix meaning three.

Triceps (TRIE-seps)

The muscle on the back of the upper arm. The triceps straightens the elbow.

tricho-

A prefix meaning hair or hairlike.

Tricuspid Atresia (trie-KUS-pid uh-TREE-zhuh)

A *congenital* heart defect in which the *tricuspid valve* (the valve between the right atrium and the right ventricle) has failed to develop. This leaves no opening from the right atrium to the right ventricle. Without the valve, blood cannot flow through the normal route to the lungs to become oxygenated. Surgery is required to repair this condition.

Tricuspid Valve

One of four valves in the heart that open and close with each heart beat to control the flow of blood. Blood exits each chamber of the heart through one of the valves. The tricuspid valve is located between the right atrium and the right ventricle of the heart. The three cusps (small flaps) of the tricuspid valve close during each heart beat to prevent blood from flowing back into the right atrium.

Compare **Aortic Valve, Mitral Valve,** *and* **Pulmonary Valve.**

Trifluoperazine (trie-floo-oe-PER-uh-zeen)

An *antipsychotic drug.*

Trimester (TRIE-mes-tuhr or trie-MES-tuhr)

One of the three periods into which pregnancy is divided. Each trimester is approximately three months long.

Refer to **Gestation.**

Trimethadione (trie-meth-uh-DIE-oen)

An *antiepileptic drug.*

Trimethoprim (trie-METH-uh-prim)
An *antibacterial drug.*

Triploid (TRIP-loid)
Having three sets of *chromosomes.*
   Compare **Diploid.**

Trisomy (TRIE-soe-mee)
The presence of an extra (a third) of a particular numbered *chromosome*
within the body's cells. (Normally, there is a pair of each numbered
chromosome.) A trisomy can occur if there is an extra chromosome in either
the egg or sperm cell that is involved in fertilization. A trisomy can also
occur as a result of a *translocation* of *genetic* material that is passed on from
parent to child. The most common trisomy is Trisomy 21 (*Down syndrome*).

Trisomy 13
The presence of a third *chromosome* number 13 in the cells of the body. This
results in a child with a *genetic* disorder characterized by severe brain malformation, *seizures, deafness, cleft lip* and/or *palate, mental retardation,* and
heart defect. Fewer than 20 percent of children with Trisomy 13 live beyond
one year of age.
   Also known as **Patau Syndrome.**
   Refer to **Trisomy.**

Trisomy 18
The presence of a third *chromosome* number 18 in the cells of the body. This
results in a child with a *genetic* disorder characterized by *failure to thrive*;
growth deficiency; *hypertonia*; facial, hand, and feet *anomalies*; severe *mental
retardation*; and heart defects. Only 10 percent of children with Trisomy 18
live beyond one year of age.
   Also known as **Edward Syndrome.**
   Refer to **Trisomy.**

Trisomy 21
   Refer to **Down Syndrome.**

trop-, tropi-
Prefixes meaning turning toward.

-trophic
A suffix meaning nourishment.

Trophic (TROF-ik)
Pertaining to nutrition or food.

-trophy
A suffix meaning nurture or nutrition.

Trunk Rotation

The ability to turn and twist the trunk. Trunk rotation is a necessary skill for walking.

Tuberculosis (TB or tb) (too-bur-kyoo-LOE-sis)

An infectious disease caused by the bacterium Mycobacterium Tuberculosis, which is transmitted by airborne droplets. Tuberculosis causes scarring of or damage to the lungs and, if the primary infection is not healed, can spread to the lymph nodes or other organs. Because the lungs are typically affected, the infection is symptomized by coughing and lung disease, and can be fatal. Tuberculosis can be prevented by administering a *vaccine* and by monitoring people who have had contact with someone who has the disease.

*Also known as **TB**.*

Tuberous Sclerosis (TOO-bur-uhs skluh-ROE-sis)

An *autosomal dominant disorder* characterized by lesions on the skin and of the brain, eyes, and kidneys; *seizures*; and often *mental retardation*. The lesions and seizures tend to develop during the early childhood years.

Tunnel Vision

A condition affecting the eyes in which the *visual field* is constricted, giving the impression of looking through a tunnel (only straight-ahead vision is possible). Tunnel vision may be caused by *glaucoma*, a disorder of the brain and optic nerve, or *retinitis pigmentosa*.

Turbinate Bone (TUR-bi-nayt)

*Refer to **Concha**.*

Turner Syndrome

A *chromosomal disorder* caused by the absence of an X chromosome in all or some of a child's body cells. Turner syndrome is characterized by *short stature*, *webbing* of the skin of the neck, a broad chest with underdeveloped breasts and widely spaced nipples, infertility, eye abnormalities such as *ptosis* (drooping of the eyelid) and *strabismus* (a condition in which the eyes do not work together), bone abnormalities, including deformity of the elbow in which it deviates away from the midline of the body (as seen when the arm is extended and the palm is facing forward), and occasionally *mental retardation* and *coarctation of the aorta* (a heart defect that causes the heart to work harder than normal). Turner syndrome only affects females.

*Also known as **XO Syndrome**.*

Twister Cables

Cable-type devices that extend from a pelvic band to the child's shoes or short leg braces to assist the child with walking. The cables help control leg rotation, a problem common to some *neurological disorders*.

Tympanic Membrane™ (tim-PAN-ik)
The fibrous membrane that carries sound vibrations to the inner ear via the bones of the middle ear. It is located at the innermost end of the ear canal (the ear canal leads inward from the outer ear) and separates it from the middle ear.
*Also known as the **Eardrum**.*

Tympanometer (tim-puh-NOM-uh-tuhr)
An electrical instrument which measures changes in the pressure and mobility of the eardrum to detect middle ear fluid.
*Refer to **Impedance Audiometry**.*

Tympanometry (tim-puh-NOM-uh-tree)
*Refer to **Impedance Audiometry**.*

Tympanostomy Tube (tim-puh-NOS-tuh-mee)
*Refer to **Ear Tube**.*

Tympanum (TIM-puh-nuhm)
The cavity of the middle ear.

Tyrosine (TIE-roe-seen or TIE-roe-sin or tie-ROE-sin)
An *amino acid*. When the body is unable to convert phenylalanine (another amino acid) to tyrosine (due to a defective enzyme), the disorder *PKU* results.

UAC
The abbreviation for umbilical artery catheter.
Refer to **Umbilical Catheter**.

UAL
The abbreviation for umbilical artery line.
Refer to **Umbilical Catheter**.

UE
The abbreviation for upper extremity.

Ulcer
An open sore on the skin or on a mucous membrane. An ulcer may be small and shallow or deep and crater-like. Ulcers are caused by tissue death resulting from an inflammation, infection, decreased blood supply (usually to a limb), constant pressure to an area, or *malignancy*.

Ulna (UL-nuh)
The long bone on the little finger (fifth finger) side of the forearm, extending from the elbow to the wrist. It is the larger of the two lower arm bones. (The other bone is the radius.)

Ulnar (UL-nuhr)
Pertaining to the side of the hand and arm nearest the little finger (fifth finger).

Ulnar Palmar Grasp
Grasp of an object using the ring finger and little finger and the palm of the hand. The ulnar palmar grasp usually develops around four months of age.
Refer to **Grasp**.

ultra-
A prefix meaning beyond or excess.

Ultrasonography (ul-truh-suh-NOG-ruh-fee)
Refer to **Ultrasound Scanning**.

Ultrasound Scanning
A diagnostic procedure in which echoes of high frequency sound waves produce a picture of internal organs or of a fetus in the uterus.
Also known as **Ultrasonography** *and* **Sonography**.

Umbilical Catheter (uhm-BIL-i-kuhl)
A *catheter* (tube) placed in a blood vessel in the baby's *umbilicus*.
Refer to **Catheter**.

Umbilical Hernia

A common condition in newborn infants in which there is a soft protrusion of bowel or *peritoneum* at the *umbilicus* caused by a weakness in the abdominal wall. Umbilical hernias usually disappear around two years of age, although sometimes they remain throughout life.

Umbilicus (um-BIL-i-kuhs or um-bi-LIE-kuhs)

The site on the abdomen where the umbilical cord was attached.
  *Also known as the **Navel**.*

Umbrella Stroller

A stroller that has a hammock-type seat. The umbrella stroller is useful with the child who stiffens into extension and needs to be in a more flexed position, as well as with the child who has low *muscle tone* and needs some support of his head and trunk.

Undescended Testes

A condition in which one or both of the testes have not moved down into the scrotum.
  *Also known as **Cryptorchidism**.*

uni-

A prefix meaning one.

Unifactorial Disorder

A disorder caused by a defective *gene* or gene pair. Unifactorial *genetic* disorders are classified as either autosomal disorders (the defective gene is on one of the 22 pairs of *autosomes*) or X-linked (the defective gene is on the *sex chromosomes*).
  *Compare **Multifactorial Disorder** and **Chromosomal Abnormality**.*
  *Refer to **Autosomal Dominant Disorder**, **Autosomal Recessive Disorder**, **X-Linked Dominant Disorder**, and **X-Linked Recessive Disorder**.*

Unilateral

Affecting or occurring on only one side of the body.

Unilateral Hearing Impairment

Hearing impairment in only one ear.

Unilateral Reaching

Reaching with only one arm.

UO

The abbreviation for of undetermined origin.

Upper GI

  *Refer to **Barium Swallow**.*

Upper Respiratory Infection (URI)

A cold, or any infection affecting the nose, throat, sinuses, ears, and larynx (voice box).

Compare **Lower Respiratory Infection.**

ure-

A prefix meaning urine.

Urea (yoo-REE-uh)

A substance produced in the liver. It is the chief end-product of nitrogen metabolism.

Refer to **Uremia.**

Uremia (yoo-REE-mee-uh)

A condition in which an excessive amount of *urea* is in the blood. It is a sign of kidney failure.

Ureter (YOOR-uh-tuhr or yoo-REE-tuhr)

One of two tubes (one per kidney) that transport urine from the kidneys to the bladder. The ureters are located behind the abdominal organs.

Urethra (yoo-REE-thruh)

The tube leading from the bladder through which urine is excreted from the body.

URI

The abbreviation for upper respiratory infection.

uri-, uric-, urico-

Prefixes meaning uric acid.

-uria

A suffix meaning urine.

Uric Acid

A crystalline compound found in urine.

Urinary Catheter

Refer to **Urinary Catheterization** *and* **Catheter.**

Urinary Catheterization

A procedure in which a *catheter* is inserted through the urethra into the bladder to drain urine.

Refer to **Catheter.**

urino-, uro-

Prefixes meaning urine.

Urologist (yoo-ROL-uh-jist)
A doctor who specializes in the care of the urinary tract in males and females, and of the male genital tract. The urologist treats urinary tract diseases.

Urticaria (ur-ti-KAR-ee-uh)
A skin condition characterized by an itchy, white rash with central swelling, surrounded by red inflammation. It is usually caused by an allergic reaction, but often the cause is unknown. Attempts to pinpoint the cause should be made so that it can be avoided. Treatment with antihistamines often gives the best symptomatic relief.
Also known as **Hives**.

Usher's Syndrome
An *autosomal recessive disorder* characterized by hearing loss and *retinitis pigmentosa*. The progressive hearing loss is evident at four to six years of age and the progressive visual impairment (which may lead to blindness) is evident by nine years of age.

utero-
A prefix meaning uterus.

Uterus (YOO-tuhr-uhs)
The female organ located in the pelvis between the bladder and the rectum. It is within the uterus that the fetus develops.
Also known as the **Womb**.

UTI
The abbreviation for urinary tract infection.

UVC
The abbreviation for umbilical venous catheter.
Refer to **Umbilical Catheter**.

UVL
The abbreviation for umbilical venous line.
Refer to **Umbilical Catheter**.

Uvula (YOO-vyoo-luh)
The tissue hanging from the middle of the back of the mouth (from the edge of the soft palate). It assists in closing the nasal cavity during the production of certain speech sounds.

Vaccination (vak-si-NAY-shuhn)
Refer to **Immunization**.

Vaccine (vak-SEEN)
A solution containing a killed or weakened bacteria or virus, given to boost the body's *immunity* (resistance) against an infectious disease caused by the bacteria or virus. Most vaccines are given by injection.

Valgus (VAL-guhs)
A bending or twisting outward of a body part, such as the lower leg in *genu valgum* (knock-knee).

Validity
The extent to which a test instrument measures what it is designed to measure.

Valium™
Refer to **Diazepam**.

Valproic Acid
An *antiepileptic drug*.

Valvuloplasty (VAL-vyoo-loe-plas-tee)
A surgical procedure to repair or reconstruct a heart valve.

Vancomycin (VAN-koe-mie-sin)
An *antibiotic drug* used to treat infections, primarily *staphylococcal* infections resistant to other antibiotics.

Varicella (var-i-SEL-uh)
Refer to **Chicken Pox**.

Varus (VAY-ruhs)
A bending or twisting inward of a body part, such as the lower leg in *genu varum* (bowleg).

vas-, vaso-
Prefixes meaning vessel.

Vascular (VAS-kyuh-luhr)
Pertaining to vessels.

VCUG
The abbreviation for voiding cystourethrogram.

VD
The abbreviation for venereal disease.

Vein
A blood vessel carrying non-oxygenated blood from the body to the right side of the heart. The two exceptions to this are the pulmonary veins, which carry oxygenated blood from the lungs to the left side of the heart, and the portal vein, which transports blood from the intestines to the liver.

Velum (VEE-luhm)
Refer to Soft Palate.

Vena Cava (VEE-nuh KAY-vuh)
One of two large veins that return deoxygenated blood from the body to the right atrium of the heart. The two venae cavae are called the inferior vena cava (which returns blood to the heart from the parts of the body below the diaphragm) and the superior vena cava (which returns blood to the heart from the diaphragm and the parts of the body above the diaphragm).

Venae Cavae
Plural of vena cava.

vene-
A prefix meaning vein.

Venereal Disease (VD) (vuh-NEER-ee-uhl)
Refer to Sexually Transmitted Disease.

Venous (VEE-nuhs)
Of or pertaining to the veins.

Venous Catheter/Venous Line
A *catheter* placed in a vein to give nutrients, medication, or blood, or to withdraw blood.
Refer to Catheter.

Ventilation
The part of respiration that includes inhalation and exhalation.

Ventilation Tube
Refer to Ear Tube.

Ventilator
A mechanical device used to provide assisted breathing for the child who cannot breathe on his own. The ventilator pumps humidified air (with a measured amount of oxygen) into the lungs via an *endotracheal tube* or *tracheostomy tube*. The elasticity of the lungs allows the air to be expelled.
Also known as a Respirator or a Life Support Machine.

Ventral (VEN-truhl)
Relating to a position toward the front of the body.
Also known as **Anterior.**
Compare **Dorsal.**

Ventral Suspension
A position of holding an infant horizontally in the air (supporting her around the trunk) with her face downward. The infant is held in this position to observe the degree to which she can hold up her head, and, then later as she develops, her back, hips, and legs.

Ventricle
A small chamber, as in the ventricles of the heart or the ventricles of the brain. The heart has two ventricles, or pumping (lower) chambers. (The two upper chambers are the atria.) Blood flows from the atria to the ventricles, where it is then pumped to the lungs and the rest of the body. The brain has four ventricles. It is within the ventricles of the brain that *cerebrospinal fluid* is made and circulated.

Ventricular Septal Defect (VSD) (ven-TRIK-yuh-luhr)
A heart defect in which there is an abnormal opening in the wall (the septum) that separates the right and left ventricles. Depending on the size of the hole (which typically allows blood to leak through from the left ventricle to the right ventricle), the heart may ultimately be forced to work harder to pump blood to the rest of the body. A large hole may need to be corrected surgically, but a small hole may close on its own.

Ventriculitis (ven-trik-yuh-LIE-tuhs)
An infection of the ventricles in the brain, sometimes associated with *spina bifida.*

Ventriculoatrial Shunt (ven-trik-yuh-loe-AY-tree-uhl)
A diversion to drain excess *cerebrospinal fluid* from the ventricles of the brain via a *catheter* that runs from the ventricles through the skull, down the outside of the skull (under the scalp) to the jugular vein in the neck and into the right atrium of the heart, where it joins the bloodstream.
Compare **Ventriculojugular Shunt** *and* **Ventriculoperitoneal Shunt.**
Refer to **Shunt.**

Ventriculojugular Shunt (ven-trik-yuh-loe-JUG-yuh-luhr)
A diversion to drain excess *cerebrospinal fluid* from the ventricles of the brain via a *catheter* that runs from the ventricles through the skull, down the outside of the skull (under the scalp) to the jugular vein in the neck, where it joins the bloodstream.

Ventriculoperitoneal Shunt (VP Shunt) (ven-trik-yuh-loe-per-i-toe-NEE-uhl)

A diversion to drain excess *cerebrospinal fluid* from the ventricles of the brain via a *catheter* that runs from the ventricles through the skull, down the outside of the skull (under the scalp), along the neck and chest (under the skin) and into the abdomen, where it is absorbed by the peritoneum (the membrane lining the abdominal cavity and covering the abdominal organs).

Compare **Ventriculoatrial Shunt**.
Refer to **Shunt**.

Venule (VEN-yool)

One of many small blood vessels that join together to form *veins*. Venules receive deoxygenated blood from *capillaries* and carry it on to the veins.

Verbalize

To express words vocally.
Compare **Vocalize**.

Vernix (VUR-niks)

The pale, fatty substance that protects the fetus's skin and insulates the baby *in utero*.

Vertebra (VUR-tuh-bruh)

Any of the 33 bones that form the spine (spinal column). The first seven vertebrae form the cervical spine (in the neck area). The first cervical vertebra is called the atlas and the second cervical vertebra is called the axis. These two vertebrae enable the head to turn. The next 12 vertebrae form the thoracic spine (in the chest area). The next five vertebrae form the lumbar spine (in the lower back area). The next five vertebrae are fused together and form the sacrum. The last four vertebrae are fused together and form the coccyx (the tailbone). The vertebrae are separated by spongy disks called intervertebral disks.

Refer to **Spinal Column**.

Vertebrae (VUR-tuh-bray)

Plural of vertebra.

Vertebral Column

Refer to **Spinal Column**.

Vertex Presentation (VUR-teks)

The birth (delivery) of a baby in which the top of the head emerges first. (The fetus is lying in the uterus with her head downward.)
Refer to **Fetal Presentation**.

Vertical Talus

Refer to **Congenital Rocker-Bottom Foot**.

Vertigo (VUR-ti-goe or vur-TIE-goe)
A feeling that one's surroundings, or one's own body, is spinning. Vertigo is caused by a disturbance of the vestibular apparatus contained in the *labyrinth* (inner ear).

Vesicle
1. A small sac within the body that contains liquid.
2. A small blister that contains clear fluid.

vesico-
A prefix meaning bladder.

Vesicostomy (ves-uh-KOS-tuh-mee)
A surgically created opening of the bladder and abdomen through which urine can drain. This procedure is done if *urinary catheterization* is not useful in resolving the problem of a *neurogenic bladder*.
   Also known as a **Cutaneous Vesicostomy**.

Vesicoureteral Reflux (ves-i-koe-yoo-REE-tuhr-uhl)
A condition in which urine flows back from the bladder into the ureter or ureters and sometimes up as far as the kidney. It may be due to blockage in the urinary tract, which may be a *congenital* condition, or may be caused by a urinary infection. It may occur due to an anatomic abnormality or secondary to infection not related to blockage. Persistent urinary reflux can cause kidney damage.
   Refer to **Reflux**.

Vesiculation (vuh-sik-yuh-LAY-shuhn)
The presence or formation of vesicles (small sacs that contain liquid).

Vestibular (ves-TIB-yoo-luhr)
Pertaining to the sensory system (the vestibular apparatus), located in the inner ear, that responds to the position of the head in relation to gravity and to movement. This sensory system allows the body to maintain balance and to enjoyably participate in movement such as swinging and roughhousing.

Vestibular Apparatus
   Refer to **Labyrinth**.

Vestibular Board
A large platform on rockers that may be used as a *vestibular stimulation* exercise to encourage the development of the child's balance reactions. The child is placed on her abdomen on the board, which is then tilted, changing the child's body position in space.

Vestibular Stimulation

An activity that stimulates the vestibular apparatus (the structures contained in the inner ear that provide the sense of balance) and helps the child develop awareness of her body position while moving in space, as well as her balance reactions. Examples of vestibular stimulation include rocking on a *vestibular board* and swinging.

Refer to **Labyrinth**.

Vestibulocochlear Nerve (ves-tib-yoo-loe-KOK-lee-uhr)

Refer to **Auditory Nerve**.

Viable (VIE-uh-buhl)

Capable of sustaining life outside of the uterus.

Vibrotactile Hearing Aid (vie-broe-TAK-til)

A device used with hearing impaired children that changes sound stimuli to vibratory stimuli. The vibration is transmitted to the inside of the wrist. This type of hearing aid helps the child with total hearing loss to feel the rhythm, or pattern, of speech. (The child with no measurable hearing does not benefit from regular hearing aids, which make sound louder.)

Compare **Hearing Aid**.

Refer to **Auditory Impairment**.

Vineland Adaptive Behavior Scales

A standardized evaluation tool used to assess the communication skills, daily living skills, socialization skills, fine motor skills, and gross motor skills of the birth to 30–year-old. Typically, the Vineland is administered by a professional with a minimum of a college degree. A parent interview format is used.

Formerly known as the **Vineland Social Maturity Scale**.

Vineland Social Maturity Scale

Refer to **Vineland Adaptive Behavior Scales**.

Virus (VIE-ruhs)

The tiniest of known infectious organisms that is obligated to live inside body cells. Viruses invade the body in several ways, including through airborne droplets which are inhaled, through contaminated food sources, through an insect or animal bite, through a needle, through the *conjunctiva* of the eye, and through direct contact with the membranes lining the genital tract during sexual intercourse. A virus may cause nuisance infections, such as the common cold, or serious infections, such as *AIDS*, or anything in between. For the most part, there is no treatment for viral infections, except to alleviate discomfort.

Also known as a **Germ**.

Compare **Bacteria**.

Viscera (VIS-uhr-uh)
1. A term that collectively refers to the internal organs, especially the abdominal organs.
2. Plural of viscus.

Viscus (VIS-kuhs)
Any large internal organ, especially in the abdomen.

Vision
The sense of sight. Vision is a process involving both the eyes and the brain. For vision to occur, light waves from the object being viewed must enter through the pupil of the eye. The cornea and the lens make it possible to focus the light waves at precisely the right spot (thus forming an image) on the retina. The retina then transmits the visual data via the optic nerves to the brain. Lastly, the vision center of the brain analyzes the data in order to interpret a visual image. Because some of the optic nerve fibers cross over in the brain, both sides of the brain normally receive information from both eyes. The measurement of normal vision is 20/20, which means that the eye can see at a distance of 20 feet (this is the numerator, or first "20") what the normal eye is supposed to see at 20 feet (this is the denominator, or second "20"). Visual impairment may occur if there is damage to the eye, to the optic nerve or nerve pathways that connect the optic nerves to the brain, or to the brain itself.
Refer to **Eye** *and* **Blindness**.

Vision Therapist
A specialist who works with people with visual impairment to help them learn to use their remaining vision as effectively as possible.

Visual Acuity
The ability of the eye to see clearly, specifically to perceive objects and to distinguish detail within central (straight-ahead) vision. It is expressed in 20/x terms, such as 20/20, 20/80, or 20/200 (meaning that at 20 feet, the eye can see as well as an eye with normal acuity can see at the distance expressed by the denominator).
Refer to **Vision**.

Visual Evoked Potential
A procedure to test vision that involves recording the brain's response to visual stimulation via *electrodes* placed on the head. This procedure is useful for testing the vision of infants and nonverbal children.

Visual Field
The total area that can be seen without moving the eyes or head. More area can be seen by the visual fields to either side of central vision than can be seen by the visual fields above and below central vision.

Visual Field Defect
A defect in an area of vision that moves with the eye, as the eye turns in different directions. A visual field defect may be caused by brain damage, optic nerve damage, injury to the eye, or disease of the eye.

Visual Learner
Referring to a person who learns best by what she sees, especially compared to what she hears. For example, the visual learner responds better to watching a demonstration of a task, such as stacking blocks, rather than to listening to an explanation of how it is done.

Visual-Motor Coordination
The ability to successfully engage in activity that involves both visual and motor skills, such as putting a puzzle piece into a puzzle board.

Visual Regard
The act of looking or gazing.

Visual Response Audiometry (VRA)
A method of testing an infant's hearing in which a visual reinforcer (such as a toy that lights up) is activated each time the baby turns her head to sound stimulation. This type of hearing test can be used with infants as young as six months of age.
   Also known as **Conditioned Orientation Reflex.**

Visual Sequential Memory
The ability to remember a sequence of pictures that is seen.

Visual Tracking
Following a moving object with the eyes.

Vital Capacity
The volume of air one can take in with maximum inhalation.

Vital Signs
Body temperature, heart rate, blood pressure, and rate of breathing.

Vitamin
One of many complex chemical nutrients needed in small amounts for normal bodily functions and maintenance of health. Vitamins are obtained through the diet and sometimes through vitamin supplements. Vitamins are classified as either fat-soluble vitamins (these include vitamins A, D, E, and K), which are absorbed with fats and stored, or water-soluble (these include vitamins C, B_{12}, and the B-complex vitamins), which are stored in the body for a short length of time and then excreted in the urine. (The exception is vitamin B_{12}, which the body stores for a longer period of time.)

Vitreous Body (VIT-ree-uhs)
Refer to **Vitreous Humor**.

Vitreous Humor
The gel-like substance of the eye located between the lens and the retina (the area within the inside of the eyeball).
Refer to **Eye**.

Vocalize
To produce consonant or vowel speech sounds, but not necessarily actual words.
Compare **Verbalize**.

Voice Disorders
Conditions that result in abnormal phonation (speech sounds), such as excessive hoarseness, a nasal voice, a high-pitched voice, or a too soft voice.

Voiding Cystourethrography (VCUG)
Refer to **Cystourethrography**.

Volar (VOE-luhr)
Pertaining to the palm or the sole.

Vomer (VOE-muhr)
The bone that forms part of the nasal septum (wall) separating the two sides of the nose.

von Recklinghausen Disease (von REK-ling-hou-zen)
Refer to **Neurofibromatosis**.

Vowel
One of the letters of the alphabet that is not a consonant. The vowels include a, e, i, o, u. (Sometimes y functions as a vowel.) Vowels are produced when air flows over the vocal cords and through the mouth. (Air flow is not obstructed as it is when producing consonant sounds.) Vowels are produced at the front of the mouth or at the back of the mouth, and are produced with the tongue in various (high and low) positions. Vowel sounds that are produced at the back of the mouth are the easiest (and thus the first) sounds a baby makes (other than crying). For example, the /o/ sound in "hot" is a low back vowel and the /i/ sound in "hit" is a high front vowel. Vowels are also described as being open vowel sounds (such as "aah") or closed vowel sounds (such as "ee"). *Diphthongs* are the last vowel sounds a baby produces.
Compare **Consonant**.

VP Shunt
The abbreviation for ventriculoperitoneal shunt.

VRA
The abbreviation for Visual Response Audiometry.

VSD
The abbreviation for ventricular septal defect.

Waardenburg Syndrome
An *autosomal dominant disorder* characterized by wide spacing between the eyes, partial *albinism* (a white hair forelock, decreased pigmentation of the skin, and *isochromic* eyes), a wide and high nose bridge, and sometimes *congenital* deafness.

Walker
An ambulation (walking) aid used with children who can balance independently while in a standing position. Walkers come with or without wheels and are either pushed or lifted and placed.

Walking Reflex
*Refer to **Stepping Reflex**.*

Wall-Eye
*Refer to **Exotropia**.*

Waterston Shunt™
A type of *shunt* placed between the ascending aorta and the right pulmonary artery. It functions to allow increased pulmonary circulation in cyanotic heart disease such as *tetralogy of Fallot*, which involves a narrowed pulmonary valve.

WBC
The abbreviation for white blood cell.

WDWN
The abbreviation for well-developed, well-nourished.

Webbing
A *congenital anomaly* in which there is a membrane or flap of skin between two or more adjoining fingers or toes. Webbing can also occur on the neck.

Wechsler Preschool and Primary Scale of Intelligence-Revised (WPPSI-R)
A standardized test used to evaluate the intelligence (verbal and performance skills) of the two- to six-and-one-half-year-old. This test may be used as an indicator of academic readiness. Typically, it is administered by a professional who holds a Ph.D. in psychology or education.

Wedge
A wedge-shaped platform, usually made of foam, that assists the child in maintaining correct positioning while *prone*. The child is placed on the wedge on his abdomen with his head and arms over the thicker (higher)

end. In this position he is able to work on his head control and his *weight bearing* on his hands and arms.

Weight Bearing
To support some or all of the weight of the body while in various positions, such as on the hands while *prone,* or on the feet while standing.

Weight Shifting
Moving the placement of weight from one body part to another. Examples include shifting weight from one hand to the other while *prone* in order to grasp a toy, or shifting weight from one foot to the other while walking. Weight shifting involves movement that changes the body's center of gravity.

Welfare
*Refer to **Department of Public Social Services**.*

Werdnig-Hoffmann Disease (VERD-nig HOF-muhn)
The most severe form of *spinal muscular atrophy* (a *neuromuscular disorder*), characterized by increasing weakness and floppiness, lack of stretch reflexes, and *paralysis,* especially of the trunk and limbs. The lack of muscle control associated with Werdnig-Hoffmann Disease results from degeneration of the motor *neurons* in the spinal cord, but the cause of the actual degeneration is unknown. This disease usually results in death in early life.
*Also known as **Infantile Muscular Atrophy**.*

Wernicke's Aphasia
*Refer to **Aphasia**.*

Wheezing
A whistling, rattling, noisy sound made during breathing, caused by air flowing through narrowed airways.

White Blood Cell (WBC)
One of three types of blood cells. They protect the body by destroying harmful or foreign substances such as bacteria, viruses, and fungi.
*Also known as a **Leukocyte**.*

Whooping Cough (HOOP-ing kof)
*Refer to **Pertussis**.*

WIC
The abbreviation for the Women, Infants, and Children Program.

Williams Syndrome
A sporadically-occurring *congenital* disorder characterized by small size, mild *microcephaly, epicanthal folds* (vertical skin folds at the inner corners of

the eyes), prominent lips, heart *anomalies*, a hoarse voice, and mild *mental retardation*.

Windpipe
Refer to **Trachea**.

Withdrawal Position
Simultaneous flexion (bending and bringing together) of the arms and legs while supine (lying on the back).

WNL
The abbreviation for within normal limits.

Wolf-Hirschhorn Syndrome
Refer to **4p- Syndrome**.

Womb
Refer to **Uterus**.

Women, Infants, and Children Program (WIC)
A federally-funded program that provides pregnant women, new mothers, infants, and young children (who qualify) with food vouchers, nutrition counseling, and referrals to health care.

Worms
A common term for *parasites* that live in the gastrointestinal tract, blood, or other organs of the body. Infestation occurs by eating undercooked or infected meats, by ingesting contaminated water, or by coming in contact with contaminated soil, and may cause acute illness or may not be recognized for years. An example of a type of worm is the *pinworm*, which causes itching of the skin around the anus where the pinworm eggs are laid.

WPPSI-R
The abbreviation for Wechsler Preschool and Primary Scale of Intelligence-Revised.

Wryneck
Refer to **Torticollis**.

"W" Sitting Position
Sitting on the buttocks between the heels of the feet. (The knees are bent, forming a "W.") Children with high tone often assume this position, but it should be discouraged because it hinders motor development and increases *spasticity*. It also encourages hip joint malformation and structural strain on the knee and ankle.

Wt
The abbreviation for weight.

X

X Chromosome
A *sex chromosome* that in humans is present in both sexes. Females have two and males have one in the cells of their body.

Xeroderma (zeer-oe-DUR-muh)
A rare, *inherited* skin condition in which the skin is very dry, rough, wrinkled, freckled, and prematurely aged (by about 5 years of age), due to extreme sensitivity to UV (ultraviolet) rays in sunlight.

X-Linked Dominant Disorder
A disorder transmitted by an abnormal *dominant gene* on the X *chromosome*. Children who *inherit* the abnormal gene from an affected parent are always born with the traits of the condition; however, children of an affected parent who receive a normal chromosome are not affected. Normal children of an affected parent have normal offspring.
   Refer to **Sex-Linked Disorder**.

X-Linked Recessive Disorder
A disorder transmitted by an abnormal *recessive gene* on the X *chromosome*. The mother usually does not have the disorder (because she has a normal X chromosome and is a *carrier*), but her sons have a 50% chance of being affected and her daughters have a 50% chance of carrying the gene (but not having the disorder themselves). In rare instances a female child of an affected father and a carrier mother might be affected. Examples of X-linked recessive disorders include *Duchenne muscular dystrophy* and *hemophilia*.
   Refer to **Sex-Linked Disorder**.

XO Syndrome
   Refer to **Turner Syndrome**.

X-ray
A radiological technique that produces images of internal body structures by passing low doses of X-rays (high-energy, invisible electromagnetic waves) through the body to strike an X-ray film or fluorescent screen. X-ray radiation may also be used to destroy diseased tissue.

XX
The normal *sex chromosome* complement in females.

XXY Syndrome (XXXY Syndrome, etc.)
   Refer to **Klinefelter Syndrome**.

XY
The normal *sex chromosome* complement in males.

Y Chromosome
A *sex chromosome* that in humans is present only in the male.

Yeast
A microscopic fungus that can cause infection. An example of a yeast is *candida albicans*.

Zarontin™ (zuh-RON-tin)
Refer to **Ethosuximide**.

Zero Reject
The principle that no child with a disability should be refused a free, appropriate, education if other children the same age are being served.

Zinc
An essential nutrient in the body. Zinc is necessary for healing, cellular immunity, and normal growth.

Zygomatic Bone (zie-goe-MAT-ik)
The cheekbone.
*Also known as the **Malar**.*

Zygote (ZIE-gote)
The cell produced when a sperm (male sex cell) fertilizes an ovum (egg, or female sex cell). The zygote contains all the *genetic* information about the new individual that will develop.

Numerals

4p- Syndrome

A *chromosomal* disorder in which part of the short arm of chromosome number 4 is deleted. This disorder is characterized by *microcephaly* (an abnormally small head size), profound *mental retardation*, *seizures*, growth deficiency, *hypotonia* (decreased *muscle tone*), eye *anomalies*, *strabismus* (a condition in which the eyes do not work together), *cleft lip* and/or *palate*, cranial and facial abnormalities, *clubfoot*, genital abnormalities, and heart anomaly. Children with 4p- syndrome often do not survive beyond early childhood.

   *Also known as **Wolf-Hirschhorn Syndrome**.*

5p- Syndrome

   *Refer to **Cri du Chat Syndrome**.*

13q- Syndrome

A *chromosomal disorder* that occurs when part of the long arm of a chromosome number 13 is deleted. This syndrome is characterized by *mental retardation* and growth deficiency and sometimes *microcephaly*; a high nasal bridge; eye *anomalies*, including *hypertelorism* (an abnormally wide space between the eyes), *ptosis* (drooping of the upper eyelid), *epicanthal folds* (a vertical skin fold at the inner corner of the eyes), abnormally small eyeballs, and *retinoblastoma* (a malignant tumor of the retina); a small lower jaw; low-set ears; a *webbed* and short neck; *clubfoot;* small or absent thumbs; heart defect; and genital anomalies, including *hypospadias* and *undescended testes*. Children with 13q- syndrome usually die before reaching adulthood.

20/20 Vision

   *Refer to **Vision** and **Visual Acuity**.*

Appendices

APPENDIX I
GROWTH CHARTS

WEIGHT

NATIONAL CENTER FOR HEALTH STATISTICS

Weight by age percentiles for girls aged birth-36 months.

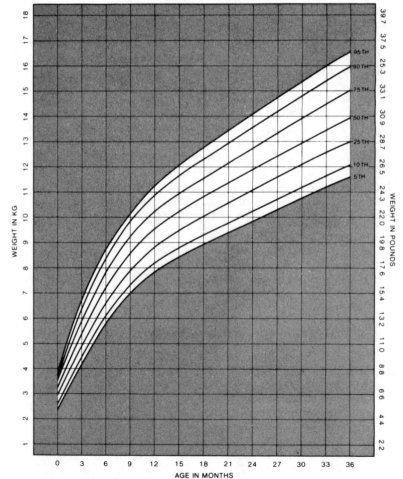

GIRLS

WEIGHT

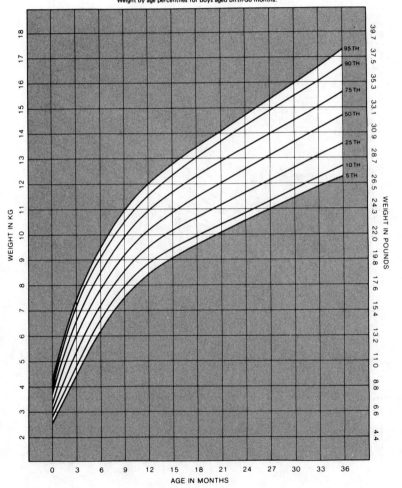

NATIONAL CENTER FOR HEALTH STATISTICS

Weight by age percentiles for boys aged birth-36 months.

BOYS

LENGTH

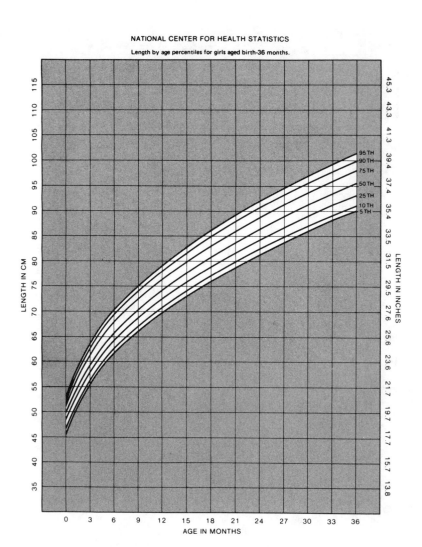

NATIONAL CENTER FOR HEALTH STATISTICS

Length by age percentiles for girls aged birth-36 months.

GIRLS

LENGTH

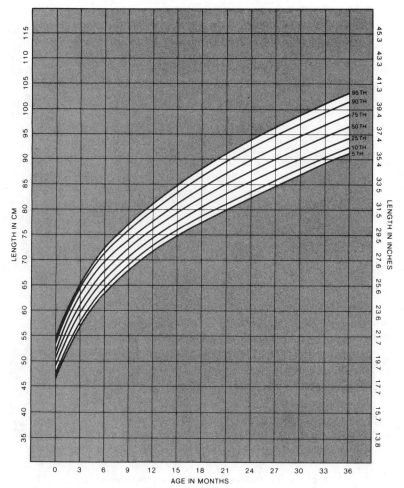

NATIONAL CENTER FOR HEALTH STATISTICS

Length by age percentiles for boys aged birth-36 months.

BOYS

HEAD CIRCUMFERENCE

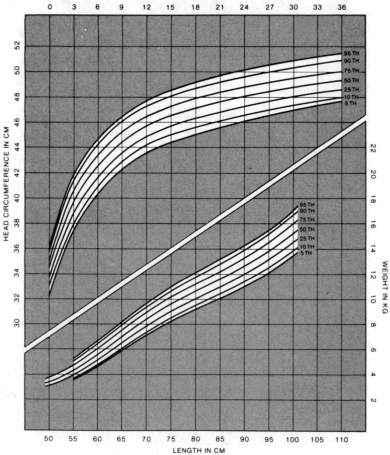

NATIONAL CENTER FOR HEALTH STATISTICS

Head circumference by age percentiles for girls aged birth-36 months.

Weight by length percentiles for girls aged birth-36 months.

GIRLS

HEAD CIRCUMFERENCE

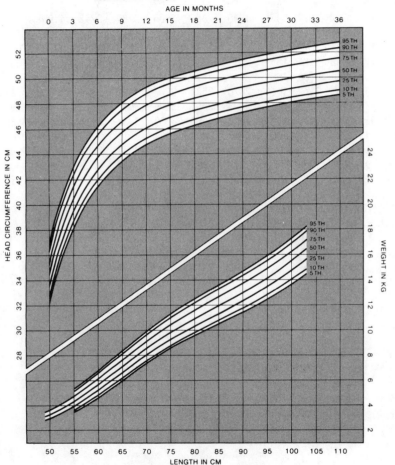

NATIONAL CENTER FOR HEALTH STATISTICS

Head circumference by age percentiles for boys aged birth-36 months.

Weight by length percentiles for boys aged birth-36 months.

BOYS

APPENDIX II
CONVERSION CHARTS: POUNDS and OUNCES TO GRAMS

		0	1	2	3	4	*Pounds* 5	6	7	8	9	10
	0	—	454	907	1361	1814	2268	2722	3175	3629	4082	4536
Oz.	1	28	482	936	1389	1843	2296	2750	3203	3657	4111	4564
	2	57	510	964	1417	1871	2325	2778	3232	3685	4139	4593
	3	85	539	992	1446	1899	2353	2807	3260	3714	4167	4621
	4	113	567	1021	1474	1928	2381	2835	3289	3742	4196	4649
	5	142	595	1049	1503	1956	2410	2863	3317	3770	4224	4678
	6	170	624	1077	1531	1984	2438	2892	3345	3799	4252	4706
	7	198	652	1106	1559	2013	2466	2920	3374	3827	4281	4734
	8	227	680	1134	1588	2041	2495	2948	3402	3856	4309	4763
	9	255	709	1162	1616	2070	2523	2977	3430	3884	4337	4791
	10	283	737	1191	1644	2098	2551	3005	3459	3912	4366	4819
	11	312	765	1219	1673	2126	2580	3033	3487	3941	4394	4848
	12	340	794	1247	1701	2155	2608	3062	3515	3969	4423	4876
	13	369	822	1276	1729	2183	2637	3090	3544	3997	4451	4904
	14	397	850	1304	1758	2211	2665	3118	3572	4026	4479	4933
	15	425	879	1332	1786	2240	2693	3147	3600	4054	4508	4961

INCHES TO CENTIMETERS

Inches	Centimeters	Inches	Centimeters
10	25.4	20.5	52.1
10.5	26.7	21	53.3
11	27.9	21.5	54.6
11.5	29.2	22	55.9
12	30.5	22.5	57.2
12.5	31.8	23	58.4
13	33.0	23.5	59.7
13.5	34.3	24	61.0
14	35.6	24.5	62.2
14.5	36.8	25	63.5
15	38.1	25.5	64.8
15.5	39.4	26	66.1
16	40.6	26.5	67.4
16.5	41.9	27	68.7
17	43.2	27.5	69.9
17.5	44.4	28	71.2
18	45.7	28.5	72.5
18.5	47.0	29	73.8
19	48.3	29.5	75.1
19.5	49.5	30	76.4
20	50.8	30.5	77.6

APPENDIX III

APGAR SCORING CHART

	0	1	2
COLOR	blue-pale	hands and feet blue, body pink	completely pink
HEART RATE	absent	below 100 beats per minute	over 100 beats per minute
BREATHING EFFORT	absent	irregular, weak, slow	good, crying
REFLEX IRRITABILITY (when a catheter is placed in a nostril)	absent	grimace	sneeze, cough
(when foot is flicked)	absent	movement, crying	vigorous crying
MUSCLE TONE	limp	some flexion of arms	active motion

APPENDIX IV
NUTRITIONAL INTAKE & FEEDING STYLE FOR INFANTS

Age	Food	Feeding Style/Positioning
0–4 mo.	• Breast milk or formula	• Child held by parent or caretaker in semi-reclined position
4–6 mo.	• Breast milk or formula • Smooth solids (strained or pureed foods)	• Child held by parent or caretaker in more upright manner • Child fed with feeder spoon (small, narrow spoon with long handle)
8 mo.	• Breast milk or formula • Finger foods (baby cookies, crackers) • Lumpy solids (ground junior foods or mashed foods)	• Child seated in high chair or other feeder chair • Given choice of bottle so child can hold independently • Cup drinking introduced
12 mo.	• Milk • Meat sticks, fruit, vegetables • Coarsely chopped table food	• Child seated in high chair, or other feeder chair • Child is now active participant in feeding process • Uses fingers to feed and is introduced to spoon feeding (child-sized spoon) • Drinks mealtime liquid from cup
18 mo.	• Coarsely chopped table food • Most meats	• Child seated in high chair or youth chair at table • Independent spoon feeding (messy) • Drinks all liquid from cup

(Elaine Geralis, ed., *Children with Cerebral Palsy: A Parent's Guide*. Rockville, MD: Woodbine House, 1991, p. 116.)

APPENDIX V
RECOMMENDED IMMUNIZATION SCHEDULES

Recommended Age	Immunization(s)
2 months	DTP, OPV, HIb
4 months	DTP, OPV, HIb
6 months	DTP, HIb
12 months	MMR
15 months	HIb
18 months	DTP, OPV
4½–6 years (before starting school)	DTP, OPV, MMR, TB

DTP (also referred to as DPT)—diphtheria and tetanus toxoids (a toxin that has been treated to decrease its poisonous effect but keep its power to stimulate the formation of antibodies) with pertussis vaccine

OPV—oral poliovirus vaccine

HIb—Hemophilus Influenzae type b

MMR—live measles, mumps, and rubella viruses

TB—tuberculosis (tuberculin test)

About the author

Since 1984, Jeanine G. Coleman, M.Ed., has been the Program Director of Advance Infant Development in Claremont, CA, a program for at-risk and developmentally disabled infants from birth to three years of age. Her responsibilities include training and supervising a staff of infant educators, and working with various state, therapy, and educational agencies. She speaks frequently at seminars and conferences and to child development center staffs on such topics as full inclusion of children with special needs, identifying developmental delays, and effective behavior management techniques. Coleman also designs toys for children who have special needs. She and her husband live in Chino Hills, California.